James E.C. Welldon

The Nicomachean Ethics of Aristotle

James E.C. Welldon

The Nicomachean Ethics of Aristotle

ISBN/EAN: 9783337038113

Printed in Europe, USA, Canada, Australia, Japan

Cover: Foto ©Thomas Meinert / pixelio.de

More available books at **www.hansebooks.com**

THE NICOMACHEAN ETHICS

OF

ARISTOTLE

TRANSLATED

WITH AN ANALYSIS AND CRITICAL NOTES

BY

J. E. C. WELLDON, M.A.

HEAD MASTER OF HARROW SCHOOL.

London:

MACMILLAN AND CO.

AND NEW YORK.

1892

Cambridge:

PRINTED BY C. J. CLAY, M.A. & SONS,

AT THE UNIVERSITY PRESS.

PREFACE.

AFTER an interval of four years it is permitted me to follow up my translations of the *Politics* and *Rhetoric* of Aristotle with a translation of his *Nicomachean Ethics*. I have had a good deal of work to do in those four years at Harrow and elsewhere, and it is, I fear, only too likely that the translation will exhibit some traces of the broken manner in which it has been written. But it has been a help to me in teaching my pupils the art of translation to be myself a translator, and the pleasure of entering into the mind of Aristotle, as none but a translator of his writings can, is a sufficient reward for the pains which it is necessary to take in translating them.

It hardly falls within the province of a translator to give his reasons for the view which he takes of particular passages. But if I feel some confidence that in adopting my own view I have not ignored the views of others who have gone before me, it is in part at least because I have had the good fortune of submitting my proof-sheets as they were passing through the press to the careful and thoughtful criticism of my friend Mr A. H. Cruickshank, one of my colleagues at Harrow, and Fellow of New College, Oxford, to whom I owe, and desire to express, my sincere thanks. In translating the *Nicomachean Ethics* I have, I think, made use of all the recent editions and commentaries (they are not very numerous), though Mr Bywater's latest contributions to the study of Aristotle were not within my reach during the earlier portion of my work. It is perhaps right to say that I refrained from consulting such translations as had already been published in England until I had finished my own independently; but in revising it I have not scrupled to refer to them and occasionally to borrow a hint from them. Thus to Mr Williams and to Mr Peters, different as their translations are, I am alike indebted. Perhaps the object which I have chiefly kept in view has been to make each sentence of my translation as clear as possible; the rendering may be wrong or right in various passages, but at least I hope it is intelligible. It may be well to add that

I have deliberately rejected the principle of trying to translate the same Greek word by the same word in English, and that, where circumstances seemed to call for it, I have sometimes used two English words to represent one word of the Greek. But when all is said, the difficulty of translating Aristotle remains great; nobody knows it so well as he who has felt it by actual trial; but I cherish the hope that this translation may be the means of bringing the master-treatise upon Ethics into the hands of some one who has not known or appreciated it before.

J. E. C. WELLDON.

Harrow School,
October 14, 1892.

N.B. The text from which this translation is made is that of Bekker's Octavo Edition, published in 1881. The marginal references are to the pages of the translation, the references in the footnotes to passages of the *Nicomachean Ethics* are to the pages and lines of Bekker's text. In referring to other works of Aristotle than the *Nicomachean Ethics* I have quoted the pages and lines of the Berlin Edition.

Where the words of the translation are printed in italics, they have generally been inserted for the sake of elucidating the sense.

b 2

ANALYSIS.

BOOK I.

CHAPTER I.

EVERY art, every science, every action or purpose, aims at some good.

The good (τἀγαθόν) is that at which all things aim.

The ends are either activities (ἐνέργειαι) or results (ἔργα) beyond the activities. Where the result is an end beyond the activity, the result is superior to the activity.

As there are various actions, arts and sciences, the ends are also various. The ends of the architectonic arts or sciences are more desirable than those of the subordinate arts and sciences.

The end which we wish for its own sake, and for the sake of which we wish everything else, is the good, or the supreme good (τὸ ἄριστον).

The knowledge of the supreme good is of great importance as regulating the aim or object of human life.

The architectonic science or faculty is the political. Its end comprehends the ends of all other sciences and is therefore the true good of mankind.

Ethics becomes then a department of Politics. It is not an exact science. Ethical truth can be ascertained only roughly and generally; it must always admit of dispute.

The young, having no experience of life, are ill judges of ethical reasonings, which are conclusions from the premisses of fact.

CHAPTER II.

The supreme good is admitted on all hands to be happiness (εὐδαιμονία). But happiness is differently conceived. By some it is defined as a visible and palpable good, e.g. pleasure, wealth or honour; by others as an absolute or abstract good, which is the cause of goodness in all other goods.

All reasoning is either deductive or inductive. Ethical reasoning starts from ascertained and known facts. But facts may be known either absolutely or relatively to the persons who know them. It is facts relatively known which form the basis of Ethics.

Hence the importance of a good moral training, as supplying the first principles of ethical reasoning.

CHAPTER III.

The lives of men may be described as (1) sensual (2) political (3) speculative.

The sensual life is the choice of slavish or brutish men.

The political life aims at honour. But honour is not identifiable with happiness, as it depends more upon the people who pay it than upon the person to whom it is paid, and is therefore not something proper to the person himself.

Nor again are virtue (ἀρετή) and happiness (εὐδαιμονία) identical, as virtue is consistent with a life of torpor or misfortune.

The speculative life will be investigated hereafter.

CHAPTER IV.

Objections to the Platonic theory of the universal good.

(1) Plato did not recognise ideas of things of which priority and posteriority are predicable. But good is predicated of relation as well as of essence, and the relative is necessarily posterior to the essential.

(2) Good is predicated in all the categories. But if so it cannot be a common universal idea.

(3) There is no single science of all good things, as there would be if the idea of good were single.

(4) Good would not become more good by being eternal, if it were a universal idea.

The Pythagorean doctrine that unity is a good is more reasonable than the Platonic doctrine that the good is a unity.

It has been suggested that the Platonic theory does not apply to all goods and that there are two kinds of goods, viz. (1) absolute (2) secondary.

But what are absolute goods ?

If nothing is an absolute good except the idea (ἰδέα), the idea will comprise no particulars. If the particulars are absolute goods, the conception of the good will be the same in them all, But it is not the same, e.g. in honour, wisdom, and pleasure. Good then is not a common term falling under one idea.

✴ CHAPTER V.

The practicable good is different in different actions or arts. e.g. in medicine, strategy, etc.

But in each it is that for the sake of which all else is done.

If then there is a certain end of all action, it will be this. which is the practicable good; or if there are several such ends, it will be these.

Happiness answers to this description of the supreme good; for whereas other goods are desired partly for their own sakes and partly as means to happiness, happiness is always desired for its own sake.

Also the final good may be assumed to be self-sufficient, and happiness is pre-eminently self-sufficient.

Also happiness is distinct from other good things, as being the end or object of them.

✴ CHAPTER VI.

The nature of happiness depends on the proper function of Man. As every part of Man, e.g. his eye, his hand, his foot, has its function, so has Man himself.

What is his function ?

Not the life of nutrition and increase (ἡ θρεπτικὴ καὶ αὐξητικὴ ζωή), for that is common to man with the plants; nor the life of sensation (ἡ αἰσθητική), for that is common to man with the lower animals. It is the practical life of the rational part of man's being (πρακτική τις τοῦ λόγον ἔχοντος).

The function of man defined as an activity of soul in accordance with reason or not independently of reason (ψυχῆς ἐνέργεια κατὰ λόγον ἢ οὐκ ἄνευ λόγου).

But the functions of a person of a certain kind, and of a person who is good of his kind, e.g. of a harpist and a good harpist, are the same.

The function of the good man then will be an activity of soul in accordance with virtue, or if there are several virtues, in accordance with the best and most complete virtue, that activity being exhibited not in a chance period of time but in a complete life (ἐν βίῳ τελείῳ).

CHAPTER VII.

The degree of accuracy attainable in Ethics is not greater than is proper to the subject. We must be content with such accuracy as is attainable.

Ethical science proceeds from first principles, and these principles are discovered sometimes by induction, sometimes by perception, sometimes by habituation and so on.

CHAPTER VIII.

Goods are divisible into three classes viz. (1) External goods, (2) Goods of the soul, (3) Goods of the body.

Of these the goods of the soul are goods in the strictest sense.

The end of human life then will be some good of the soul.

Accordingly the happy man will live well and do well, as happiness is a kind of living and doing well (εὐζωία τις καὶ εὐπραξία).

CHAPTER IX.

This definition of happiness embraces and includes the conceptions of happiness as prudence or wisdom whether (a) absolute or (b) associated with pleasure or external prosperity. For if happiness is activity in accordance with virtue, it implies virtue.

N.B. Happiness must be an activity rather than a moral state (ἕξις), as a moral state may exist and yet may be unproductive, but activity implies action.

Activity in accordance with virtue implies pleasure, as if a person is good, he finds pleasure in noble actions.

Lastly, activity in accordance with virtue implies nobleness.

Happiness then is the best and pleasantest and noblest thing in the world. But it requires the addition of external goods, as nobleness of action is impossible without external means.

CHAPTER X.

It is questioned whether happiness can be learnt or acquired, or is a gift of Heaven.

Happiness, as being the best of human things, may be reasonably supposed to be a divine gift; for how can the best of things be left to chance?

But even if it can be acquired by learning or discipline, still in its nature it is divine.

It is also of wide extent, as being capable of realization in all persons, except such as are morally deformed.

The definition of happiness agrees with the end of political science as already defined; for the end of political science is to produce a character of goodness in the citizens.

The lower animals are incapable of happiness, as being incapable of virtuous activity.

Children are incapable of happiness, except prospectively, for happiness requires complete virtue and a complete life.

CHAPTER XI.

Can a man be called happy so long as he is alive?

The Solonian *dictum* that it is necessary to look to the end would seem to forbid the ascription of happiness to any one

until after he is dead. But if happiness is a species of activity,
how can a person be happy not in his life time, but after his
death ?   Nor is it right to conceive a person to be happy after
his death, as being at last exempt from the changes and chances
of life; for it may reasonably be believed that the dead are
affected more or less by such good or evil as occurs to their
children and descendants.

To call a person happy after his death is to predicate happiness of him, not when the happiness exists, but when it has
existed and is past.

Again, to make happiness dependent upon the fortune of the
moment is to destroy its stability and completeness. But no
human function is so constant or stable as activity in accordance
with virtue.

The conclusion is that happiness possesses the element of
stability. It is not affected by petty incidents of good or ill
fortune, nor is it destroyed, although it may be impeded, by
serious pains and calamities.

Happiness being determined by virtuous activity the happy
man can never become miserable, as he will never commit mean
actions. His happiness will be seldom disturbed, but if disturbed,
as e.g. by heavy misfortune, will be only slowly restored.

The happy man then is one whose activity accords with
perfect virtue, and who is adequately furnished with external
goods, not for a casual period of time, but for a complete lifetime.

It is probable that a person after death is affected, but not
affected to any great extent, by the fortunes of his descendants
or friends, i.e. they do not create or destroy his happiness.

CHAPTER XII.

Is happiness properly an object of praise or an object of
honour ?

Praise implies a certain character and a certain relation to
somebody or something else in the object of praise. Hence
praise is inapplicable to the Gods, as they stand above comparison.

It follows that praise is inapplicable to the highest goods.

Happiness then, as being the supreme good, is an object, not of praise, but of something higher than praise, viz. honour.

From another point of view happiness, as being a first principle (ἀρχή), is equally an object of honour.

✠ CHAPTER XIII.

Happiness being an activity of soul in accordance with complete or perfect virtue, the consideration of virtue affords the best insight into happiness.

Human excellence or virtue is not that of the body but that of the soul.

Now the soul has two parts, one irrational (ἄλογον) the other rational (λόγον ἔχον). The rational part is also capable of division into

(1) the vegetative part which is common to man with all living things, and is removed from the sphere of virtue

(2) the emotional or concupiscent part, which is irrational, and yet may be said to partake of reason, not as possessing or understanding reason, but as being capable of obedience to reason.

There are therefore in man

(1) Intellectual virtues (διανοητικαὶ ἀρεταί) i.e. virtues of the rational part of his soul, e.g. wisdom and prudence,

(2) Moral virtues (ἠθικαὶ ἀρεταί) i.e. virtues of the irrational part of his soul when acting in obedience to reason, e.g. liberality and temperance.

BOOK II.

CHAPTER I.

VIRTUE or excellence (ἀρετή) then is twofold, viz.

(1) Intellectual

(2) Moral

Intellectual virtue is originated and fostered mainly by teaching; it therefore demands time and experience.

✗ Moral virtue is created by habit. It follows that moral virtue is not implanted by nature, as a law of nature cannot be altered by habituation.

Nature affords the capacity for virtue, and that capacity is perfected by habit.

There is a marked difference between the natural powers or faculties (δυνάμεις) of man and his virtues.

The faculties are acquired before the corresponding activities are displayed. Thus the faculty of sight or hearing precedes its active exercise. But the virtues are acquired by their exercise; justice by just action, temperance by temperate action, and so on.

Legislation aims at making the citizens good by discipline of the habits.

It is true of virtue as of art that the causes and means by which it is produced, and by which it is destroyed, are the same. A person becomes a good or bad musician by practising music well or badly. Similarly he becomes brave or cowardly by acting rightly or wrongly in the face of danger.

In a word, moral states are the results of activities corresponding to the moral states themselves. Hence the serious importance of the training of the habits from early days.

✗ CHAPTER II.

ɣ. The study of Ethics is not speculative only but practical. Our object is not merely to know the nature of virtue, but to become ourselves virtuous.

It is necessary therefore to consider the principle of right action. But reasoning upon practical matters cannot be scientifically exact; it can only be tentative or approximate.

Excess and deficiency are alike fatal in conduct. Excess or deficiency of gymnastic exercise is fatal to strength, excess or deficiency of meat and drink to health. Similarly in respect of courage, temperance, and the other virtues, excess or deficiency is destructive, the mean or intermediate state is preservative, of the virtues.

As the causes and agencies which produce, increase, and destroy the moral states are the same, so is the sphere of their activity the same also. Strength e.g. is produced by taking food and undergoing toil; but nobody can take so much food or undergo so much toil as the strong man. The same is true of courage or temperance. The pleasure or pain which follows upon actions is the test of a person's moral state.

The essential quality of courage lies in facing dangers with pleasure, or of temperance in abstaining from physical gratifications with pleasure. Hence the importance of such a training as produces pleasure and pain in presence of the right objects. This is the true education.

The connexion of virtue with pleasures and pains follows

(1) because the virtues are concerned with actions and emotions, and every action or emotion is attended by pleasure and pain .

(2) because the employment of pains as means of punishment implies the pleasantness of the condition which punishments are intended to remedy.

Certain philosophers, e.g. the Cynics, seeing the influence of pleasures and pains upon conduct, have been led to define the virtues as apathetic states.

Moral virtue then tends to produce the best action in respect of pleasures and pains.

Again, there are three natural objects of desire, viz. the noble, the expedient, and the pleasant, and three natural objects of avoidance, viz. the shameful, the injurious, and the painful. It follows that the good man will take a right line in respect of all these, but especially of pleasure, as pleasure is an element of nobleness and expediency.

Also pleasure is a sentiment fostered in men from early childhood. Pleasure and pain too are in a greater or less degree the standards of human action.

The study of Ethics then is throughout concerned with pleasures and pains, as right or wrong pleasures and pains have a material influence upon actions.

CHAPTER III.

When it is said that a person becomes just by just action, or temperate by temperate action, justice and temperance as qualities imply not only the corresponding actions but the corresponding knowledge or motive.

In order to just or temperate actions it is necessary

(1) that a person should know what he is doing

(2) that he should deliberately choose to do it

(3) that he should choose to do it for its own sake

(4) that it should be an instance or evidence of a fixed and immutable moral state.

Hence virtue, as necessitating these conditions, differs from art, which requires none of these conditions or only the condition of knowledge.

CHAPTER IV.

THE NATURE OF VIRTUE.

The qualities of the soul are three (viz.)

(1) emotions ($\pi\acute{a}\theta\eta$)

(2) faculties ($\delta\upsilon\nu\acute{a}\mu\epsilon\iota\varsigma$)

(3) moral states ($\H{\epsilon}\xi\epsilon\iota\varsigma$).

Virtue then must be one of these three.

But the virtues like the vices are not emotions, for

(1) praise and blame attach to virtues or vices but not to emotions

(2) the virtues imply, but the emotions do not imply, deliberate purpose

(3) a person is said to be moved ($\kappa\iota\nu\epsilon\hat{\iota}\sigma\theta\alpha\iota$) in respect of his emotions, but to have a certain disposition ($\delta\iota\alpha\kappa\epsilon\hat{\iota}\sigma\theta\alpha\acute{\iota}\ \pi\omega\varsigma$) in respect of his virtues or vices.

Nor again are the virtues faculties, for

(1) it is not an abstract capacity for emotion which is the subject of praise or censure

(2) the faculties are gifts of nature, the virtues are not.

If then the virtues are neither emotions nor faculties, they must be moral states.

CHAPTER V.

It is not enough to show that virtue is a moral state, it is necessary to describe the character of that moral state.

Every virtue or excellence has the effect of producing a good condition of that of which it is a virtue or excellence, and of enabling it to perform its function well. The excellence of the eye e.g. makes the eye good and its function good. Similarly the excellence or virtue of a man will be such a moral state as makes him good and able to perform his proper function well.

In everything there is

    (1) a greater

    (2) a smaller

    (3) an equal

whether

    (a) absolute or

    (b) relative to ourselves.

The equal is a mean between excess and deficiency. The absolute mean is equally distant from both extremes, the relative mean is neither too much nor too little for ourselves.

In practical matters the wise man seeks and chooses the relative mean.

Every science or art, if it is to perform its function well, must regard the mean and refer its productions to the mean. Accordingly, successful productions are those to which nothing can be added, and from which nothing can be taken. But virtue is superior to any science or art. Virtue therefore will aim at the mean.

All emotions and actions admit of excess and deficiency, they admit also of the mean.

To experience emotions at the right times, on the right occasions, towards the right persons, for the right causes, and in the right manner is the mean, or the supreme good, and this is characteristic of virtue.

Virtue then is a mean state as aiming at the mean.

Again, there are many different ways of going wrong, but there is only one way of going right. Evil is infinite, good finite; hence excess and deficiency are characteristics of vice, and the mean state is characteristic of virtue.

CHAPTER VI.

DEFINITION OF VIRTUE.

Virtue is a state of deliberate moral purpose, consisting in a mean that is relative to ourselves, the mean being determined by reason or as a prudent man would determine it (ἕξις προαιρετική, ἐν μεσότητι οὖσα τῇ πρὸς ἡμᾶς, ὡρισμένῃ λόγῳ καὶ ὡς ἂν ὁ φρόνιμος ὁρίσειεν).

It is a mean state

(1) as lying between the two vices of excess and deficiency

(2) as discovering and embracing the mean in emotions and actions.

But while virtue is a mean state if regarded in its essence, it is an extreme if regarded from the point of view of the supreme good.

It is not every action or every emotion that admits of a mean state.

Some emotions, e.g. malice and envy, some actions, e.g. theft and murder, are intrinsically wicked. These actions and emotions are in themselves excesses or deficiencies; they do not therefore admit of a mean state.

CHAPTER VII.

PARTICULAR VIRTUES AS EXEMPLIFICATIONS OF THE MEAN STATE.

Excess	Mean State	Deficiency
(ὑπερβολή)	(μεσότης)	(ἔλλειψις)
Foolhardiness	Courage	Cowardice
(θράσος)	(ἀνδρεία)	(δειλία)
Licentiousness	Temperance	Insensibility
(ἀκολασία)	(σωφροσύνη)	(ἀναισθησία)
Prodigality	Liberality	Illiberality
(ἀσωτία)	(ἐλευθεριότης)	(ἀνελευθερία)
Vulgarity	Magnificence	Meanness
(βαναυσία)	(μεγαλοπρέπεια)	(μικροπρέπεια)
Vanity	Highmindedness	Littlemindedness
(χαυνότης)	(μεγαλοψυχία)	(μικροψυχία)

N.B. Magnificence differs from liberality as having to do with large sums of money.

Excess	Mean State	Deficiency
Ambition		Lack of ambition
(φιλοτιμία)		(ἀφιλοτιμία)

N.B. There is no name for the mean state; hence sometimes ambition, sometimes lack of ambition is praised.

Excess	Mean State	Deficiency
Passionateness	Gentleness	Impassivity
(ὀργιλότης)	(πραότης)	(ἀοργησία)
Boastfulness	Truthfulness	Self-depreciation
(ἀλαζονεία)	(ἀλήθεια)	or Irony (εἰρωνεία)
Buffoonery	Wittiness	Boorishness
(βωμολοχία)	(εὐτραπελία)	(ἀγροικία)
Obsequiousness (if disinterested (ἀρεσκεία) or Flattery (if interested) (κολακεία)	Friendliness (φιλία)	Quarrelsomeness (δυσκολία)
Bashfulness	Modesty	Shamelessness
(? κατάπληξις)	(αἰδώς)	(ἀναισχυντία)
Envy	Righteous Indigna-	Malice
(φθόνος)	tion (νέμεσις)	(ἐπιχαιρεκακία)

N.B. This last example is inexact, as Aristotle saw in his *Rhetoric*. Envy and Malice are not opposites, but compatible and co-existent.

CHAPTER VIII.

The extremes are opposed both to the mean and to each other; the mean is opposed to the extremes. [But the opposition between the two extremes is greater than that between either extreme and the mean.

In some cases the excess, in others the deficiency, is the more opposed to the mean. Foolhardiness e.g. is more opposed to courage than cowardice, licentiousness is more opposed to temperance than insensibility. The reason of this greater opposition lies partly in the nature of the thing itself, partly in the greater inclination of human nature to one extreme than to the other.

W. N. E.   C

CHAPTER IX.

Moral virtue then is a mean state as lying between two vices, and as aiming at the mean in the emotions and actions. Hence the difficulty of virtuous living, as it is always difficult to find the mean.

PRACTICAL RULES FOR HUMAN LIFE.

(1) To depart from that extreme which is the more opposed to the mean.

(2) To pull ourselves in the direction opposite to our natural inclination.

(3) Where the attainment of the mean is impossible, to choose the lesser of two evils.

Beyond these rules it is impossible to go. No theory will define the limits of right conduct.

BOOK III.

CHAPTER I.

VIRTUE being concerned with emotions and actions, and voluntary emotions and actions being subjects of praise and blame, but involuntary emotions and actions the subjects of pardon or pity, it is necessary to distinguish what is voluntary from what is involuntary.

Actions done under compulsion or from ignorance are involuntary. But an action is compulsory if its origin is external to the person who does it, e.g. if the wind carries him out of his course.

It is sometimes difficult to decide whether a particular action is voluntary or involuntary, e.g. if a person does some shameful action at a tyrant's command to save the lives of his parents or children, or if he throws his goods overboard to save his ship. Such actions may be said to be voluntary, as being chosen by the person at the time of doing them, but in the abstract they are involuntary.

They may be either laudable or censurable or simply pardonable. Yet there are probably some actions which a good man could not be compelled to do ; he would rather die any death, however dreadful.

As a general rule it is a mistake to lay the blame of wrong actions upon external causes rather than upon our own moral weakness.

CHAPTER II.

An action which is due to ignorance is non-voluntary, but it is not involuntary unless it is followed by a feeling of pain and regret.

To act *from* ignorance is one thing, to act *in* ignorance is another. A person e.g. who is intoxicated acts not from ignorance, but from intoxication, but he acts in ignorance.

Ignorance is a frequent cause of injustice. But the ignorance which is the cause of injustice is ignorance which affects the moral purpose ; it is also ignorance of the universal ; but the ignorance which is the cause of involuntary action is ignorance of particulars, i.e. of the particular circumstances and occasion of the action. This latter ignorance admits of pity and forgiveness.

The particulars of action are

(1) the agent.

(2) the action itself.

(3) its occasion, or circumstances (περὶ τί ἢ ἐν τίνι). We may add

(4) the instrument.

(5) the object (ἕνεκα τίνος).

(6) the manner of acting.

Nobody but a madman can be ignorant of all these particulars ; but a person may be said to have acted involuntarily if he was ignorant of any one of them, especially if he was ignorant of the most important particulars, although an action cannot be called involuntary in respect of such ignorance, unless it occasions pain and regret to the agent.

CHAPTER III.

Action being involuntary, if done under compulsion or from ignorance, it appears to be voluntary, if the agent originates it with a knowledge of the particular circumstances of the action.

Actions due to passion or desire are not involuntary for

(1) if they were, no lower animal would act voluntarily

(2) it cannot be supposed that nothing which is done from desire or passion is voluntary, or that noble actions are voluntary and shameful actions involuntary.

There are certain things which ought to be objects of desire, and it cannot be said that these are desired involuntarily.

Again, what is involuntary is painful, what is done from desire is pleasant.

Again, there is no difference in respect of involuntariness between errors of reason and errors of passion; it is a duty to avoid both.

CHAPTER IV.

MORAL PURPOSE (προαίρεσις).

It is closely related to virtue and is a better criterion of character than actions.

Moral purpose is voluntary (ἑκούσιον), but volition is a wider term than moral purpose for

(1) children and the lower animals have volition, but not moral purpose

(2) actions done on the spur of the moment are voluntary but lack moral purpose.

(1) Moral purpose is not desire (ἐπιθυμία), for

(a) irrational creatures are capable of desire, but not of moral purpose.

(b) Moral purpose, but not desire, is proper to continence; desire, but not moral purpose, to incontinence.

(c) desire is contrary to moral purpose, but one desire is not contrary to another

(d) pleasure is the object of desire, but not of moral purpose.

(2) Moral purpose is not passion (θυμός); for where actions are due to anger, they are not directed by moral purpose.

(3) Moral purpose is not wish (βούλησις), for .

(a) we may wish for impossibilities, e.g. immortality, but we do not purpose them

(b) we may wish for things which are possible in themselves but lie wholly beyond our own power ; but we do not purpose things, unless it is more or less in our own power to effect them.

(c) Wish is directed to the end, moral purpose to the means.

(4) Moral purpose is not opinion (δόξα), for

(a) Opinion applies to all things, i.e. to things which are eternal or impossible, as well as to things which lie within our own power ;(moral purpose is confined to things which lie within our own power.)

(b) Opinion is distinguished by being true or false, (moral purpose by being good or evil.) Nor is moral purpose opinion of a particular kind ; for character depends upon purposing good or evil, not upon holding particular opinions.

(c) Opinion relates to the nature of things, moral purpose to the duty of accepting or avoiding things.

∽ (d) Moral purpose is praised rather as being directed to a proper end than as being correct, opinion is praised as being true.

∽ (e) We purpose such things as we best know to be good ; we form an opinion of things of which we have no knowledge.

(f) The power of forming the best opinion does not imply the power of making the best moral choice ; for a person may form a good opinion, but, being vicious, may not purpose good action.

ᐳ Moral purpose is not only voluntary, but implies previous deliberation.

CHAPTER V.

What are the proper subjects of deliberation (βούλευσις)? A subject of deliberation must be understood to be that about which a sensible person would deliberate. It will not be then

(a) A thing which is eternal or immutable, e.g. the universe or the incommensurability of the diagonal and the side of a square.

(b) A thing which follows the same invariable course, e.g.. the rising and setting of the sun.

(c) A thing which is wholly irregular, e.g. the rain.

(d) A mere accident, e.g. the finding of a treasure. Nor will it be any human affair which lies beyond the control of our own action; the matters about which we deliberate are practical matters within our own power. Deliberation relates not to ends but to means. A doctor does not deliberate *whether* he shall cure his patients, but *how* he shall cure them. All deliberation is investigation (ζήτησις); but there are forms of investigation, e.g. mathematical investigations, which are not forms of deliberation. The objects of deliberation and of moral purpose are the same, except that the object of moral purpose is itself the result of deliberation.

Moral purpose then is a deliberative desire of something which it is in our power to effect (βουλευτικὴ ὄρεξις τῶν ἐφ' ἡμῖν).

CHAPTER VI.

The wish is directed to the end; but what is the end? Is it the good (τὸ ἀγαθόν), or what appears to be the good (τὸ φαινόμενον ἀγαθόν)? In an absolute sense it is the good which is the object of wish, but in reference to the individual it is that which appears to be good. The true good is good relatively to the virtuous man, as the truly wholesome is that which is wholesome to a person in a good state of health.

Pleasure is a frequent cause of erroneous moral purpose, as appearing to be, but not actually being, good.

CHAPTER VII.

Virtue and vice are both voluntary; for if it is in our power to act, it is in our power to refrain from acting, and if it is in our power to refrain from acting, it is in our power to act.

This is the justification of the rewards attached to good, and the punishments inflicted for evil, action. Ignorance itself is punishable, if it is due to vice or negligence.

A person is responsible for his own demoralization. It is no excuse for injustice or licentiousness that a person has formed the habit of unjust or licentious action; he ought not to have formed the habit.

Vices of the body, as well as of the soul, are censurable, if they are the results of intemperance or folly.

The appreciation of virtue is itself the consequence of moral discipline.

CHAPTER VIII.

Actions (πράξεις) and moral states (ἕξεις) are both voluntary, but not voluntary in the same sense or degree.

Actions are voluntary throughout, moral states are voluntary in their inception but not in their development.

CHAPTER IX.

DISCUSSION OF THE SEVERAL VIRTUES.

I. Courage (ἀνδρεία).

It has been defined as a mean state in regard to sentiments of fear and confidence (μεσότης περὶ φόβους καὶ θάρρη). All evil things are objects of fear, but they do not all afford scope for a display of courage. There are some things which it is right to fear, and disgraceful not to fear, e.g. ignominy. Poverty or sickness, as not being vicious or the consequence of vice, is not a proper object of fear, although it is an evil. A person is not necessarily courageous if he does not fear poverty or sickness, nor is he cowardly, if he fears insult offered to his wife or children. What are then the fearful things in regard to which a courageous man displays his courage? Firstly death. Secondly, the perils of death, and therefore especially the chances of war.

CHAPTER X.

II. Fear (φόβος).

There are some things which all men fear, as exceeding the power of human endurance. The things which excite fear, but do not exceed the power of endurance, are of various magnitudes and degrees. It is the manner in which a person faces these things which proves him to be courageous or cowardly. Fear may be wrong either in itself or in its manner, time, etc. The courageous man is he who faces and fears the right things for the right motive, in the right way, and at the right time. To the courageous man courage is noble ; hence nobleness is the end or object of courage. There is no name for excessive fearlessness ; excessive confidence in facing fearful things is called foolhardiness (θράσος). Foolhardiness is a species of imposture, as affecting an unreal courage. Most foolhardy people are cowards at heart. Excessive fearfulness is cowardice (δειλία), it is fear of the wrong things in the wrong way, and at the wrong time etc.

CHAPTER XI.

Courage then is a mean state in regard to the causes of confidence and fear. It chooses action, or endures pain, from love of nobleness or fear of disgrace. Suicide, as seeking refuge from evil in death, is an act not of courage but of cowardice. There are five spurious kinds of courage.

(1) Political or civil courage (πολιτικὴ ἀνδρεία), viz. courage engendered by penalties which the laws inflict or honours which they confer. It resembles true courage, as its motive is a sense of honour. Similar to it is the courage of compulsion, as when soldiers are flogged into battle.

(2) Experience (ἐμπειρία). In war regular troops, having greater experience, are more courageous than raw recruits. On the other hand regular troops in the face of overpowering danger are the first to flee. Experience then is courage only in certain circumstances.

(3) Passion (θυμός) spurs men like wild beasts to encounter perils. But nobleness, not passion, is the motive of true courage. The courage of passion must be reinforced by right purpose, if it is to become true courage.

(4) Sanguineness (τὸ εὔελπι). It resembles courage in respect of its confidence, but it differs from courage inasmuch as the confidence of the courageous is due to nobleness, and that of the sanguine to the belief in their own superiority and in their probable immunity from suffering. Sanguine people turn tail, but

courageous people do not, if the result does not correspond with their expectation. Courage in meeting unforeseen perils is an evidence of the moral state.

(5) Ignorance (ἄγνοια). Ignorance is shortlived courage, as it is generally destroyed by enlightenment.

CHAPTER XII.

Courage in its nature is painful, as it is especially seen in the endurance of painful things ; but the end which courage proposes to itself is pleasant. If the circumstances in which courage is displayed are painful, courage sees through the circumstances to the end. Still the happier a man is, the greater will be his pain at the prospect of death, and the greater his courage in meeting it bravely.

CHAPTER XIII.

III. *Temperance* (σωφροσύνη).

Temperance is a mean state in respect of pleasures (μεσότης περὶ ἡδονάς); it is not equally concerned with pains. What are these pleasures ? They are not mental pleasures such as ambition or the love of learning, neither are they innocent pleasures such as the pleasures of conversation. Temperance applies to bodily pleasures exclusively, but not to all bodily pleasures. A person is not called intemperate or licentious for taking pleasure in the gratification of the sight or hearing, or, as a rule, of the smell. The lower animals are generally incapable of the pleasures of these senses. Temperance and licentiousness (ἀκολασία) have to do with such pleasures as the lower animals generally are capable of, i.e. with the pleasures of the touch and the taste, especially of the touch. The touch is the most universal of the senses and it is this of which incontinence is predicable. It is because the pleasures of touch are shared by man with the lower animals that such pleasures are called brutish.

Desires are

(1) universal (κοιναί) and natural (φυσικαί).

(2) individual (ἴδιοι) and acquired (ἐπίθετοι).

The desire of food e.g. is natural, the desire of a particular food is individual and may be acquired. In respect of the natural desires mistakes are rare, and they always take the form of excess. In respect of individual pleasures many people go wrong, and they go wrong in many different ways. Excess in respect of pleasures is licentiousness (ἀκολασία).

CHAPTER XIV.

The licentious man then desires all pleasures or the greatest pleasures, and desires them above all else. Deficiency in the love of pleasures is non-existent. Temperance is the mean state in respect of pleasures. The temperate man is eager in a moderate and right spirit for all such things as are pleasant and wholesome, and for all other pleasures, so long as they are not prejudicial to these, or inconsistent with noble conduct, or extravagant beyond his means.

CHAPTER XV.

Licentiousness is more strictly voluntary action than cowardice, as the former is due to pleasure the latter to pain, for

(1) we choose pleasure but avoid pain

(2) pain distracts our nature, pleasure leaves it free.

Cowardice as a moral state is less voluntary than particular acts of cowardice. Particular acts of licentiousness are more voluntary than licentiousness as a moral state. The term licentiousness is applicable to the faults of children as well as to those of grown up people ; hence the necessity of producing an obedient disposition in children.

In the temperate man the concupiscent element (τὸ ἐπιθυμητικόν) lives in harmony with the reason.

BOOK IV.

CHAPTER I.

IV. Liberality (ἐλευθεριότης)

LIBERALITY is a mean state in regard to property (μεσότης περὶ χρήματα) i.e. in regard to the giving and taking of property, particularly in giving it. All such things as have their value measured by money (νόμισμα) are property. Prodigality (ἀσωτία) and illiberality (ἀνελευθερία) are excesses and deficiencies in regard to property.

Things which admit of use may be used either well or badly, but riches are a useful thing. He will make the best use of riches who possesses the virtue appropriate to property, i.e. the liberal man. Right giving is more truly distinctive of the liberal man than right taking, for

(1) virtue is better seen in the author than in the recipient of benefactions

(2) gratitude is the reward of giving rather than that of not taking

(3) there is less virtue in not taking than in giving

(4) giving is a sign of liberality, not taking is rather a sign of justice.

Of all forms of virtue liberality is the best beloved.

CHAPTER II.

The liberal man gives from a noble motive and in a right spirit, i.e. he gives the right amount to the right persons and at the right time; also his giving is done with pleasure or without pain. He does not take from wrong sources, nor is he inclined to ask favours; his taking is only a means to subsequent giving; he is careful of his own property as being anxious to employ it in relieving others; he refrains from giving indiscriminately in order to have the means of giving aright. Excessive liberality is pre-judicial to a person's own interest.

Liberality consists not in the amount of the money given, but in the moral state of the giver. People who have inherited money are more liberal than people who have made it. The liberal man values wealth not for its own sake but as affording an opportunity of giving; but he does not give to the wrong people, or on the wrong occasion etc. The liberal man may be defined as one who spends in proportion to his substance and who spends upon the right objects; he takes too from the right sources and to the right amount; he is easy to deal with in money matters, for if he spends more than is right, it is less painful to him than if he does not spend enough.

CHAPTER III.

Prodigality (ἀσωτία) exceeds in giving and in not taking but is deficient in taking.

Illiberality (ἀνελευθερία) is deficient in giving and exceeds in taking, but on a small scale.

The two characteristics of prodigality, viz. giving and not taking, can seldom be combined in the same person; for the one naturally prevents the other.

A prodigal is a liberal man who has run wild; let him be reformed, and he will become liberal. The fault of his nature is not vice but folly. But a prodigal often does more harm than good, as he spends his money recklessly, and his extravagant spending leads to unscrupulous taking. Thus the prodigal becomes selfish and licentious. But while prodigality may be cured, illiberality is incurable; it is more natural to man than prodigality, it is of wide extent too, and assumes numerous forms. But the characteristics of illiberality, viz. deficient giving and excessive taking, are not always found together.

Some people, e.g. misers, are deficient in giving, but they do not covet other people's property; others again, while naturally abstaining from giving, are induced by fear to abstain from taking.

Others are unscrupulous as to the sources from which they take; but if people take large sums from wrong sources, e.g. by sacking cities or plundering temples, they are called wicked and impious rather than illiberal.

The essence of illiberality is a sordid love of gain.

Illiberality may be regarded as the opposite of liberality, and as being a greater and more natural evil than prodigality.

CHAPTER IV.

V. *Magnificence* (μεγαλοπρέπεια).

It resembles liberality as having to do with property or having to do with the use of property, but differs from it in scale.

Magnificence is suitable expenditure upon a great scale (ἐν μεγέθει πρέπουσα δαπάνη), but the greatness is relative to the person, occasion, and circumstances.

The deficiency corresponding to magnificence is meanness (μικροπρέπεια), the excess vulgarity (βαναυσία).

It is essential to magnificence that the result as well as the occasion should be worthy of the large expenditure.

The nature of magnificence is nobleness, its spirit is cheerful and lavish; in a word magnificence is excellence of work on a great scale.

CHAPTER V.

It follows that a poor man is incapable of magnificence. A rich man may display magnificence

(a) in the ceremonial of divine worship.

(b) in liturgies (λειτουργίαι) or services rendered to the state.

(c) on private occasions of rare occurrence, e.g. marriage.

(d) on any occasion of peculiar interest to the state or the upper classes.

Magnificence in all cases presupposes propriety.

CHAPTER VI.

Vulgarity consists in excessive expenditure, i.e. in expenditure disproportionate to the occasion. Its motive is ostentation not nobleness.

Meanness is deficiency of expenditure; it often ruins a great work for the sake of petty economy.

CHAPTER VII.

VI. *High-Mindedness* (μεγαλοψυχία).

A highminded person is one who regards himself as worthy of high things and who is worthy of them (ὁ μεγάλων αὐτὸν ἀξιῶν ἄξιος ὤν). He is distinguished from

(a) a person who is worthy of small things and who regards himself as worthy of them.

(b) a person who regards himself as worthy of high things and is unworthy of them.

(c) a person who takes too low a view of his own worth.

The highminded person, as estimating his own desert neither too highly nor too lowly, occupies an intermediate position. The thing for which he cares most is honour. Meanmindedness (μικροψυχία) is an under-estimate, conceit (χαυνότης) an overestimate, of one's personal desert.

The highminded man, as being worthy of the highest things, must be in the highest degree good. Highmindedness then is, as it were, the crown of the virtues (κόσμος τις τῶν ἀρετῶν).

While caring principally, but not inordinately, for honour, the highminded man takes a moderate view of wealth, political power etc.; he is not excessively elated by good, nor excessively depressed by illfortune.

CHAPTER VIII.

The gifts of fortune contribute to highmindedness, as high birth and great political power or wealth are considered to be titles to honour; but virtue constitutes the sole true title to honour.

People who possess wealth, power etc. without virtue are apt to become supercilious and insolent.

The highminded man alone is justified in his contempt for others.

Characteristics of highmindedness

(a) To shrink from encountering small dangers, but to be ready to encounter great dangers.

(b) To be fond of conferring benefits but ashamed of receiving them.

(c) To try to return benefits with interest.

(d) To be unwilling to ask favours.

(e) To bear oneself with dignity towards the great, but with moderation towards the middle class.

(f) To be free from self-assertion.

(g) To avoid fussiness or hurry.

(h) To act seldom, but effectively.

(i) To be open in one's hatreds and friendships.

(*j*) To care more for reality than for reputation; therefore to be truthful.

(*k*) To eschew servility.

(*l*) To be little given to admiration.

(*m*) Not to bear grudges.

(*n*) To avoid gossip or evil speaking.

(*o*) Not to whine over what is inevitable or insignificant.

(*p*) To prefer nobleness to profit.

CHAPTER IX.

The deficiency corresponding to highmindedness is meanmindedness (μικροψυχία), the excess conceit (χαυνότης). The meanminded person is one who, being worthy of good things, deprives himself of the things of which he is worthy; his spirit is one of self-ignorance and self-depreciation. It results in deterioration of character. The conceited person aims at effect; his spirit is one of self-exaltation.

Meanmindedness, rather than conceit, is opposed to highmindedness.

CHAPTER X.

Highmindedness then has to do with honour on a large scale. The virtue which is related to highmindedness as liberality is related to magnificence, i.e. which has to do with honour on a small scale, has no name. The excessive desire of honour is called ambition (φιλοτιμία); but ambition is a neutral term, being sometimes regarded as a vice, at other times as a virtue. The opposite of ambition is lack of ambition (ἀφιλοτιμία).

CHAPTER XI.

VII. *Gentleness* (πραότης).

Gentleness, or good temper, is a mean state in respect of angry feelings (μεσότης περὶ ὀργάς); the excess is irascibility (ὀργιλότης), the deficiency may be described as a phlegmatic disposition (ἀοργησία).

The excess may take the form of

(a) irascibility (ὀργιλότης).

(b) quick temper (ἀκροχολία).

(c) sullenness (πικρότης).

(d) sternness (χαλεπότης).

The mean state, i.e. good temper, is the state of a person who does not get angry, except with the right persons, on the right occasions, in the right manner etc.

CHAPTER XII.

VIII. *Friendliness* (φιλία).

There is no name for the mean state between complaisance (ἀρεσκεία) and surliness (δυσκολία); it most nearly resembles friendliness. It is the state of a person who in association with other people is neither over-anxious to give pleasure nor over-indifferent about giving pain. If a person seeks to give pleasure without any ulterior object, it is called complaisance, if he seeks to give it for the sake of some personal advantage, it is called flattery (κολακεία).

CHAPTER XIII.

IX. *Truthfulness* (ἀλήθεια).

There is also no name for the mean state between boastfulness (ἀλαζονεία) and irony or self-depreciation (εἰρωνεία). The intermediate character is a species of truthfulness. A departure from truth on the side of exaggeration may be either pretentiousness or boastfulness; such a departure on the side of depreciation is irony or if it applies to small things, humbug ; but exaggerated deficiency, as well as excess, is a form of boastfulness.

Boastfulness is more opposed to truthfulness than irony.

CHAPTER XIV.

X. *Wittiness* (εὐτραπελία).

In respect of relaxation (ἀνάπαυσις) or diversion (διαγωγή) the excess is buffoonery (βωμολοχία), the deficiency boorishness (ἀγριότης), the mean state is wittiness (εὐτραπελία).

The characteristic of wittiness is tact (ἐπιδεξιότης).
A refined gentleman is in action and conversation a law to himself.

CHAPTER XV.

Shame (αἰδώς) is rather an emotion than a moral state. It is an emotion appropriate not to all ages, but to youth. It is virtuous only hypothetically, i.e. it is virtue subsequent to deeds which are wrong in themselves, and ought not to have been done.

BOOK V.

CHAPTER I.

JUSTICE (δικαιοσύνη) AND INJUSTICE (ἀδικία).

Justice is the moral state which makes people capable of doing what is just and makes them just in action and intention. Injustice is the opposite moral state.

The moral states (ἕξεις) are different from the sciences (ἐπιστῆμαι) and faculties (δυνάμεις); for the same faculty or science applies to contraries, but one of two contrary moral states does not apply to its contraries.

One of two contrary moral states may be ascertained from the other, or moral states may be ascertained from a consideration of their phenomena.

CHAPTER II.

The words justice and injustice are used in a plurality of senses, and the various senses being closely allied are apt to be confused. A person is said to be unjust

   (a) if he breaks the law of the land
   (b) if he takes more than his share of anything.

Similarly he is said to be just

   (a) if he keeps the law
   (b) if he acts fairly towards others.

W. N. E.   *d*

Where injustice is equivalent to unfairness, i.e. where it means taking more than one's share (πλεονεξία), it is concerned with the goods of fortune.

CHAPTER III.

The law-breaker being unjust and the law-abiding person just, it follows that whatever is lawful is in some sense just. The object of laws is the interest of the community as a whole. All that tends then to create and to conserve happiness in the body politic is in one sense just.

Justice as so defined is complete virtue in relation to one's neighbours; hence justice alone of the virtues seems to be the good of others. This justice is not a part of virtue but the whole of virtue; the corresponding injustice is not a part of vice but the whole of vice.

CHAPTER IV.

Justice then is either virtue as a whole or a part of virtue; injustice either vice as a whole or a part of vice. In the large sense justice and injustice are concerned with the whole sphere of virtuous or vicious action, in the narrow sense with the goods of fortune, i.e. honour, property etc.

CHAPTER V.

The unjust then is

(a) the illegal

(b) the unfair.

Similarly the just is

(a) the legal

(b) the fair.

But illegality stands to unfairness in the relation of the whole to its part. The partial justice and injustice then are parts of justice and injustice as wholes.

Justice and injustice as wholes are generally determinable by law; they are coextensive with the field of legal enactments. Particular justice may take two forms, viz.

(1) the distribution of honour, wealth etc. among the members of the community

(2) the correction of wrong in private transactions.

Private transactions again may be

(a) voluntary, such as buying, selling, etc.

(b) involuntary :

and, further, involuntary transactions may be

(a) secret, e.g. theft, adultery etc.

(b) violent, e.g. assault, rape, murder etc.

CHAPTER VI.

Particular injustice being equivalent to unfairness, the mean state is fairness or equality (τὸ ἴσον).

But fairness or equality implies two persons or things at least. The just then is

(1) a mean

(2) fair or equal,

(3) relative to certain persons.

Consequently the just implies four terms at least, the persons relatively to whom it is just being two, and the things in which it consists being also two. Also, if the persons are equal, the things will be equal, and where there is inequality of persons, there ought to be inequality in the shares of the things. Justice then is a sort of proportion (ἀνάλογόν τι). Proportion implies four terms ; hence the just requires four terms at least, and an equality of ratio between them. Thus, if A and B are persons, C and D things, as A is to B, so will C be to D.

CHAPTER VII.

The conjunction of A with C and of B with D will be what is just in distribution (διανομή). This justice is a mean between the violations of proportion, it is in mathematical language a geometrical proportion. Hence injustice, being disproportionate, may take the form either of excess or defect, or rather of excess on the one side and of defect on the other.

$d\,2$

Corrective justice (τὸ διορθωτικόν) occurs in private transactions, whether voluntary or involuntary. It is also a form of proportion, but it is an arithmetical not a geometrical proportion. It presupposes an injustice, i.e. an unfairness or unequality, and aims at redressing it by taking away so much from one party and adding so much to the other. Fairness or inequality in this sense is the mean between excess and defect. It is as if a line be divided into unequal segments, and the part by which the larger of the two segments exceeds the half be cut off and added to the smaller segment. It aims at placing people, after exchange, in the same position in which they stood before it.

CHAPTER VIII.

Retaliation (τὸ ἀντιπεπονθός) is not equivalent to justice whether distributive (διανεμητικόν) or corrective (διορθωτικόν). Retaliation takes no account of

(a) a person's character or office
(b) his will.

Requital may be requital either of good or evil. Proportionate requital is produced by cross conjunction (ἡ κατὰ διάμετρον σύζευξις). Suppose A is a builder, B a cobbler, C a house, D a shoe. In order that retaliation or reciprocity (ἀνταπόδοσις) may be attained, it is necessary to equate the goods, viz. the house and the shoe; in other words, the subjects of exchange must be comparable.

Money (νόμισμα) is the means of comparison or equation between objects of exchange. It serves as a single universal standard of measurement. Society rests upon the demand for mutual services. Money is the most stable of goods, its value is the most constant. Thus society implies exchange, exchange equality of goods, equality commensurability, and commensurability money.

CHAPTER IX.

Just conduct then is a mean between committing and suffering injustice. Injustice is an extreme, whether of excess or of defect, justice a mean.

CHAPTER X.

It does not follow, if a person commits injustice (ἀδικεῖ), that he is necessarily unjust (ἄδικος). To be unjust is not to commit an unjust action but to have the moral state of injustice. Justice, i.e. political justice, implies law, it can only exist where the relations of people are legally defined. A magistrate is a guardian of justice and therefore of equality. Justice as between masters and slaves or between parents and children is different from political justice.

Political justice is partly natural, partly conventional. The part of political justice which is natural is that which has the same authority everywhere and is independent of opinion. The part which is conventional is dependent upon law or custom and differs in different places. It is wrong to hold that all political justice is conventional. Every rule of justice or law stands to individual actions in the relation of the universal to particulars. Just or unjust action implies that a person acts voluntarily. Voluntary action has been defined to be such action as is in a person's power and is done by him knowingly; involuntary action such as is not done knowingly or is done knowingly but is not in a person's power or is done by him under compulsion. If a person performs just or unjust actions involuntarily, the justice or injustice is accidental, it is not inherent in the actions.

Voluntary actions are done either with or without deliberate purpose. An action done in ignorance is called a mistake (ἁμάρτημα), if the person affected or the thing done or the instrument or the effect is not such as the agent supposed. It is called a mishap (ἀτύχημα) if the hurt done is contrary to the expectation of the agent. But an unjust action done with knowledge though without deliberation, is an act of injustice (ἀδίκημα). But it is only when the action is the result of deliberate purpose that the agent deserves to be called unjust. Involuntary actions are either venial or not. They are venial, if they are committed not only *in* ignorance but *from* ignorance. They are not venial, if they are not committed from ignorance but in ignorance and from an emotion which is neither natural nor human.

CHAPTER XI.

Is it possible for a person to suffer injustice voluntarily? The answer seems to depend upon the definition of doing injustice. If to do injustice means simply to hurt somebody voluntarily, and voluntariliness implies knowledge of the person, the instrument, and the manner, then a person, e.g. an incontinent person, if he hurts himself voluntarily, may be said to suffer injustice voluntarily. But if, as is probable, to do injustice implies action contrary to the wish of the person to whom it is done, the suffering of injustice cannot be voluntary.

CHAPTER XII.

(1) Is it he who assigns to somebody else more than he deserves, or he who enjoys it, that commits injustice?

(2) Can a person do injustice to himself?

It is the distributor who commits the injustice, for his action is voluntary.

An action, unless it is voluntary, cannot be unjust.

CHAPTER XIII.

Justice is difficult of attainment, as it consists not in actions but in a moral state. Consequently the idea that it is not less characteristic of the just man to act unjustly than to act justly is absurd.

CHAPTER XIV.

EQUITY (ἐπιείκεια).

Equity is not identical with justice nor is it generically different from it. The just and the equitable are both good, but the equitable is better. The equitable is just, but it is not just in the eye of the law; it is a rectification of legal justice. For all law is couched in general terms; but there are cases upon which it is impossible to pronounce correctly in general terms, and equity applies to these cases. Equity in fact represents the mind, as opposed to the rule, of the legislator.

CHAPTER XV.

The question of acting unjustly to oneself affects the right of suicide. The suicide acts unjustly, but unjustly to the state, not to himself. This is the reason why the state punishes suicide. An act of injustice is not only voluntary and deliberate but prior in time to the injury received; but if a person can act unjustly to himself, he will be simultaneously the author and the victim of the same injustice. It is bad to suffer injustice and bad to commit it, but worse to commit it than to suffer it. Speaking metaphorically we may say that there is a justice between the different parts of a man's being; it is in respect of these different parts that a person may be said to be capable of injustice to himself.

BOOK VI.

CHAPTER I.

THE mean lies between the excess and the deficiency. It is also such as right reason decides. But it is necessary to explain this definition of the mean and to explain it by defining the nature of right reason.

CHAPTER II.

It has been laid down that the soul is divisible into two parts,

 (1) the rational (τὸ λόγον ἔχον)

 (2) the irrational (τὸ ἄλογον).

But the rational part may be similarly subdivided.
It includes

 (a) the scientific part (τὸ ἐπιστημονικόν), i.e. the part with which we contemplate such existences as have invariable principles (τὰ ὄντα ὅσων αἱ ἀρχαὶ μὴ ἐνδέχονται ἄλλως ἔχειν).

 (b) the ratiocinative part (τὸ λογιστικόν), i.e. the part with which we contemplate such existences as are variable (τὰ ἐνδεχόμενα ἄλλως ἔχειν).

It is necessary to ascertain the perfect state of each of these parts of the soul.

There are three faculties of the soul which determine action and truth, viz.

(1) Sensation (αἴσθησις)

(2) Reason (νοῦς)

(3) Appetite or Desire (ὄρεξις).

Sensation cannot originate moral action, for brutes possess sensation but are incapable of such action. But as moral virtue is a state of deliberate moral purpose, and moral purpose is deliberative desire, it follows that moral virtue implies

(a) truth of reason,

(b) rightness of desire.

Moral purpose then is the origin of action. The mere intellect by itself possesses no motive power, it must be intellect directed to a certain end, i.e. it must be practical. The moral purpose can have no relation to the past; it is the future or contingent, not the past, which is the subject of deliberation.

CHAPTER III.

There are five means by which the soul arrives at truth, viz.

(1) Art (τέχνη)

(2) Science (ἐπιστήμη)

(3) Prudence (φρόνησις)

(4) Wisdom (σοφία)

(5) Intuitive Reason (νοῦς).

(1) Whatever is the object of science is invariable and eternal. It is also capable of being learnt, whether by induction (ἐπαγωγή) or by syllogism (συλλογισμός). Science then is a demonstrative state of mind; it implies certainty.

CHAPTER IV.

(2) That which is variable includes the objects

(a) of production

(b) of action.

Art may be defined as a rationally productive state of mind; it relates to the creation of things whose existence was not necessary but contingent, and whose original cause lies in the producer himself. The end of art is production, not action. ✕

CHAPTER V.

(3) Prudence is the capacity of deliberating well upon ✕ what is good or expedient for oneself, not in a particular but in a general or comprehensive sense. But deliberation does not apply to such matters as are incapable of alteration or as lie beyond one's own power of action; its end is not production but action.

Prudence therefore is neither a science nor an art. It may be said to be a true rational and practical state of mind in the field of human good and evil. Prudence differs from art ✕

(a) as not admitting of excellence

(b) as preferring involuntary error to voluntary.

It is, in fact, virtue of the opiniative (τὸ δοξαστικόν) part of the soul.

CHAPTER VI.

(4) The first principles of scientific truth are not the subjects of science or art or prudence, neither are they the subjects of wisdom, as the wise man sometimes proceeds from premisses which are not themselves demonstrable.

(5) There remains only the intuitive reason as the means ✕ by which these principles are apprehended.

CHAPTER VII.

Wisdom is either special, as referring to a particular art, or general. General wisdom is the most consummate of the sciences. It is the union of intuitive reason and science. It is higher than statesmanship, as its subjects are, or may be, higher than Man; it is the union of science and intuitive reason in the sphere of things of the most honourable nature.

CHAPTER VIII.

Prudence deals with such things as are of human interest and admit of deliberation. It is a practical virtue, and, as being practical, has to do, not with universals only, but primarily with particulars. The architectonic or supreme form of prudence is statesmanship. But prudence in the strict sense is generally taken to relate to one's own individual interests.

CHAPTER IX.

Prudence then is the knowledge of one's own interests. Such knowledge implies experience, and experience is inconsistent with youth.

Prudence is the antithesis of intuitive reason, as dealing with particular facts which are matters not of scientific knowledge, but of perception.

CHAPTER X.

Deliberation is a particular form of investigation.

Wise deliberation is

   (a)   not science (ἐπιστήμη)

   (b)   not happy conjecture (εὐστοχία)

   (c)   not sagacity (ἀγχίνοια)

   (d)   not opinion (δόξα) of any kind.

But it necessarily implies the exercise of reason. It remains that wise deliberation must be correctness of thought in deliberation. Not that all correct deliberation is wise deliberation; for it is possible to arrive at what is good by a false syllogism. It is correctness of object, manner, and time, in matters of expediency. Also it may be either absolute or relative to a certain end; in a word it may be defined as correctness in matters of expediency with reference to a particular end.

CHAPTER XI.

Intelligence (σύνεσις) is different from opinion. If it were not, everybody would be intelligent. It is also different from prudence, although its sphere is the same. Intelligence is critical, i.e. it makes distinctions; prudence is imperative, i.e. it issues commands. Judgment or consideration (γνώμη) is a correct determination of what is equitable; hence equity is a disposition to forgiveness.

CHAPTER XII.

Intuitive reason, prudence, intelligence, and judgment may be all regarded as having the same tendency; they are all concerned with matters of action, i.e. with ultimate truths; for both the first principles and the particular facts with which intuitive reason deals are ultimate truths (ἔσχατα). Demonstration (ἀπό-δειξις) starts from the truths of intuitive reason and is throughout concerned with those truths.

CHAPTER XIII.

What is the utility of wisdom and prudence?

(a) They are desirable in themselves, as being each a virtue of one of the two parts of the soul.

(b) They are in a sense productive.

(c) They are essential to the discharge of a person's proper function. While virtue ensures the correctness of the moral purpose, prudence decides upon such means as are natural in order to give that purpose effect.

The faculty of hitting upon the means conducive to a given object is called cleverness (δεινότης). Prudence is cleverness tempered by virtue, just as virtue properly so called is natural virtue fortified by reason. Goodness then in a proper sense is impossible without prudence, prudence is impossible without moral virtue.

Prudence does not employ, but aims at producing wisdom; it does not rule wisdom but rules in the interests of wisdom.

BOOK VII.

CHAPTER I.

THERE are three species of moral character to be avoided, viz. vice (κακία) incontinence (ἀκρασία) and brutality (θηριότης). The opposite of vice is virtue; the opposite of incontinence is continence; the opposite of brutality may be called heroic or divine virtue.

CHAPTER II.

It is generally held that the continent man

(a) abides by his calculations

(b) is prevented by his reason from following his wrong desires,

and that the incontinent man

(a) departs from his calculations

(b) is led by his emotions to do what he knows to be wrong.

The relations of continence, temperance, and steadfastness (καρτερία) and again of incontinence and licentiousness, are matters of dispute.

CHAPTER III.

How is it that a person, if his conceptions of duty are right, acts incontinently?

The Socratic denial of incontinence, on the ground that nobody who has a conception of what is best acts against it, is at variance with the facts of experience. Incontinence implies the existence of strong and base desires; temperance implies the absence of such desires. Continence, although it implies adherence to opinion, does not imply adherence to every opinion; for if an opinion is wrong, it is better not to adhere to it.

Again, if there is incontinence in all things and not in regard to the sensual emotions alone, who is continent in an absolute sense?

CHAPTER IV.

Three questions necessarily arise respecting continence,

(1) Can incontinent people be said to act with knowledge, and if so, what is the nature of that knowledge?

(2) What is the sphere of continence or incontinence?

(3) Are the continent person and the steadfast person the same or different?

CHAPTER V.

The word knowledge is used in two distinct senses; it may mean

(a) that a person possesses knowledge, but does not apply it,

(b) that he applies his knowledge.

It is only when wrong action is taken after reflexion that it appears strange. An incontinent person is like a person who is asleep, or mad, or intoxicated; in one sense he possesses, but in another sense he does not possess, knowledge. Brutes are not said to be incontinent, as having no universal conceptions. The deliverance of an incontinent person from ignorance and his restoration to knowledge is similar to a person's recovery from intoxication, or his awakening after sleep. Incontinence then occurs when a person possesses not knowledge in a full sense but only such knowledge as depends on sensation.

CHAPTER VI.

Can a person be incontinent in an absolute sense, and if so what is the sphere of such a person's incontinence?

Pleasures and pains are the sphere in which continence and incontinence are displayed. But the things which produce pleasure are (a) necessary, e.g. the processes of nutrition and of sexual love, (b) not necessary but desirable in themselves, e.g. victory, honour, wealth.

If a person exceeds the limits of right reason in the latter class of things, he is not called incontinent in an absolute sense but incontinent in respect of money, honour etc. ; but if he exceeds those limits in respect of bodily or sensual enjoyments, and exceeds them not of deliberate purpose but contrary to his purpose and intelligence, he is called incontinent in an absolute sense. States of brutality, however produced, lie beyond the pale of human vice and therefore of human incontinence.

CHAPTER VII.

Incontinence in respect of angry passion is less disgraceful than incontinence in respect of sensual desire; for

(1) Passion follows reason in a sense; desire disobeys and disregards reason.

(2) Passion is more natural than the desire of excessive pleasure.

(3) Passion is less cunning than desire.

(4) Passionate action involves pain, but wantonness is associated with pleasure. Continence and incontinence then are properly concerned with bodily desires and pleasures and with such of these desires and pleasures as are human; hence brutes are not called continent or temperate.

Brutality is not so bad as vice, but it is more formidable.

CHAPTER VIII.

The licentious person is worse than the incontinent, as he acts in cold blood, or without a strong momentary desire.

Continence is preferable to steadfastness, as it implies not mere resistance to pain but victory over pleasure.

The love of amusement is rather effeminacy than licentiousness.

Incontinence assumes the form sometimes of impetuosity, at other times of weakness.

CHAPTER IX.

Licentiousness is indisposed to repentance, it is therefore incurable; incontinence is disposed to repentance, it is therefore curable. Vice may be unconscious, incontinence cannot.

Incontinence, unlike licentiousness, does not imply loss of principle.

CHAPTER X.

A person is incontinent, if he does not abide by moral purpose or reason, i.e. by right moral purpose and true reason. A person who abides by his opinion at all costs is called obstinate (ἰσχυρο-γνώμων). Obstinate people are

(1) self-opinionated (ἰδιογνώμονες).

(2) ignorant (ἀμαθεῖς).

(3) boorish (ἄγροικοι).

CHAPTER XI.

Continence is the mean state between excess and deficiency of pleasure in bodily gratifications. Both the excess and the deficiency are vicious, but the deficiency is rarely seen.

The difference between continence and temperance is that the incontinent person and the licentious person both pursue bodily pleasures, but the former does not, and the latter does, regard it as right to pursue them.

Prudence and incontinence are incompatible, as prudence implies virtuous character.

There are various kinds of incontinence. The incontinence which is the result of habit is more easily curable than the incontinence which is the result of nature.

CHAPTER XII.

Three opinions respecting pleasure,

(1) That no pleasure is a good either essentially or accidentally.

(2) That some pleasures are good, but the majority are bad.

(3) That even if every pleasure is a good, the supreme good cannot be pleasure.

(1) In general pleasure is not a good; for

(a) Every pleasure is a process to a natural state, it is not an end.

(b) Pleasure is eschewed by the temperate man.

(c) Not pleasure but painlessness is pursued by the prudent man.

(d) Pleasure is an impediment to thought.

(e) There is no art of pleasure.

(f) Children and brute beasts pursue pleasure.

(2) Pleasures are not all virtuous; for some are disreputable.

(3) Pleasure is not the supreme good, as it is not an end but a process.

CHAPTER XIII.

Good is of two kinds, viz.

(a) Absolute.

(b) Relative.

Moral states then, and also motions and processes, will be of two kinds.

The good is

(a) an activity (ἐνέργεια),

(b) a moral state (ἕξις).

Hence such processes as restore a person to his rational condition are only pleasant in an accidental sense; they are not natural or absolute pleasures.

Nor is it true that in all pleasures there is an end distinct from the pleasures themselves. Pleasure should therefore be defined as an unimpeded activity of the natural state of one's being (ἀνεμπόδιστος ἐνέργεια τῆς κατὰ φύσιν ἕξεως).

Some pleasures may be injurious, but it does not follow that all pleasures are bad.

No moral state is impeded by the pleasure which it produces; it is impeded only by alien pleasures.

If pleasure is not a product of art, neither is any other activity.

Children and brute beasts pursue pleasures, but not absolute pleasures.

CHAPTER XIV.

As pain is an evil, either absolutely or relatively, its opposite, viz. pleasure, must be a good. Also happiness is an activity and an unimpeded activity, but such unimpeded activity is pleasure.

Pleasure of some kind then is the supreme good.

External goods, and goods of fortune are necessary as accessories to happiness; they do not themselves constitute happiness.

The fact that all brutes and all men pursue pleasure is an indication that pleasure is in some sense the supreme good; but it is a mistake to identify pleasure with bodily pleasures.

CHAPTER XV.

Reasons why bodily pleasures appear more desirable than other pleasures.

(1) Such pleasures drive out pain.

(2) They are violent, and are therefore pursued by people who are incapable of other pleasures. Human nature, not being simple, requires change of pleasures. God enjoys one simple pleasure everlastingly.

BOOK VIII.

CHAPTER I.

FRIENDSHIP OR LOVE (φιλία).

(1) It is indispensable at all ages and in all the circumstances of life.

(2) It is natural, as is seen in the natural love of parents for their offspring, not only among human beings, but throughout the animal world.

(3) It is social, as being the bond which holds states together.

(4) It is noble, and is therefore the subject of praise.

CHAPTER II.

What is the nature of friendship or love?

It has been defined as a sort of likeness (ὁμοιότης). But likeness whether of temper or of occupation has been also held to be prejudicial to friendship or love.

In order to understand friendship or love it is necessary to understand what is lovable.

The lovable is that which is good or pleasant or useful, and a thing is useful if it is a means to what is good or pleasant. It is relative good, i.e. good considered not absolutely but in relation to an individual, that is lovable in his eyes. The term friendship or love is not applicable to the affection felt for inanimate things, for

(1) such things cannot reciprocate affection,

(2) we do not wish the good of such things, e.g. we cannot be said to wish the good of wine.

Friendship or love as distinguished from mere good will (εὔνοια) requires

(a) that it should be reciprocated

(b) that it should not be unknown to either person.

CHAPTER III.

As the motives of friendship are three, there will be three kinds of friendship. Where the motive is utility or pleasure, the friendship is not disinterested; it is therefore accidental and easily dissoluble. Friendships of utility are most common among the old, friendships of pleasure among the young.

CHAPTER IV.

Perfect friendship or love is the friendship or love of people who are good and alike in virtue.

(1) It implies

   (a) goodness, both absolute and relative, in the two friends,

   (b) pleasantness.

(2) It satisfies the conditions of permanency,

(3) it is rare, as such people are rare, and it takes time to know them.

CHAPTER V.

Friendships based upon pleasure or upon utility resemble the perfect friendship, as the good are both pleasant and useful to one another. But it is only the good who are friends for the friends' own sake. It is only the good whose friendship cannot be destroyed by calumnies. Other friendships than those of the good may be said to be called friendships by analogy.

CHAPTER VI.

Bad people then may be friends from motives of pleasure or utility; good people are friends from love of the persons themselves. The characteristic element of friendship or love may be either a moral state or an activity. Absence, e.g. does not destroy friendship. Friendship generally implies community of life ; hence it is difficult for old or austere people.

e 2

CHAPTER VII.

Affection (φίλησις) resembles an emotion (πάθος), friendship (φιλία) resembles a moral state (ἕξις), for

(1) the love of friends involves moral purpose

(2) the desire of a person's good for his own sake is the issue of a moral state.

These conditions are best realized in the friendship of the good.

Perfect friendship is impossible in relation to a great number of people. The friendship which is based upon pleasure more nearly resembles perfect friendship than the friendship which rests upon utility.

CHAPTER VIII.

Friendships based upon exchange of services are seldom permanent. Where friendship or love depends upon superiority, as in the relation of a father to his children, the affection ought to be proportionate to the superiority, i.e. the superior party ought to receive more affection than he gives.

CHAPTER IX.

In justice proportionate (τὸ κατ' ἀξίαν) equality is the first consideration, quantitative (τὸ κατὰ πυσόν) equality the second; in friendship quantitative equality is the first consideration, and proportionate equality the second. A vast superiority between persons precludes friendship, as in the case of the Gods.

Ambition makes people wish to be loved rather than to love others, as love is a form of honour. But honour is desired as a sign of respect or admiration, love is desired for its own sake; hence it is better to be loved than to be honoured.

CHAPTER X.

Friendship or love seems to consist rather in loving than in being loved; witness the love of mothers for their children.

A vicious friendship possesses no stability. A utilitarian friendship lasts as long as the utility lasts, but not longer; it is generally a union of opposites, e.g. of a poor man and a rich man.

CHAPTER XI.

Friendship and justice have the same occupations and the same sphere, for friendship is a form of association, and every association involves justice of some kind. As justice is of different kinds, so is friendship. All associations may be said to be parts of the political association ; hence friendship is a political virtue.

CHAPTER XII.

There are three kinds of polity, viz.

(1) Kingship (βασιλεία).

(2) Aristocracy (ἀριστοκρατία).

(3) Timocracy (τιμοκρατία), which depends upon a property qualification.

There are three perversions or corruptions (παρεκβάσεις) of these polities, viz.

(1) tyranny (τυραννίς) the perversion of kingship

(2) oligarchy (ὀλιγαρχία) the perversion of aristocracy

(3) democracy (δημοκρατία) the perversion of timocracy.

It is possible to discover models of these constitutions in households. The association of father and children takes the form of kingship ; the association of master and slave takes the form of tyranny ; the association of husband and wife takes the form of aristocracy. Where the husband is lord of everything, it is an oligarchy. The association of brothers resembles timocracy. A household in which everybody does as he chooses and there is no government resembles a democracy.

CHAPTER XIII.

There is a friendship or love which is proper to each of these several polities.

The friendship or love of a king to his subjects takes the form of superiority in benefaction; that of a father to his children is similar to it. The friendship or love of husband and wife is the same as exists in an aristocracy ; the friendship or love of brothers is similar to that which is characteristic of a timocracy. In a tyranny friendship is practically non-existent ; the relation of tyrant and subjects is like the relation of master and slaves.

CHAPTER XIV.

Parents feel affection for their children as being a part of themselves ; children feel affection for their parents as the source of their being. The friendship or love of brothers is like that of comrades (ἑταῖροι) for each other, but it is intensified. Among other kinsmen the elements of love are proportionate to the nearness of the kinship. The love of husband and wife is a natural law ; it derives strength from utility and pleasure, but also from virtue.

Children are a bond of union between parents.

CHAPTER XV.

Quarrelling arises chiefly in such friendship as depends upon utility. It seldom occurs in the friendship which depends upon pleasure. The friendship which depends upon utility is either moral (ἠθική) or legal (νομική), i.e. is based either upon character or upon stated conditions. Friendship upon stated conditions implies a definite *quid pro quo*. Where the basis of friendship is utility, the measure of the utility is the benefit done to the recipient rather than the intention of the benefactor. In friendships depending upon virtue there is no room for quarrelling.

CHAPTER XVI.

Inequality in the position or character of friends affords occasion for quarrelling. In such friendship the superior person ought to receive a larger share of honour, the needy person a larger share of profit. It is on this principle that honour is paid to the great officers of state. In extreme cases, e.g. in the relation of man to the Gods, an adequate repayment is impossible. Hence the duty of a son to his father is greater than that of a father to his son.

BOOK IX.

CHAPTER I.

HETEROGENEOUS friendships (αἱ ἀνομοιειδεῖς φιλίαι) are preserved by the principle of proportion (τὸ ἀνάλογον). The friendship of love is especially apt to be destroyed by the violation of that principle.

Is the value of a benefaction to be settled by the author or by the recipient of the benefaction ? They may clearly set different values upon it. It would seem that the recipient should settle it, but should settle it with regard to his feelings before he received it, not to his feelings when he has actually received it.

CHAPTER II.

Questions of casuistry relating to friendship, e.g. Is the respect and obedience due to a father unlimited ? Ought a person to serve a friend in preference to a virtuous man ? Ought he to repay a debt to a benefactor rather than make a present to a comrade ?

The general rule is that it is a duty to repay services in preference to conferring favours, but the rule is open to exceptions. A father does not possess a claim to unlimited respect, although his claim to the highest degree of respect is indisputable. It is an especial duty to afford parents the means of living. But generally every person or class of persons to whom we stand in relation is entitled to a particular respect, and we must pay due respect to each.

CHAPTER III.

Ought we to dissolve friendships with people whose character is no longer what it once was ?

If the motive of the friendship was utility or pleasure, the dissolution appears to be reasonable. If it was character, the dissolution is inevitable, unless indeed it appears that the vice which dissolves the friendship may be cured. Any wide moral discrepancy leads to dissolution of friendship; but he who has once been a friend cannot be altogether as a stranger.

CHAPTER IV.

The love of friends is an expansion of self-love. The characteristics of friendship are all found in the relation of the virtuous man to himself. They do not exist in the relation of a vicious man to himself; for vice destroys the sympathy of parts and unity of purpose which are indispensable to friendship or love.

CHAPTER V.

Goodwill (εὔνοια) resembles friendship (φιλία), but differs from it, as goodwill may be directed towards people who are unknown to us and who do not know that we wish them well. Goodwill differs from affection (φίλησις) for

(1) it does not imply the same intensity of feeling

(2) it may arise in a moment; it does not demand familiarity.

Goodwill may be said to be the germ of friendship or to be unproductive friendship, and to become friendship only by lapse of time and by familiarity, although not such friendship as is based on utility or pleasure; for goodwill depends on virtue or goodness.

CHAPTER VI.

Unanimity (ὁμόνοια) is a mark of friendship, unanimity not being mere unity of opinion, which may exist among people who do not know each other, but agreement in purpose and policy. Unanimity is impossible except among the virtuous; the vicious, seeking each an advantage over the other, cannot be unanimous.

CHAPTER VII.

Why is it that benefactors are better friends to the recipients of their benefactions than the recipients to their benefactors? It is not merely that benefactors are like creditors, and recipients like debtors. It is that all people feel affection for their own work, and that benefactors stand towards the recipient of their benefactions in the relation of an author or creator to his work, and also that the benefactor feels his action to be noble, that he enjoys the consciousness of activity, and that the fact of taking trouble for a person or thing is itself a motive to affection.

CHAPTER VIII.

Should a person love himself or somebody else most? Excessive self-love is generally censured. On the other hand the conditions of friendship are best realized, as has been seen, in the relation of a man to himself. The explanation seems to lie in the meaning of self-love. If a person is called a lover of self, as assigning to himself an undue share of such things as money and honour, he is open to censure. But if he is so called, as feeling affection for the supreme part of his being, i.e. for his reason, and as cultivating it to the utmost, he deserves praise. In this sense a good man ought to be a lover of self; but his self-love ought to be a spur to noble actions.

CHAPTER IX.

Does the happy man need friends? On the one hand it is said that, as being happy, he possesses all good things; therefore he has no need of friends; on the other hand, that if he possesses all good things, he must possess the greatest of all external goods, viz. friends. Beneficence too, which is the part of the good man, implies objects of beneficence, and of such objects the best are his friends. Also, Man as a social being must live in community with others and if so, must live preferentially with friends and virtuous people. The happy man does not need friends who may be useful to him, but he needs friends towards whom he may exercise his ✕ virtuous activity. Also human life is defined by the faculty of sensation or thought, but a faculty is intelligible only by reference to its activity, and the exercise of the activity implies persons towards whom it may be exercised, i.e. friends.

CHAPTER X.

What is the true limit to the number of a person's friends ?
The answer depends on the character of the friends. If expediency is the motive of friendship, the number of friends should not be larger than is sufficient for one's own life; if the motive is pleasure, the number should not be large, as a few friends are enough to sweeten life. There is not the same limitation in the case of virtuous friends, but a limitation is made by the impossibility of standing in a relation of true friendship to an unlimited number of people. It would seem that the limit of such friendships will be found to be the highest number of persons with whom one can live a common life.

CHAPTER XI.

Friendships are valuable both in prosperity and in adversity. They are nobler in prosperity, but more necessary in adversity. It is a duty to be forward in inviting friends to share one's good fortune, but slow in inviting them to share one's ill fortune.

CHAPTER XII.

The essence of friendship or love is association (κοινωνία); hence community of life is essential to friendship or love. But this community of life, while it elevates the friendship of the good, deteriorates and degrades the friendship of the wicked.

BOOK X.

CHAPTER I.

IMPORTANCE of discussing pleasure (ἡδονή), as the formation of virtuous character depends largely upon a rightly directed sense of pleasure and dislike.

Some people hold that pleasure is the good, i.e. the supreme good, others that it is something utterly bad. The latter view is inconsistent with human experience.

CHAPTER II.

It was the view of Eudoxus that pleasure is the good because

    (1) all things, whether rational or irrational, aim at pleasure.

    (2) pleasure is an end in itself

    (3) the addition of pleasure to any good renders that good more desirable.

Pleasure may be a good, yet not the highest good. It may be a good although

    (a) it is not a quality (ποιότης),

    (b) it possesses the element of indefiniteness (τὸ ἀόριστον).

It is not a process of motion (κίνησις) or production (γένεσις), as it is not characterized by quickness and slowness. It is not a satisfaction of the natural state of man's being, although the process of satisfaction may be attended with pleasure. It is the pleasures of eating and drinking which have given rise to the theory that pleasure is a process of satisfaction; but other pleasures, e.g. the pleasures of mathematics, have no antecedent pain. There are immoral, as well as moral pleasures, but they do not prove pleasure to be a bad thing, as they are not pleasant except to people who are in a bad condition. The truth seems to be this : Pleasure is not the good, nor are all pleasures desirable, but only such pleasures as are not immoral in their origin.

CHAPTER III.

NATURE OR CHARACTER OF PLEASURE.

Pleasure, like sight, is perfect at any time; it is not made more perfect by increased duration of time. Hence pleasure is not a motion, as every motion takes a certain time. Pleasure is a whole, it is not divisible into parts; it is therefore not a motion or process of production.

CHAPTER IV.

Every sense exercises its activity upon its own object and the perfection of the activity implies

(1)   that the sense should be in itself in a sound condition

(2)   that the object should be the noblest that falls within its domain.

When this is the case, the activity is not only most perfect, but most pleasant.

Every sense has its proper pleasure. Pleasure perfects the activity not as something inherent in it, but as something superadded to it.

The impossibility of feeling pleasure continuously arises from the incapacity of human nature for continuous activity. Pleasure, as perfecting the activities, perfects life.

CHAPTER V.

Pleasures are of different kinds, e.g. the pleasures of the intellect and the different pleasures of the senses. Pleasure increases activity, but the pleasures of one activity may be impediments to the exercise of another. Alien pleasures have much the same effect upon a particular activity as pains. As activities differ in goodness and badness, so do pleasures. Not only are the pleasures of beings who are different in kind themselves different, but different beings of the same kind have different pleasures; thus what is pleasant to one man is unpleasant to another. It is the pleasures of the virtuous man which are true pleasures. The pleasures belonging to the activity or activities of the perfect man are perfect pleasures.

CHAPTER VI.

Happiness, as has been said, is not a moral state (ἕξις) but an activity (ἐνέργεια). It is also an activity desirable in itself. Happiness does not consist in amusement or in relaxation but in virtuous activity.

CHAPTER VII.

Happiness is therefore the activity of the highest part of Man's nature. It is a speculative rather than practical activity, for

(1) it is the activity of the intuitive reason (νοῦς), which is the highest human faculty

(2) it is the most continuous form of activity

(3) it is the most pleasant form of activity

(4) it possesses in a preeminent degree the character of self-sufficiency (αὐτάρκεια).

Leisure is essential to happiness.

The activity of the intuitive reason is the highest, as it does not aim at any end beyond itself. It possesses its proper pleasure, and this pleasure enhances the activity. This then is the perfect happiness of man, if a perfect or complete length of life is given it. The reason being divine in comparison with the rest of man's nature, the life which accords with reason will be divine in comparison with human life in general. A man's reason, as being the supreme part of his nature, may be called his true self.

CHAPTER VIII.

Non-speculative virtue is happy only in a secondary sense. The moral virtues are inseparably allied to the emotions and so to the physical organization of human nature. But the happiness which consists in the exercise of the reason is independent of the emotions. It needs external resources, but does not need them to the same extent as moral virtue. Virtue implies both moral purpose and moral performance. Perfect happiness is a species of speculative activity, as appears from the conception of the Gods, who are *ex hypothesi* preeminently happy, and whose happiness displays itself in activity, but who cannot be supposed to perform moral actions. The lower animals, being incapable of speculative activity, are incapable of happiness.

CHAPTER IX.

Man requires external prosperity, but only so much prosperity as is requisite for virtue. Excessive prosperity is rather prejudicial than helpful to happiness. It is activity directed by reason which constitutes the best title to the favour of Heaven.

CHAPTER X.

It is not the knowledge but the practice of virtue which is the end of ethical study. Mere theory is impotent to make men good. It has been held that men are made good

(1) by nature ($\phi\acute{v}\sigma\epsilon\iota$)

(2) by habit ($\H\H\H$)

(3) by teaching ($\delta\iota\delta\alpha\chi\hat{\eta}$).

Virtue presupposes a certain suitability of character; but the character needs education under virtuous laws. It needs also the habitual practice of what is right in after-life. Hence the importance of education and of the rewards and punishments appointed by law. It is only in Sparta and a few other states that education or the discipline of the character has been understood to fall within the province of legislation. In education individual methods are superior to general, as it demands the study of individual character. But this individual study must itself be based upon an understanding of principles. The principles of legislation are taught not by statesmen but by sophists, but the sophists are ignorant of the true nature of statesmanship. It is necessary therefore to investigate legislation and for that purpose to collect and compare political constitutions, to consider their merits and defects, and to determine the means by which they are preserved or destroyed. Thus Ethics leads up to Politics.

THE NICOMACHEAN ETHICS

OF ARISTOTLE.

BOOK I.

EVERY art and every scientific inquiry, and similarly ᴄʜᴀᴘ. I. every action and purpose, may be said to aim at some Nature of the good. good. Hence the good has been well defined as that at which all things aim. But it is clear that there is a difference in the ends; for the ends are sometimes Difference activities, and sometimes results beyond the mere in the ends. activities. Also, where there are certain ends beyond the actions, the results are naturally superior to the activities.

As there are various actions, arts, and sciences, it Subor-follows that the ends are also various. Thus health dination of arts and is the end of medicine, a vessel of shipbuilding, victory sciences. of strategy, and wealth of domestic economy. It often happens that there are a number of such arts or sciences which fall under a single faculty, as the art of making bridles, and all such other arts as make the instruments of horsemanship, under horsemanship, and this again as well as every military action under strategy, and in the same way other arts or sciences under other faculties. But in all these cases the ends of the architectonic arts or sciences, whatever they may be, are more desirable than those of the subordinate arts or sciences, as it is for the sake of the former that the latter are themselves sought after. It makes no difference to the argument whether the activities themselves are the ends of the actions, or something else beyond the activities as in the above mentioned sciences.

If it is true that in the sphere of action there is an end which we wish for its own sake, and for the sake of which we wish everything else, and that we do not desire all things for the sake of something else (for, if that is so, the process will go on *ad infinitum*, and our desire will be idle and futile) it is clear that this will be the good or the supreme good.

Import-ance of knowing the su-preme good.

Does it not follow then that the knowledge of this supreme good is of great importance for the conduct of life, and that, *if we know it*, we shall be like archers who have a mark at which to aim, we shall have a better chance of attaining what we want? But, if this is the case, we must endeavour to comprehend, at least in outline, its nature, and the science or faculty to which it belongs.

Science or faculty of the su-preme good. Ethics a department of Politics.

It would seem that this is the most authoritative or architectonic science or faculty, and such is evidently the political; for it is the political science or faculty which determines what sciences are necessary in states, and what kind of sciences should be learnt,

and how far they should be (learnt by particular)
people. We perceive too that the faculties which are
held in the highest esteem, e.g. strategy, domestic
economy, and rhetoric, are subordinate to it. But
as it makes use of the other practical sciences, and
also legislates upon the things to be done and the
things to be left undone, it follows that its end will
comprehend the ends of all the other sciences, and
will therefore be the true good of mankind. For
although the good of an individual is identical with the
good of a state, yet the good of the state, whether in
attainment or in preservation, is evidently greater
and more perfect. For while in an individual by
himself it is something to be thankful for, it is nobler
and more divine in a nation or state.

These then are the objects at which the present
inquiry aims, and it is in a sense a political[1] inquiry.
But our statement of the case will be adequate, if it
be made with all such clearness as the subject-matter
admits; for it would be as wrong to expect the same
degree of accuracy in all reasonings as in all manu-
factures. Things noble and just, which are the
subjects of investigation in political science, exhibit
so great a diversity and uncertainty that they are
sometimes thought to have only a conventional, and
not a natural, existence. There is the same sort of
uncertainty in regard to good things, as it often
happens that injuries result from them; thus there
have been cases in which people were ruined by

Ethics not
an exact
science.

---

[1] It is characteristic of Aristotle's philosophy to treat Ethics
as a branch or department of Politics.

wealth, or again by courage. As our subjects then and our premisses are of this nature, we must be content to indicate the truth roughly and in outline ; and as our subjects and premisses are true generally *but not universally,* we must be content to arrive at conclusions which are only generally true. It is right to receive the particular statements which are made in the same spirit ; for an educated person will expect accuracy in each subject only so far as the nature of the subject allows ; he might as well accept probable reasoning from a mathematician as require demonstrative proofs from a rhetorician. But everybody is competent to judge the subjects which he understands, and is a good judge of them. It follows that in particular subjects it is a person of *special* education, and in general a person of universal education, who is a good judge. Hence the young[1] are not proper students of political science, as they have no experience of the actions of life which form the premisses and subjects of the reasonings. Also it may be added that from their tendency to follow their emotions they will not study the subject to any purpose or profit, as its end is not knowledge but action. It makes no difference whether a person is young in years or youthful in character ; for the defect *of which I speak* is not one of time but is due to the emotional character of his

The young not qualified to be students of Ethics.

---

[1] This is believed to be the passage which Shakespeare had in mind, though the reference to it is put in Hector's mouth,

"young men, whom Aristotle thought
Unfit to hear moral philosophy."
  Troilus and Cressida, Act ii. Scene 2.

life and pursuits. Knowledge is as useless to such a person as it is to an intemperate person. But where the desires and actions of people are regulated by reason the knowledge of these subjects will be extremely valuable.)

But having said so much by way of preface as to CHAP. II. the students of political science, the spirit in which it should be studied, and the object which we set before ourselves, let us resume our argument as follows :

⌐ As every knowledge and moral purpose aspires to some good, what is in our view the good at which the political science aims, and what is the highest of all The end of practical goods ? As to its name there is, I may say, science. a general agreement. The masses and the cultured classes agree in calling it happiness, and conceive Happiness. that "to live well" or "to do well" is the same thing as "to be happy." But as to the nature of happiness Nature of they do not agree, nor do the masses give the same happiness. account of it as the philosophers. The former define it as something visible and palpable, e.g. pleasure, wealth, or honour; different people give different definitions of it, and often the same person gives different definitions at different times ; for when a person has been ill, it is health, when he is poor, it is wealth, and, if he is conscious of his own ignorance, he envies people who use grand language above his own comprehension. Some *philosophers*[1] on the other hand have held that, besides these various goods, there is an absolute good which is the cause of goodness in them all. It would perhaps be a waste of time to examine all these opinions, it will be

[1] Aristotle is thinking of the Platonic "ideas."

enough to examine such as are most popular or as
seem to be more or less reasonable.

Deductive and inductive reasoning: first principles. But we must not fail to observe the distinction
between the reasonings which proceed from first
principles and the reasonings which lead up to first
principles. For Plato[1] was right in raising the
difficult question whether the *true* way was from first
principles or to first principles, as in the race-course
from the judges to the goal, or *vice versa*. We must
begin then with such facts as are known. But facts
may be known in two ways, i.e. either relatively to
ourselves or absolutely. It is probable then that *we*
must begin with such facts as are known to us, *i.e.*
relatively. It is necessary therefore, if a person is
to be a competent student of what is noble and just
and of politics in general, that he should have received a good moral training. For the fact that a
thing is so is a first principle or starting-point[2],
and, if the fact is sufficiently clear, it will not be
necessary to go on to ask the reason of it. / But a
person who has received a good moral training either
possesses first principles, or will have no difficulty
in acquiring them. But if he does not possess them,
and cannot acquire them, he had better lay to heart
Hesiod's lines[3]:

[1] The reference is probably not to any special passage in
the dialogues of Plato, but to the general drift or scope of the
Socratic dialectics.

[2] Aristotle's reasoning depends in part on the double meaning
of ἀρχή viz. (1) starting-point or beginning, (2) first principle or
axiomatic truth.

[3] Ἔργα καὶ Ἡμέραι 291—295.

"Far best is he who is himself all-wise,
And he, too, good who listens to wise words;
But whoso is not wise nor lays to heart
Another's wisdom is a useless man."

But to return from our digression : It seems not Chap. III.
unreasonable that people should derive their concep- Different conception of the good or of happiness from men's lives. tions of happiness.
Thus ordinary or vulgar people conceive it to be
pleasure, and accordingly approve a life of enjoyment.
For there are practically three prominent lives, the
sensual, the political, and, thirdly, the speculative.
Now the mass of men present an absolutely slavish
appearance, as choosing the life of brute beasts, but they
meet with consideration because so many persons in
authority share the tastes of Sardanapalus[1]. Cultivated
and practical people, on the other hand, identify
happiness with honour, as honour is the general end
of political life. But this appears too superficial for
our present purpose ; for honour seems to depend
more upon the people who pay it than upon the
person to whom it is paid, and we have an intuitive
feeling that the good is something which is proper to
a man himself and cannot easily be taken away from
him. It seems too that the reason why men seek
honour is that they may be confident of their own
goodness. Accordingly they seek it at the hands of
the wise and of those who know them well, and they
seek it on the ground of virtue ; hence it is clear that
in their judgment at any rate virtue is superior to
honour. It would perhaps be right then to look
upon virtue rather than honour as being the end of

[1] The most luxurious, and the last, Assyrian monarch.

the political life. Yet virtue again, it appears, lacks completeness; for it seems that a man may possess virtue and yet be asleep or inactive throughout life, and, not only so but he may experience the greatest calamities and misfortunes. But nobody would call such a life a life of happiness, unless he were maintaining a paradox. It is not necessary to dwell further on this subject, as it is sufficiently discussed in the popular philosophical treatises[1]. The third life is the speculative which we will investigate hereafter[2].

The life of money-making is in a sense a life of constraint, and it is clear that wealth is not the good of which we are in quest; for it is useful in part as a means to something else. It would be a more reasonable view therefore that the things mentioned before, viz. *sensual pleasure, honour and virtue*, are ends than that wealth is, as they are things which are desired on their own account. Yet these too are apparently not ends, although much argument has been employed[3] to show that they are.

Chap. IV.
The universal good.

We may now dismiss this subject; but it will perhaps be best to consider the universal *good*, and to discuss the meaning in which the phrase is used,

---

[1] The "popular philosophical treatises" τὰ ἐγκύκλια φιλοσο-φήματα as they are called περὶ οὐρανοῦ i. ch. 9, p. 279 A₃₀ represent, as I suppose, the discussions and conclusions of thinkers outside the Aristotelian school and are in fact the same as the ἐξωτερικοὶ λόγοι.

[2] The investigation of the speculative life occurs in Book x.

[3] The usage of Aristotle is in favour of taking καταβέβληνται to mean "has been employed" rather than "has been wasted"; see especially περὶ Κόσμου ch. 6, p. 397 B₁₉.

although there is this difficulty in such an enquiry, that the *doctrine of* ideas has been introduced by our friends[1]. Yet it will perhaps seem the best, and indeed the right course, at least when the truth is at stake, to go so far as to sacrifice what is near and dear to us, especially as we are philosophers. For friends and truth are both dear to us, but it is a sacred duty to prefer the truth.

Now the authors of this theory did not make ideas of things in which they predicated priority and posteriority. Hence they did not constitute an idea of numbers. But good is predicated equally of substance, quality and relation, and the absolute or essential, *i.e. substance*, is in its nature prior to the relative, as relativity is like an offshoot or accident of existence ; hence there cannot be an idea which is common to them both. Again, there are as many ways of predicating good as of predicating existence ; for it is predicated of substance as e.g. of God or the mind, or of quality as of the virtues, or of quantity as of the mean, or of relativity as of the useful, or of time as of opportunity, or of place as of a habitation, and so on. It is clear then that it cannot be a common universal idea or a unity; otherwise it would not be predicated in all the categories[2] but only in one. Thirdly, as there is a single science of all such things as fall under a single idea, there would have been a single science of all good things, *if the idea of "good" were single ;* but in fact there are many sciences even of such good things as fall under

[Side note: Doctrine of ideas.]

[Side note: No universal idea of "good."]

---

[1] In reference, of course, to Plato.

[2] For the "categories", see Κατηγορίαι ch. 4.

a single category, strategy, e.g. being the science
of opportunity in war, and medicine the science of
opportunity in disease, medicine again being the
science of the mean in respect of food, and gymnastic
the science of the mean in respect of exercise. It
would be difficult, too, to say what is meant by the
"absolute" in anything, if in "absolute man" and in
"man" there is one and the same conception of man.
For there will be no difference between them in
respect of manhood, and, if so, neither will there be
any difference between "absolute good" and "good"
in respect of goodness. (Nor again will good be
more good if it is eternal, since a white thing which
lasts for a long time is not whiter than that which
lasts for a single day.) There seems to be more
plausibility in the doctrine of the Pythagoreans[1]
who place unity in the catalogue of goods, and
Speusippus[2] apparently agrees with them. However these are questions which may be deferred
to another occasion ; but there is an objection to my
arguments which suggests itself, viz. that the *Platonic*
theory does not apply to every good, that the things
which in themselves are sought after and welcomed
are reckoned as one species and the things which
tend to produce or in any sense preserve these or to
prevent their opposites are reckoned as goods in a
secondary sense as being means to these. It is clear

---

[1] The point is that it is apparently more reasonable to describe
unity as a good than to describe good as a unity. The Pythagoreans, or some of them, drew up catalogues of opposites
(συστοιχίαι), as Aristotle explains *Metaph.* i. ch. 5.

[2] Plato's nephew and successor in the Academy.

then that there will be two kinds of goods, some Two kinds
being absolute goods, and others secondary. Let us of "good": ideal and
then separate goods which are merely serviceable practic-
from absolute goods and consider if they are conceived able.
as falling under a single idea. But what kind of
things is it that may be defined as absolute goods?
Will it be all such as are sought after independently
of their consequences, e.g. wisdom, sight, and certain
pleasures and honours? For granting that we seek
after these sometimes as means to something else,
still we may define them as absolute goods. Or is
none of these things an absolute good, nor anything
else except the idea? But then the type *or idea*
will be purposeless, *i.e. it will not comprise any
particulars.* If, on the other hand, these things too
are absolute goods, the conception of the good will
necessarily appear the same in them all, as the
conception of whiteness appears the same in snow
and in white lead. But the conception of honour,
wisdom and pleasure, are distinct and different in
respect of goodness. "Good" then is not a common
term falling under one idea. But in what sense is
the term used? For it does not seem to be an
accidental homonymy[1]. Is it because all goods issue
from one source or all tend to one end; or is it
rather a case of analogy? for as the sight is to the
body, so is the mind to the soul, *i.e. the mind may be
called the eye of the soul, and so on.* But it will

---

[1] What is meant by an "accidental homonymy" or equivo-
cation is easily seen in the various senses of a single English word
such as *bull.*

perhaps be well to leave this subject for the present, as an exact discussion of it would belong rather to a different branch of philosophy. But the same is true of the idea ; for even if there is some one good which is predicated of all these things, or some abstract and absolute good, it will plainly not be such as a man finds practicable and attainable, and therefore will not be such a good as we are in search of. It will possibly be held, however, that it is worth while to apprehend this *universal good,* as having a relation to the goods which are attainable and practicable ; for if we have this as a model, we shall be better able to know the things which are good relatively to ourselves, and, knowing them, to acquire them. Now although there is a certain plausibility in this theory, it seems not to harmonize with scientific experience ; for while all sciences aim at a certain good and seek to supply a deficiency, they omit the knowledge of the universal good. Yet it is not reasonable to suppose that what would be so extremely helpful is ignored, and not sought at all by artists generally. But it is difficult to see what benefit a cobbler or carpenter will get in reference to his art by knowing the absolute good, or how the contemplation of the absolute idea will make a person a better physician or general. For it appears that a physician does not regard health abstractedly, but regards the health of man or rather perhaps of a particular man, as he gives his medicine to individuals.

CHAP. V.
Nature of
the prac-
ticable
good.

But leaving this subject for the present let us revert to the good of which we are in quest and consider what its nature may be. For it is clearly different in different actions or arts ; it is one thing in medicine, another in strategy, and so on. What then is the good in each of these instances ? It is presumably that for the sake of which all else is done. This in medicine is health, in strategy, victory, in domestic architecture, a house, and so on. But in every action and purpose it is the end, as it is for the sake of the end that people all do everything else. If then there is a certain end of all action, it will be this which is the practicable good, and if there are several such ends it will be these.

Our argument has arrived by a different path at the same conclusion as before ; but we must endeavour to elucidate it still further. As it appears that there are more ends than one and some of these, e.g. wealth, flutes, and instruments generally we desire as means to something else, it is evident that they are not all final ends. But the highest good is clearly something final. Hence if there is only one final end, Final good. this will be the object of which we are in search, and if there are more than one, it will be the most final of them. We speak of that which is sought after for its own sake as more final than that which is sought after as a means to something else ; we speak of that which is never desired as a means to something else as more final than the things which are desired both in themselves and as means to something else ; and we speak of a thing as absolutely final, if it is always desired in itself and never as a means to something else.

It seems that happiness preeminently answers to Happiness

the final
good.

this description, as we always desire happiness for its own sake and never as a means to something else, whereas we desire honour, pleasure, intellect, and every virtue, partly for their own sakes (for we should desire them independently of what might result from them) but partly also as being means to happiness, because we suppose they will prove the instruments of happiness. Happiness, on the other hand, nobody desires for the sake of these things, nor indeed as a means to anything else at all.

We come to the same conclusion if we start from the consideration of self-sufficiency, if it may be assumed that the final good is self-sufficient. But when we speak of self-sufficiency, we do not mean that a person leads a solitary life all by himself, but that he has parents, children, wife, and friends, and fellow-citizens in general, as man is naturally a social being. But here it is necessary to prescribe some limit; for if the circle be extended so as to include parents, descendants, and friends' friends, it will go on indefinitely. Leaving this point, however, for future investigation, we define the self-sufficient as that which, taken by itself, makes life desirable, and wholly free from want, and this is our conception of happiness.

Again, we conceive happiness to be the most desirable of all things, and that not merely as one among other good things. If it were one among other good things, the addition of the smallest good would increase its desirableness; for the accession makes a superiority of goods, and the greater of two goods is always the more desirable. It appears then that happiness is something final and self-sufficient, being the end of all action.

Perhaps, however, it seems a truth which is Chap. VI. generally admitted, that happiness is the supreme good; what is wanted is to define its nature a little Nature of happiness. more clearly. The best way of arriving at such a definition will probably be to ascertain the function of Man. For, as with a flute-player, a statuary, or any artisan, or in fact anybody who has a definite function and action, his goodness, or excellence seems to lie in his function, so it would seem to be with Man, if indeed he has a definite function. Can it be said then that, while a carpenter and a cobbler have definite functions and actions, Man, unlike them, is naturally functionless? The reasonable view is that, as the eye, the hand, the foot, and similarly each several part of the body has a definite function, so Man_may be regarded as having a definite function apart from all these. What then, can this function be? It is not life; for life is apparently something which man shares with the plants; and it is something peculiar to him that we are looking for. We must exclude therefore the life of nutrition and increase. There is next what may be called the life of sensation. But this too, is apparently shared by Man with horses, cattle, and all other animals. There remains what I may call the practical life of the rational part *of Man's being*. But the rational part is twofold; it is rational partly in the sense of being obedient to reason, and partly in the sense of possessing reason and intelligence. The practical life too may be conceived of in two ways[1], *viz., either as a moral state, or as a moral activity:* but we must understand by it the life of activity, as this seems to be the truer form of the conception.

Function of Man.

The function of Man then is an activity of soul in accordance with reason, or not independently of reason. Again the functions of a person of a certain kind, and of such a person who is good of his kind e.g. of a harpist and a good harpist, are in our view generically the same, and this view is true of people of all kinds without exception, the superior excellence being only an addition to the function ; for it is the function of a harpist to play the harp, and of a good harpist to play the harp well. This being so, if we define the function of Man as a kind of life, and this life as an activity of soul, or a course of action in conformity with reason, if the function of a good man is such activity or action of a good and noble kind, and if everything is successfully performed when it is performed in accordance with its proper excellence,

Definition of the good of Man.

it follows that the good of Man is an activity of soul in accordance with virtue or, if there are more virtues than one, in accordance with the best and most complete virtue. But it is necessary to add the words "in a complete life." For as one swallow or one day does not make a spring, so one day or a short time does not make a fortunate or happy man.

CHAP. VII.

This may be taken as a sufficiently accurate sketch of the good; for it is right, I think, to draw the

---

[1] In other words life may be taken to mean either the mere possession of certain faculties or their active exercise.

outlines first and afterwards to fill in the details. It would seem that anybody can carry on and complete what has been satisfactorily sketched in outline, and that time is a good inventor or cooperator in so doing. This is the way in which the arts have made their advances, as anybody can supply a deficiency.

But bearing in mind what has been already said, we must not look for the same degree of accuracy in all subjects; we must be content in each class of subjects with accuracy of such a kind as the subject-matter allows, and to such an extent as is proper to the inquiry. For while a carpenter and a geometrician both want to find a right angle, they do not want to find it in the same sense; the one wants only such an approximation to it as will serve his practical purpose, the other, as being concerned with truth, wants to know its nature or character. We must follow the same course in other subjects, or we shall sacrifice the main points to such as are subordinate. Again, we must not insist with equal emphasis in all subjects upon ascertaining the reason of things. We must sometimes e.g. in dealing with first principles be content with the proper evidence of a fact; the fact itself is a first point or principle. But there are various ways of discovering first principles; some are discovered by induction, others by perception, others by what may be called habituation, and so on. We must try to apprehend them all in the natural *or appropriate* way, and must take pains to define them satisfactorily, as they have a vital influence upon all that follows from them. For it seems that the first

Degree of accuracy attainable in Ethics. p. 3.

principle or beginning is more than half[1] the whole,
and is the means of arriving at a clear conception of
many points which are under investigation.

CHAP.VIII.   In considering the first principle we must pay
regard not only to the conclusion and the premisses
of our argument, but also to such views as are
popularly held about it. /For while all experience
harmonizes with the truth, it is never long before
truth clashes with falsehood.

Classifica-   Goods have been divided into three classes, viz.
tion of
goods.   external goods as they are called, goods of the soul
and goods of the body. Of these three classes we
consider the goods of the soul to be goods in the
strictest or most literal sense. But it is to the soul
that we ascribe psychical[2] actions and activities.
Thus our definition is a good one, at least according
to this theory, which is not only ancient but is
accepted by students of philosophy at the present
time. It is right too, inasmuch as certain actions and
activities are said to be the end ; for thus it appears
that the end is some good of the soul and not an
external good. It is in harmony with this definition
that the happy man should live well and do well, as
p. 5.   happiness, it has been said, is in fact a kind of living
and doing well.

CHAP. IX.   It appears too that the requisite characteristics of
happiness are all contained in the definition ; for some
people hold that happiness is virtue, others that it is

---

[1] In allusion to the adage ἀρχὴ ἥμισυ παντός, in which however
ἀρχή means "beginning."

[2] It is a pity that the English language does not possess a
word which stands to "soul" in the relation of ψυχικός to ψυχή.

prudence[1], others that it is wisdom of some kind, Concep-
others that it is these things or one of them conjoined happiness.
with pleasure or not dissociated from pleasure, others
again include external prosperity. Some of these
views are held by many ancient thinkers, others by a
few thinkers of high repute. It is probable that
neither side is altogether wrong, but that in some
one point, if not in most points, they are both right.

Now the definition is in harmony with the view of Happiness
those who hold that happiness is virtue or excellence preme
of some sort; for activity in accordance with virtue good.
implies virtue. But it would seem that there is a
considerable difference between taking the supreme
good to consist in acquisition or in use, in a moral
state or in an activity. For a moral state, although
it exists, may produce nothing good, e.g. if a person
is asleep, or has in any other way become inactive.
But this cannot be the case with an activity, as
activity implies action and good action. As in the
Olympian games it is not the most beautiful and
strongest persons who receive the crown but they
who actually enter the lists as combatants—for it is
some of these who become victors—so it is they
who act rightly that attain to what is noble and good
in life. Again, their life is pleasant in itself. For
pleasure is a psychical fact, and whatever a man is said
to be fond of is pleasant to him, e.g. a horse to one
who is fond of horses, a spectacle to one who is fond

---

[1] The difference between φρόνησις "prudence" or "practical
wisdom" and σοφία "speculative" or "theoretical wisdom" is
commonly assumed by Aristotle.

of spectacles, and similarly just actions to a lover of
justice, and virtuous actions in general to a lover of
virtue. Now most men find a sense of discord in
their pleasures, because their pleasures are not such
as are naturally pleasant. But to the lovers of
nobleness natural pleasures are pleasant. It is actions
in accordance with virtue that are naturally pleasant.
Such actions then are pleasant both relatively to
these persons and in themselves. Nor does their life
need that pleasure should be attached to it as a sort
of amulet ; it possesses pleasure in itself. For it may
be added that a person is not good, if he does not
take delight in noble actions, as nobody would call a
person just if he did not take delight in just actions,
or liberal if he did not take delight in liberal actions,
and so on. But if this is so, it follows that actions in
accordance with virtue are pleasant in themselves.
But they are also good and noble, and good and
noble in the highest degree, if the judgment of the
virtuous man upon them is right, his judgment being
such as we have described. Happiness then is the
best and noblest and pleasantest thing in the world,
nor is there any such distinction between goodness,
nobleness, and pleasure as the epigram at Delos
suggests :

> "Justice is noblest, Health is best,
> To gain one's end is pleasantest."

For these are all essential characteristics of the
best activities, and we hold that happiness consists in
these or in one and the noblest of these. Still it is
clear that happiness requires the addition of external
goods, as we said ; for it is impossible, or at least

difficult for a person to do what is noble unless he is
furnished with external means. For there are many
things which can only be done through the instrumentality of friends or wealth or political power, and
there are some things the lack of which must mar
felicity, e.g. noble birth, a prosperous family, and
personal beauty. For a person is incapable of happiness if he is absolutely ugly in appearance, or low
born, or solitary and childless, and perhaps still more
so, if he has exceedingly bad children or friends, or
has had good children or friends and has lost them
by death. As we said, then, it seems that prosperity
of this kind is an indispensable addition to virtue. It
is for this reason that some persons identify good
fortune, and others virtue, with happiness.

The question is consequently raised whether hap- CHAP. X.
piness is something that can be learnt or acquired by Can happiness be
habit or discipline of any other kind, or whether it learnt or
acquired?
comes by some divine dispensation or even by chance.

Now if there is anything in the world that is a Happiness
a gift of
gift of the Gods to men, it is reasonable to suppose the Gods.
that happiness is a divine gift, especially as it is the
best of human things. This however is perhaps a
point which is more appropriate to another investigation than the present. But even if happiness is not
sent by the Gods but is the result of virtue and of
learning or discipline of some kind, it is apparently
one of the most divine things in the world ; for it
would appear that that which is the prize and end of
virtue is the supreme good and is in its nature divine
and blessed. It will also be widely extended ; for it
will be capable of being produced in all persons,

except such as are morally deformed, by a process of study or care. And if it is better that happiness should be produced in this way than by chance, it may reasonably be supposed that it is so produced, as the order of things is the best possible in Nature and so too in art, and in causation generally, and most of all in the highest kind of causation. But it would be altogether inconsistent to leave what is greatest and noblest to chance. But the definition *of happiness* itself helps to clear up the question ; for happiness has been defined as a certain kind of activity of the soul in accordance with virtue. Of the other goods, *i.e. of goods besides those of the soul*, some are necessary as antecedent conditions of happiness, others are in their nature co-operative and service-able as instruments of happiness.

The conclusion at which we have arrived agrees with our original position. For we laid it down that the end of political science is the supreme good ; and

Object of political science.

political science is concerned with nothing so much as with producing a certain character in the citizens, or in other words with making them good, and

Animals, and the young, incapable of happi-ness.

capable of performing noble actions. It is reasonable then not to speak of an ox, or a horse, or any other animal as happy ; for none of them is capable of participating in activity as so defined. For the same reason no child can be happy, as the age of a child makes it impossible for him to display this activity at present, and if a child is ever said to be happy, the ground of the felicitation is his promise, *rather than his actual performance.* For happiness demands, as

p. 16.

we said, a complete virtue and a complete life.) For

there are all sorts of changes and chances in life, and it is possible that the most prosperous of men will, in his old age, fall into extreme calamities as is told of Priam in the heroic legends. But if a person has experienced such chances, and has died a miserable death, nobody calls him happy.

Is it the case then that nobody in the world may be called happy so long as he is alive? Must we adopt Solon's[1] rule of looking to the end? and, if we follow Solon, can it be said that a man is really happy after his death? Surely such a view is wholly absurd, especially for us who define happiness as a species of activity. But if we do not speak of one who is dead as happy, and if Solon's meaning is not this but rather that it is only when a man is dead that it is safe to call him fortunate as being exempt at last from evils and calamities, this again is a view which is open to some objection. For it seems that one who is dead is capable of being affected both by good and by evil in the same way as one who is living but unconscious, e.g. by honours and dishonours and by the successes or reverses of his children and his descendants generally. But here again a difficulty occurs. For if a person has lived a fortunate life up to old age, and has died a fortunate death, it is possible that he may experience many vicissitudes of fortune in the persons of his descendants. Some of them may be good and may enjoy such a life as they deserve ; others may be bad and may have a bad life.

---

[1] Herodotus I. ch. 32 is the authority for the celebrated warning which Solon is said to have addressed to Crœsus.

It is clear, too, that descendants may stand in all sorts of different degrees of relationship to their ancestor. It would be an extraordinary result, if the dead man were to share the vicissitudes of their fortune and to become happy at one time and miserable at another, *as they became either happy or miserable*. But it would be equally extraordinary, if the future of descendants should not affect their parents at all or for a certain time. It will be best, however, to revert to the difficulty which was raised before, as it will perhaps afford an answer to the present question. If it is right to look to the end, and when the end comes to felicitate a person not as being fortunate but as having been so before, surely it is an extraordinary thing that at the time when he is happy we should not speak the truth about him, because we do not wish to call the living happy in view of the vicissitudes to which they are liable and because we have formed a conception of happiness as something that is permanent and exempt from the possibility of change and because the same persons are liable to many revolutions of fortune. For it is clear that, if we follow the changes of fortune, we shall often call the same person happy at one time, and miserable at another, representing the happy man as "a[1] sort of chameleon without any stability of position." It cannot be right to follow the changes of fortune. It is not upon these that good or evil depends; they are necessary accessories of human life, as we said; but it is a man's activities in accord-

p. 20.

---

[1] Apparently an Iambic line.

ance with virtue that constitute his happiness and the opposite activities that constitute his misery. The difficulty which has now been discussed is itself a witness that this is the true view. For there is no human function so constant as the activities in accordance with virtue ; they seem to be more permanent than the sciences themselves. Among these activities, too, it is the most honourable which are the most permanent, as it is in them that the life of the fortunate chiefly and most continuously consists. For this is apparently the reason why such activities are not liable to be forgotten[1].

Constancy of the virtuous activities.

The element of permanency which is required will be found in the happy man, and he will preserve his character throughout life ; for he will constantly or in a preeminent degree pursue such actions and speculations as accord with virtue ; nor is there anybody who will bear the chances of life so nobly, with such a perfect and complete harmony, as he who is truly good and "foursquare without a flaw[2]." Now

[1] Aristotle means that it is comparatively easy to forget scientific truths, when they have once been learnt, but it is difficult, if not impossible, to lose the habit of virtuous activity. In other words, he means that knowledge is less stable, and therefore less valuable, than character.

[2] The phrase "foursquare without a flaw" is taken from Simonides, as Plato says in his *Protagoras* p. 339, B, where the passage in which the phrase occurs is quoted at length. Cp. *Rhetoric* III. ch. 11 p. 1411 B_{27}. In a similar, but not identical sense a modern poet speaks of the great Duke of Wellington as

"that tower of strength
Which stood foursquare to all the winds that blew."

the events of chance are numerous and of different
magnitudes. It is clear then that small incidents. of
good fortune, or the reverse, do not turn the scale of
life, but that such incidents as are great and numerous augment the felicity of life, if they are fortunate,
as they tend naturally to embellish it and the use of
them is noble and virtuous, and on the other hand, if
they are of a contrary character, mar and mutilate its
felicity by causing pains and hindrances to various
activities. Still even in these circumstances nobility
shines out, when a person bears the weight of accu-
mulated misfortunes with calmness, not from insensibility but from innate dignity and magnanimity.

The happy
man in-
capable of
misery.
p. 24.

But if it is the activities which determine the
life, as we said, nobody who is fortunate can become
miserable ; for he will never do what is hateful and
mean. For our conception of the truly good and
sensible man is that he bears all the chances of life
with decorum and always does what is noblest in the
circumstances, as a good general uses the forces at
his command to the best advantage in war, a good
cobbler makes the best shoe with the leather that is
given him, and so on through the whole series of the arts.
If this is so, it follows that the happy man can never
become miserable ; I do not say that he will be
fortunate, if he meets such chances of life as Priam.
Yet he will not be variable or liable to frequent
change, as he will not be moved from his happiness easily or by ordinary misfortunes but only by
such misfortunes as are great and numerous ; and
after them it will not be soon that he will regain his
happiness, but, if he regains it at all, it will be only in

a long and complete period of time and after attaining in it to great and noble results.

(We may safely then define a happy man as one whose activity accords with perfect virtue and who is adequately furnished with external goods, not for a casual period of time but for a complete or perfect lifetime.) But perhaps we ought to add, that he will always live so, and will die as he lives ; for it is not given us to foresee the future, but we take happiness to be an end, and to be altogether perfect and complete, and, this being so, we shall call people fortunate during their lifetime, if they possess and will possess these characteristics, but fortunate only so far as men may be fortunate. *Definition of happiness.*

But to leave the discussion of this subject : The idea that the fortunes of one's descendants and of one's friends generally have no influence at all upon oneself seems exceedingly harsh, and contrary to received opinions. But as the events of life are numerous and present all sorts of differences, and some are of more concern to us than others, it would be clearly a long, if not an infinite task, to define them individually ; we must, I think, be content to describe them generally and in outline. Now, as in personal misfortunes some have a certain weight and influence upon our life, and others, it seems, are comparatively light, so it is with such misfortunes as affect our friends generally. But as the difference between the experiences of the living or the dead is far greater than the difference between terrible crimes when enacted upon the stage in tragedies and the same crimes when merely assumed to have already *The fortunes of the living as affecting the dead.*

occurred, it is necessary to take account of this
difference also, and still more perhaps of the serious
doubt which has been raised as to the participation
of the dead in any good or evil. For it is probable in
this view that if anything, whether good or evil,
reaches the dead at all, it is feeble and insignificant,
either absolutely, or in relation to them, or if not, is
of such a magnitude and character as to be incapable
of making people happy if they are not happy or of
depriving them of their felicity, if they are.

It would seem then that the dead are affected or
influenced in some way by the prosperity and the
adversity of their friends, but that the influence is of
such a kind and degree as not to make people happy,
if they are not happy, nor to have any similar effect.

CHAP. XII.
Is happi-
ness an
object of
praise or of
honour?

Having determined these points, let us consider
whether happiness belongs rather to such things as
are objects of praise or to such things as are objects
of honour. For it is clearly not a mere potential
good.

It appears that whatever is an object of praise is
praised as possessing a certain character, and standing
in a certain relation to something. For we praise
one who is just and manly and good in any way, or
we praise virtue, because of their actions and productions. We praise one who is strong and swift and
so on, as naturally possessing a certain character and
standing in a certain relation to something that is
itself good and estimable. The truth of this statement
becomes clear, if we take the case of praises bestowed
upon the Gods. Such praise appears ridiculous as
implying a reference to ourselves, and there must be

such a reference, because, as we said, praise invariably implies a reference *to a higher standard*. But if this is the nature of praise, it is clear that it is not praise but something greater and better which is appropriate to all that is best, as indeed is evident; for we speak of the Gods as "blessed" and "happy" *rather than as* "*praiseworthy*" and we speak of the most godlike men as "blessed." It is the same with goods ; for nobody praises happiness as he praises justice, but he calls it blessed, as being in its nature better and more divine. It is sometimes held on these grounds that Eudoxus[1] was right in advocating the supremacy of pleasure ; for the fact that pleasure is a good and yet is not praised, indicates, as he thought, that it is higher than the objects of praise, as God and the good are higher, these being the standards to which everything else is referred. For praises[2] are appropriate to virtue, as it is virtue which makes us capable of noble deeds ; but panegyrics to accomplished results, whether they be results of the body or of the soul. But it may be said that an exact discussion of these points belongs more properly to the special study of panegyrics. We see clearly, however, from what has been said, that happiness is something

---

[1] A pupil of Plato, whose personal character is favourably noticed by Aristotle in Book x. ch. 2. He was an astronomer as well as a philosopher.

[2] The distinction between the ἕξις of virtue as deserving praise (ἔπαινος) and the ἔργον as deserving panegyric (ἐγκώμιον) which is drawn out in the *Rhetoric* Book III. ch. 9 is introduced a little awkwardly here, where the point is that virtue, as being a subject of praise, was in the Eudoxian view inferior to pleasure.

honourable and final. And that it is so seems to follow also from the fact that it is a first principle; for it is for the sake of happiness that we all do everything else, and the first principle or the cause of all that is good we regard as something honourable and divine.

CHAP.XIII.
Virtue as an element of happiness.

Inasmuch as happiness is an activity of soul in accordance with complete or perfect virtue, it is necessary to consider virtue, as this will perhaps be the best way of studying happiness.

It appears that virtue is the object upon which the true statesman has expended the largest amount of trouble, as it is his wish to make the citizens virtuous and obedient to the laws. We have instances of such statesmen in the legislators of Crete and Lacedaemon and such other legislators as have resembled them. But if this inquiry is proper to political science, it will clearly accord with our original purpose to pursue it. But it is clear that it is human virtue which we have to consider; for the good of

p. 16.

which we are in search is, as we said, human good, and the happiness, human happiness. By human virtue or excellence we mean not that of the body, but that of the soul, and by happiness we mean an activity of the soul.

Importance of psychology to the statesman.

If this is so, it is clearly necessary for statesmen to have some knowledge of the nature of the soul in the same way as it is necessary for one who is to treat the eye or any part of the body, to have some knowledge of it, and all the more as political science is better and more honourable than medical science. Clever doctors take a great deal of trouble to understand the body, and similarly the statesman must make a study of the soul. But he must study it with a view to his particular object and so far only as his object requires; for to elaborate the study of it further would, I think, be to aggravate unduly the labour of our present undertaking. ⌐

There are some facts concerning the soul which are adequately stated in the popular or exoterical discourses, and these we may rightly adopt. It is stated e.g. that the soul has two parts, one irrational and the other possessing reason. But whether these parts are distinguished like the parts of the body and like everything that is itself divisible, or whether they are theoretically distinct, but in fact inseparable, as convex and concave in the circumference of a circle, is of no importance to the present inquiry. *Analysis of the soul.*

Again, it seems that of the irrational part of the soul one part is common, *i.e. shared by man with all living things,* and vegetative; I mean the part which is the cause of nutrition and increase. For we may assume such a faculty of the soul to exist in all things that receive nutrition, even in embryos, and the same faculty to exist in things that are full grown, as it is more reasonable to suppose that it is the same faculty than that it is different. It is clear then that the virtue or excellence of this faculty is not distinctively human but is shared by man with all living things; for it seems that this part and this faculty are especially active in sleep, whereas good and bad people are never so little distinguishable as in sleep— whence the saying that there is no difference between the happy and the miserable during half their lifetime. And this is only natural ; for sleep is an inactivity of the soul in respect of its virtue or vice, except in so far as certain impulses affect it to a slight extent, and make the visions of the virtuous better than those of ordinary people. But enough has been said on this point, and we must now leave the principle of nutrition, as it possesses no natural share in human virtue.

It seems that there is another natural principle of the soul which is irrational and yet in a sense partakes of reason. For in a continent or incontinent person, we praise the reason, and that part of the soul which possesses reason, as it exhorts men rightly and exhorts them to the best conduct. But it is clear that there is in them another principle which is naturally different from reason and fights and contends against reason. For just as the paralysed parts of the body, when we intend to move them to the right, are drawn away in a contrary direction to the left, so it is with the soul ; the impulses of incontinent people run counter to reason. But there is this difference, however, that while in the body we see the part which is drawn astray, in the soul we do not see it. But it is probably right to suppose with equal certainty that there is in the soul too something different from reason, which opposes and thwarts it, although the sense in which it is distinct from reason is immaterial. But it appears that this part too partakes of reason, as we said ; at all events in a continent person it obeys reason, while in a temperate or courageous person it is probably still more obedient, as being absolutely harmonious with reason.

It appears then that the irrational part of the soul
is itself twofold ; for the vegetative faculty does not
participate at all in reason, but the faculty of desire
or general concupiscence participates in it more or
less, in so far as it is submissive and obedient to
reason. But *it is obedient* in the sense in which we
speak of "paying attention to a father" or "to
friends," but not in the sense in which we speak of
'paying attention to mathematics." All correction,
rebuke and exhortation is a witness that the irrational part of the soul is in a sense subject to the
influence of reason. But if we are to say that this
part too possesses reason, then the part which
possesses reason will have two divisions, one possessing reason absolutely and in itself, the other listening
to it as a child listens to its father.

Virtue or excellence again, admits of a distinction
which depends on this difference. For we speak of
some virtues as intellectual and of others as moral, Intellectual
wisdom, intelligence and prudence, being intellectual, and moral
liberality and temperance being moral, virtues. For virtues.
when we describe a person's character, we do not say
that he is wise or intelligent but that he is gentle
or temperate. Yet we praise a wise man too in
respect of his mental state, and such mental states
as deserve to be praised we call virtuous.

BOOK II.

VIRTUE or excellence being twofold, partly intellectual and partly moral, intellectual virtue is both originated and fostered mainly by teaching; it therefore demands experience and time. Moral[1] virtue on the other hand is the outcome of habit, and accordingly its name (ἠθικὴ ἀρετή) is derived by a slight deflexion from habit (ἔθος)[2]. From this fact it is clear that no moral virtue is implanted in us by nature; a law of nature cannot be altered by habituation. Thus a stone naturally tends to fall downwards, and it cannot be habituated or trained to rise upwards, even if we were to habituate it by throwing it upwards ten thousand times; nor again can fire be trained to sink downwards, nor anything else that follows one natural law be habituated or trained to follow another. It is neither by nature then nor in defiance of nature that virtues are im-

Genesis of moral virtue.

---

[1] The student of Aristotle must familiarize himself with the conception of intellectual as well as of moral virtues, although it is not the rule in modern philosophy to speak of the "virtues" of the intellect.

[2] The approximation of ἔθος (habit) and ἦθος (character) cannot be represented in English.

planted in us. Nature gives us the capacity of receiving them, and that capacity is perfected by habit.

Again, if we take the various natural powers which
belong to us, we first acquire the proper faculties
and afterwards display the activities. It is clearly so
with the senses. It was not by seeing frequently
or hearing frequently that we acquired the senses
of seeing or hearing ; on the contrary it was because
we possessed the senses that we made use of them,
not by making use of them that we obtained them.
But the virtues we acquire by first exercising them,
as is the case with all the arts, for it is by doing what
we ought to do when we have learnt the arts that
we learn the arts themselves ; we become e.g. builders
by building and harpists by playing the harp. Similarly it is by doing just acts that we become just, by
doing temperate acts that we become temperate, by
doing courageous acts that we become courageous.
The experience of states is a witness to this truth, for
it is by training the habits that legislators make the
citizens good. This is the object which all legislators
have at heart ; if a legislator does not succeed in it,
he fails of his purpose, and it constitutes the distinction between a good polity and a bad one.

Again, the causes and means by which any virtue
is produced and by which it is destroyed are the
same ; and it is equally so with any art ; for it is by
playing the harp that both good and bad harpists are
produced and the case of builders and all other
artisans is similar, as it is by building well that they
will be good builders and by building badly that they
will be bad builders. If it were not so, there would

3—2

be no need of anybody to teach them ; they would all be born good or bad *in their several trades.* The case of the virtues is the same. It is by acting in such transactions as take place between man and man that we become either just or unjust. It is by acting in the face of danger and by habituating ourselves to fear or courage that we become either cowardly or courageous. It is much the same with our desires and angry passions. Some people become temperate and gentle, others become licentious and passionate, according as they conduct themselves in one way or another way in particular circumstances. In a word moral states are the results of activities corresponding to the moral states themselves. It is our duty therefore to give a certain character to the activities, as the moral states depend upon the differences of the activities. Accordingly the difference between one training of the habits and another from early days is not a light matter, but is serious or rather all-important.

CHAP. II.
Actions
conducing
to virtue.

p. 35.

Our present study is not, like other studies[1], purely speculative in its intention ; for the object of our enquiry is not to know the nature of virtue but to become ourselves virtuous, as that is the sole benefit which it conveys. It is necessary therefore to consider the right way of performing actions, for it is actions as we have said that determine the character of the resulting moral states.

That we should act in accordance with right

---

[1] i.e. such studies as generally occupied the attention of the Aristotelian school.

reason is a common general principle, which may here
be taken for granted. The nature of right reason,
and its relation to the virtues generally, will be
subjects of discussion hereafter. But it must be
admitted at the outset that all reasoning upon practical matters must be like a sketch in outline, it cannot
be scientifically exact. We began by laying down the *Scientific exactitude impossible.*
principle that the kind of reasoning demanded in any
subject must be such as the subject-matter itself
allows ; and questions of practice and expediency no
more admit of invariable rules than questions of
health.

But if this is true of general reasoning *upon
Ethics,* still more true is it that scientific exactitude is
impossible in reasoning upon particular *ethical* cases.
They do not fall under any art or any law, but the
agents themselves are always bound to pay regard to
the circumstances of the moment as much as in
medicine or navigation.

Still, although such is the nature of the present
argument, we must try to make the best of it.

The first point to be observed then is that in such
matters as we are considering deficiency and excess *Deficiency and excess both fatal.*
are equally fatal. It is so, as we observe, in regard
to health and strength; for we must judge of what
we cannot see by the evidence of what we do see.
Excess or deficiency of gymnastic exercise is fatal to
strength. Similarly an excess or deficiency of meat
and drink is fatal to health, whereas a suitable
amount produces, augments and sustains it. It is the
same then with temperance, courage, and the other
virtues. A person who avoids and is afraid of every-

thing and faces nothing becomes a coward ; a person who is not afraid of anything but is ready to face everything becomes foolhardy.⟩ Similarly he who enjoys every pleasure and never abstains from any pleasure is licentious ; he who eschews all pleasures like a boor is an insensible sort of person. For temperance and courage are destroyed by excess and deficiency but preserved by the mean state.

Again, not only are the causes and the agencies of production, increase and destruction in the moral states the same, but the sphere of their activity will be proved to be the same also. It is so in other instances which are more conspicuous, e.g. in strength ; for strength is produced by taking a great deal of food and undergoing a great deal of labour, and it is the strong man who is able to take most food and to undergo most labour. The same is the case with the virtues. It is by abstinence from pleasures that we become temperate, and, when we have become temperate, we are best able to abstain from them. So too with courage; it is by habituating ourselves to despise and face alarms that we become courageous, and, when we have become courageous, we shall be best able to face them.

The pleasure or pain which follows upon actions may be regarded as a test of a person's moral state. He who abstains from physical pleasures and feels delight in so doing is temperate ; but he who feels pain at so doing is licentious. He who faces dangers with pleasure, or at least without pain, is courageous ; **Virtue in relation to pleasures and pains.** but he who feels pain at facing them is a coward. For moral virtue is concerned with pleasures and pains. It is pleasure which makes us do what is base, and pain which makes us abstain from doing what is noble. Hence the importance of having had a certain training from very early days, as Plato[1] says, such a training as produces pleasure and pain at the right objects ; for this is the true education.

Again, if the virtues are concerned with actions and emotions, and every action and every emotion is attended by pleasure and pain, this will be another reason why virtue should be concerned with pleasures and pains. There is also a proof of this fact in the use of pleasure and pain as means of punishment ; for punishments are in a sense remedial measures, and the means employed as remedies are naturally the opposites of the diseases to which they are applied. p. 35. Again, as we said before, every moral state of the soul is in its nature relative to, and concerned with, the thing by which it is naturally made better or worse. But it is pleasures and pains which produce vicious moral states, if we pursue and avoid such pleasures and pains as are wrong, or pursue and avoid them at the wrong time or in the wrong manner, or in any other of the various ways in which it is logically possible to do wrong. Hence it is that people[2] actually define the virtues as certain apathetic or quiescent states ; but they are wrong in using this absolute language, and not qualifying it by the addition of the right or wrong manner, time and so on.

It may be assumed then that moral virtue tends

[1] *Laws* II. p. 653 A—c.
[2] As e.g. the Cynics.

to produce the best action in respect of pleasures and
pains, and that vice is its opposite. But there is
another way in which we may see the same truth.
There are three things which influence us to desire
them, viz. the noble[1], the expedient, and the pleasant;
and three opposite things which influence us to eschew
them, viz. the shameful, the injurious, and the painful.
The good man then will be likely to take a right line,
and the bad man to take a wrong one, in respect of
all these, but especially in respect of pleasure ; for
pleasure is felt not by Man only but by the lower
animals, and is associated with all things that are
matters of desire, as the noble and the expedient
alike appear pleasant. Pleasure too is fostered in us
all from early childhood, so that it is difficult to get
rid of the emotion of pleasure, as it is deeply ingrain-
ed in our life. Again, we make pleasure and pain in
a greater or less degree the standard of our actions.
It is inevitable therefore that our present study
should be concerned from first to last with pleasures
and pains ; for right or wrong feelings of pleasure
or pain have a material influence upon actions.
Again, it is more difficult to contend against pleasure
than against anger, as Heraclitus[2] says, and it is *not
what is easy but* what is comparatively difficult that

---

[1] It must be remembered that τὸ καλόν and τὸ αἰσχρόν may
mean "the beautiful" and "the ugly" as well as "the noble" and
the "shameful," but it is the moral meaning which preponderates
here.

[2] The saying of Heraclitus, as given in *Eudem. Eth.* II. 7, p.
1223 B₂₃, is simply χαλεπὸν θυμῷ μάχεσθαι· ψυχῆς γὰρ ὠνεῖται, the
last words meaning that a person will gratify his anger even at
the risk of his life.

is in all cases the sphere of art or virtue, as the value
of success is proportionate to the difficulty. This
then is another reason why moral virtue and political
science should be exclusively occupied with pleasures
and pains; for to make a good use of pleasures and
pains is to be a good man, and to make a bad use
of them is to be a bad man.

We may regard it then as established that virtue
is concerned with pleasures and pains, that the causes
which produce it are also the means by which it is
augmented, or, if they assume a different character,
is destroyed, and that the sphere of its activity is the
things which were themselves the causes of its
production.

But it may be asked what we mean by saying that Chap. III.
people must become just by doing what is just and Comparison of
temperate by doing what is temperate. For if they virtues and
acts.
do what is just and temperate, they are *ipso facto*
proved, it will be said, to be just and temperate in
the same way as, if they practise grammar and music,
they are proved to be grammarians and musicians.

But is not the answer that the case of the arts
is not the same? For a person may do something
that is grammatical either by chance or at the sug-
gestion of somebody else; hence he will not be a
grammarian unless he not only does what is grammatical but does it in a grammatical manner, i.e.
in virtue of the grammatical knowledge which he
possesses.

There is another point too of difference between
the arts and the virtues. The productions of art
have their excellence in themselves. It is enough

therefore that, when they are produced, they should
be of a certain character. But actions in accordance
with virtue are not e.g. justly or temperately performed because they are in themselves just or
temperate. It is necessary that the agent at the
time of performing them should satisfy certain
conditions, i.e. in the first place that he should know
what he is doing, secondly that he should deliberately
choose to do it and to do it for its own sake, and
thirdly that he should do it as an instance of a settled
and immutable moral state. If it be a question
whether a person possesses any art, these conditions,
except indeed the condition of knowledge, are not
taken into account; but if it be a question of
possessing the virtues, the mere knowledge is of little
or no avail, and it is the other conditions, which are
the results of frequently performing just and temperate actions, that are not of slight but of absolute
importance. Accordingly deeds are said to be just
and temperate, when they are such as a just or
temperate person would do, and a just and temperate
person is not merely one who does these deeds but
one who does them in the spirit of the just and the
temperate.

It may fairly be said then that a just man becomes
just by doing what is just and a temperate man
becomes temperate by doing what is temperate, and
if a man did not so act, he would not have so much as
a chance of becoming good. But most people, instead
of doing such actions, take refuge in theorizing; they
imagine that they are philosophers and that philosophy will make them virtuous ; in fact they behave

like people who listen attentively to their doctors but never do anything that their doctors tell them. But it is as improbable that a healthy state of the soul will be produced by this kind of philosophizing as that a healthy state of the body will be produced by this kind of medical treatment.

We have next to consider the nature of virtue. Now, as the qualities of the soul are three, viz. emotions, faculties and moral states, it follows that virtue must be one of the three. By the emotions I mean desire, anger, fear, courage, envy, joy, love, hatred, regret, emulation, pity, in a word whatever is attended by pleasure or pain. I call those faculties in respect of which we are said to be capable of experiencing these emotions, e.g. capable of getting angry or being pained or feeling pity. And I call those moral states in respect of which we are well or ill disposed towards the emotions, ill-disposed e.g. towards the passion of anger, if our anger be too violent or too feeble, and well-disposed, if it be duly moderated, and similarly towards the other emotions.

Now neither the virtues nor the vices are emotions ; for we are not called good or evil in respect of our emotions but in respect of our virtues or vices. Again, we are not praised or blamed in respect of our emotions ; a person is not praised for being afraid or being angry, nor blamed for being angry in an absolute sense, but only for being angry in a certain way ; but we are praised or blamed in respect of our virtues or vices. Again, whereas we are angry or afraid without deliberate purpose, the virtues are in some sense deliberate purposes, or do not exist in the

Marginal notes:

CHAP. IV.

Virtue not an emotion nor a faculty but a moral state.

absence of deliberate purpose. It may be added that while we are said to be moved in respect of our emotions, in respect of our virtues or vices we are not said to be moved but to have a certain disposition.

These reasons also prove that the virtues are not faculties. For we are not called either good or bad, nor are we praised or blamed, as having an abstract capacity for emotion. Also while Nature gives us our faculties, it is not Nature that makes us good or p. 35. bad, but this is a point which we have already discussed. If then the virtues are neither emotions nor faculties, it remains that they must be moral states.

CHAP. V. The nature of virtue has been now generically

Virtue not only a moral state but a particular moral state. described. But it is not enough to state merely that virtue is a moral state, we must also describe the character of that moral state.

It must be laid down then that every virtue or .excellence has the effect of producing a good condition of that of which it is a virtue or excellence, and of enabling it to perform its function well. Thus the excellence of the eye makes the eye good and its function good, as it is by the excellence of the eye that we see well. Similarly, the excellence of the horse makes a horse excellent and good at racing, at carrying its rider and at facing the enemy.

If then this is universally true, the virtue or excellence of man will be such a moral state as makes a man good and able to perform his proper function p. 16. well. We have already explained how this will be the case, but another way of making it clear will be to study the nature or character of this virtue.

Now in everything, whether it be continuous or
discrete[1], it is possible to take a greater, a smaller, or
an equal amount, and this either absolutely or in
relation to ourselves, the equal being a mean between
excess and deficiency. By the mean in respect of the
thing itself, or the absolute mean, I understand that
which is equally distinct from both extremes ; and
this is one and the same thing for everybody. By the
mean considered relatively to ourselves I understand
that which is neither too much nor too little ; but
this is not one thing, nor is it the same for everybody.
Thus if 10 be too much and 2 too little we take 6 as a
mean in respect of the thing itself ; for 6 is as much
greater than 2 as it is less than 10, and this is a mean
in arithmetical proportion. But the mean considered
relatively to ourselves must not be ascertained in this
way. It does not follow that if 10 pounds *of meat* be
too much and 2 be too little for a man to eat, a
trainer will order him 6 pounds, as this may itself be
too much or too little for the person who is to take
it ; it will be too little e.g. for Milo[2], but too much
for a beginner in gymnastics. It will be the same
with running and wrestling ; *the right amount will
vary with the individual.* This being so, everybody
who understands his business avoids alike excess and
deficiency ; he seeks and chooses the mean, not the
absolute mean, but the mean considered relatively to
ourselves.

Doctrine of the mean.

---

[1] In Aristotelian language, as Mr Peters says, a straight line
is a " continuous quantity " but a rouleau of sovereigns a " discrete
quantity."

[2] The famous Crotoniate wrestler.

Every science then performs its function well, if it regards the mean and refers the works which it produces to the mean. This is the reason why it is usually said of successful works that it is impossible to take anything from them or to add anything to them, which implies that excess or deficiency is fatal to excellence but that the mean state ensures it. Good[1] artists too, as we say, have an eye to the mean in their works. But virtue, like Nature herself, is more accurate and better than any art; virtue therefore will aim at the mean ;—I speak of moral virtue, as it is moral virtue which is concerned with emotions and actions, and it is these which admit of excess and deficiency and the mean. Thus it is possible to go too far, or not to go far enough, in respect of fear, courage, desire, anger, pity, and pleasure and pain generally, and the excess and the deficiency are alike wrong; but to experience these emotions at the right times and on the right occasions and towards the right persons and for the right causes and in the right manner is the mean or the supreme good, which is characteristic of virtue. Similarly there may be excess, deficiency, or the mean, in regard to actions. But virtue is concerned with emotions and actions, and here excess is an error and deficiency a fault, whereas the mean is successful and laudable, and success and merit are both characteristics of virtue.

Virtue a mean or intermediate state.

It appears then that virtue is a mean state, so far at least as it aims at the mean.

---

[1] In the Greek text the parenthesis should be continued to the words πρὸς τοῦτο βλέποντες ἐργάζονται.

Again, there are many different ways of going wrong; for evil is in its nature infinite, to use the Pythagorean[1] figure, but good is finite. But there is only one possible way of going right. Accordingly the former is easy and the latter difficult ; it is easy to miss the mark but difficult to hit it. This again is a reason why excess and deficiency are characteristics of vice and the mean state a characteristic of virtue.

"For good is simple, evil manifold[2]."

Virtue then is a state of deliberate moral purpose consisting in a mean that is relative to ourselves, the mean being determined[3] by reason, or as a prudent man would determine it. CHAP. VI. Definition of Virtue.

It is a mean state *firstly as lying* between two vices, the vice of excess on the one hand, and the vice of deficiency on the other, and secondly because, whereas the vices either fall short of or go beyond what is proper in the emotions and actions, virtue not only discovers but embraces the mean.

Accordingly, virtue, if regarded in its essence or theoretical conception, is a mean state, but, if regarded from the point of view of the highest good, or of excellence, it is an extreme. Virtue both a mean and an extreme.

But it is not every action or every emotion that

---

[1] The Pythagoreans, starting from the mystical significance of number, took the opposite principles of "the finite" (τὸ πέρας or τὸ πεπερασμένον) and "the infinite" (τὸ ἄπειρον) to represent good and evil.

[2] A line—perhaps Pythagorean—of unknown authorship.

[3] The superior authority of the MSS. is in favour of ὡρισμένη, but ὡρισμένῃ, which has the support of the Old Translation and of Aspasius, accords better with the Aristotelian conception of virtue. Cp. p. 29, ll. 30—32.

admits of a mean state. There are some whose very
name implies wickedness, as e.g. malice, shamelessness,
and envy, among emotions, or adultery, theft, and
murder, among actions. All these, and others like
them, are censured as being intrinsically wicked, not
merely the excesses or deficiencies of them. It is
never possible then to be right in respect of them;
they are always sinful. Right or wrong in such
actions as adultery does not depend on our committing them with the right person, at the right time or
in the right manner; on the contrary it is sinful to do
anything of the kind at all. It would be equally
wrong then to suppose that there can be a mean state
or an excess or deficiency in unjust, cowardly or licentious conduct; for, if it were so, there would be a mean
state of an excess or of a deficiency, an excess of an
excess and a deficiency of a deficiency. But as in
temperance and courage there can be no excess or deficiency because the mean is, in a sense, an extreme, so
too in these cases there cannot be a mean or an excess
or deficiency, but, however the acts may be done, they
are wrong. For it is a general rule that an excess or
deficiency does not admit of a mean state, nor a mean
state of an excess or deficiency.

CHAP. VII.   But it is not enough to lay down this as a general
rule; it is necessary to apply it to particular cases, as
in reasonings upon actions general statements, although they are broader[1], are less exact than particular
statements. For all action refers to particulars, and
it is essential that our theories should harmonize with
the particular cases to which they apply.

[1] Reading κοινότεροι, with the majority of MSS.

We must take particular virtues then from the catalogue[1] *of virtues.*

In regard to feelings of fear and confidence, courage is a mean state. On the side of excess, he whose fearlessness is excessive has no name, as often happens, but he whose confidence is excessive is foolhardy, while he whose timidity is excessive and whose confidence is deficient is a coward.

In respect of pleasures and pains, although not indeed of all pleasures and pains, and to a less extent in respect of pains than of pleasures, the mean state is temperance[2], the excess is licentiousness. We never find people who are deficient in regard to pleasures; accordingly such people again have not received a name, but we may call them insensible.

As regards the giving and taking of money, the mean state is liberality, the excess and deficiency arc prodigality and illiberality. Here the excess and deficiency take opposite forms; for while the prodigal man is excessive in spending and deficient in taking, the illiberal man is excessive in taking and deficient in spending.

(For the present we are giving only a rough and summary account *of the virtues,* and that is sufficient for our purpose; we will hereafter determine their character more exactly[3].)

The doctrine of the mean in its application to particular virtues.

Courage.

Temperance.

Liberality.

[1] It would seem that a catalogue of virtues (διαγραφή or ὑπογραφή) must have been recognized in the Aristotelian school. Cp. *Eud. Eth.* ii. ch. 3.

[2] It is well worth while, if it be possible, to restore the word "temperance" to its true meaning, as the English equivalent of σωφροσύνη.

[3] I have placed this sentence in a parenthesis, as it interrupts the argument respecting the right use of money.

W. N. E. 4

In respect of money there are other dispositions *Magnifi-cence.* as well. There is the mean state which is magnificence; for the magnificent man, as having to do with large sums of money, differs from the liberal man who has to do only with small sums; and the excess *corresponding to it* is bad taste or vulgarity, the deficiency is meanness. These are different from the excess and deficiency of liberality; what the difference is *p. 107.* will be explained hereafter.

Highmind-edness. In respect of honour and dishonour the mean state is highmindedness, the excess is what is called vanity, the deficiency littlemindedness. Corresponding to liberality, which, as we said, differs from magnificence as having to do *not with great but* with small sums of money, there is a moral state which has to do with petty honour and is related to highmindedness which has to do with great honour; for it is possible to aspire to honour in the right way, or in a way which is excessive or insufficient, and if a person's aspirations are excessive, he is called ambitious, if they are deficient, he is called unambitious, while if they are between the two, he has no name. The dispositions too are nameless, except that the disposition of the ambitious person is called ambition. The consequence is that the extremes lay claim to the mean or intermediate place. We ourselves speak of one who observes the mean sometimes as ambitious, and at other times as unambitious; we sometimes praise an ambitious, and at other times an unambitious person. The reason for our doing so will be stated in due course, but let us now discuss the other virtues in accordance with the method which we have followed hitherto.

Anger, like other emotions, has its excess, its Anger.
deficiency, and its mean state. It may be said that
they have no names, but as we call one who observes
the mean gentle, we will call the mean state gentleness. Among the extremes, if a person errs on the
side of excess, he may be called passionate and his
vice passionateness, if on that of deficiency, he may be
called impassive and his deficiency impassivity.

There are also three other mean states with a
certain resemblance to each other, and yet with a
difference. For while they are all concerned with
intercourse in speech and action, they are different in
that one of them is concerned with truth in such
intercourse, and the others with pleasantness, one
with pleasantness in amusement and the other with
pleasantness in the various circumstances of life. We
must therefore discuss these states in order to make
it clear that in all cases it is the mean state which is
an object of praise, and the extremes are neither right
nor laudable but censurable. It is true that these mean
and extreme states are generally nameless, but we
must do our best here as elsewhere to give them a
name, so that our argument may be clear and easy to
follow.

In the matter of truth then, he who observes the Truth-
mean may be called truthful, and the mean state fulness.
truthfulness. Pretence, if it takes the form of exaggeration, is boastfulness, and one who is guilty of
pretence is a boaster; but if it takes the form of
depreciation it is irony, and he who is guilty of it
is ironical.

As regards pleasantness in amusement, he who Wittiness.

4—2

observes the mean is witty, and his disposition wittiness; the excess is buffoonery, and he who is guilty
of it a buffoon, whereas he who is deficient in wit may
be called a boor and his moral state boorishness.

Friendli-
ness.

As to the other kind of pleasantness, viz. pleasantness in life, he who is pleasant in a proper way is
friendly, and his mean state friendliness; but he who
goes too far, if he has no ulterior object in view, is
obsequious, while if his object is self interest, he is
a flatterer, and he who does not go far enough and
always makes himself unpleasant is a quarrelsome
and morose sort of person.

Mean states
of the
emotions.
Modesty.

There are also mean states in the emotions[1] and
in the expression of the emotions. For although
modesty is not a virtue, yet a modest person is
praised as if he were virtuous; for here too one
person is said to observe the mean and another to
exceed it, as e.g. the bashful man who is never
anything but modest, whereas a person who has
insufficient modesty or no modesty at all is called
shameless, and one who observes the mean modest.

Righteous
indigna-
tion.

Righteous indignation, again, is a mean state
between envy and malice[2]. They are all concerned
with the pain and pleasure which we feel at the
fortunes of our neighbours. A person who is right-

---

[1] The distinction, it seems, is between those mean or intermediate states (μεσότητες) which take the form of action and
those which are simply emotional.

[2] Sir Alexander Grant points out that in the *Rhetoric* ii. ch.
9 the two vices between which righteous indignation (νέμεσις) is
here said to lie are recognized as identical or as co-existing in
the same person ὁ γὰρ αὐτός ἐστιν ἐπιχαιρέκακος καὶ φθονερός.

eously indignant is pained at the prosperity of the undeserving ; but the envious person goes further and is pained at anybody's prosperity, and the malicious person is so far from being pained that he actually rejoices *at misfortunes.*

We shall have another opportunity[1] however of discussing these matters. But in regard to justice, as the word is used in various senses, we will afterwards[2] define those senses and explain how each of them is a mean state. And we will follow the same course with the intellectual virtues[3].

There are then three dispositions, two being vices, CHAP.VIII. viz. one the vice of excess and the other that of deficiency, and one virtue, which is the mean state between them ; and they are all in a sense mutually opposed. For the extremes are opposed both to the *The extremes opposed both* mean and to each other, and the mean is opposed to *posed both* the extremes. For as the equal if compared with the *to the mean and to each* less is greater but if compared with the greater is *other.* less, so the mean states, whether in the emotions or in actions, if compared with the deficiencies, are excessive, but if compared with the excesses are deficient. Thus the courageous man appears foolhardy as compared with the coward, but cowardly as compared with the foolhardy. Similarly, the temperate man appears licentious as compared with the insensible but insensible as compared with the licentious, and the liberal man appears prodigal as compared with the illiberal, but illiberal as compared

[1] In Book iii. ch. 9—end of Book iv.
[2] In Book v.
[3] In Book vi.

with the prodigal. The result is that the extremes
mutually repel and reject the mean ; the coward
calls the courageous man foolhardy, but the foolhardy
man calls him cowardly, and so on in the other cases.

But while there is this mutual opposition between
the extremes and the mean, there is greater opposition between the two extremes than between either
extreme and the mean ; for they are further removed
from each other than from the mean, as the great
from the small and the small from the great than
both from the equal. Again, while some extremes
exhibit more or less similarity to the mean, as
foolhardiness to courage and prodigality to liberality,
there is the greatest possible dissimilarity between
the extremes. But things which are furthest removed
from each other are defined to be opposites ; hence
the further things are removed, the greater is the
opposition between them.

It is in some cases the deficiency and in others
the excess which is the more opposed to the mean.
Thus it is not foolhardiness the excess, but cowardice
the deficiency which is the more opposed to courage,
nor is it insensibility the deficiency, but licentiousness
the excess which is the more opposed to temperance.
There are two reasons why this should be so. One
lies in the nature of the thing itself ; for as one of
the two extremes is the nearer and more similar to
the mean, it is not this extreme, but its opposite,
that we chiefly set against the mean. For instance,
as it appears that foolhardiness is more similar and
nearer to courage than cowardice, it is cowardice that
we chiefly set against courage ; for things which are

further removed from the mean seem to be more opposite to it. This being one reason which lies in the nature of the thing itself, there is a second which lies in our own nature. It is the things to which we ourselves are naturally more inclined that appear more opposed to the mean. Thus we are ourselves naturally more inclined to pleasures *than to their oppo-sites*, and are more prone therefore to licentiousness than to decorum. Accordingly we speak of those things, in which we are more likely to run to great lengths, as being more opposed to the mean. Hence it follows that licentiousness which is an excess is more opposed to temperance than insensibility.

It has now been sufficiently shown that moral CHAP. IX. virtue is a mean state, and in what sense it is a mean Definition of virtue state; it is a mean state as lying between two vices, as a mean a vice of excess on the one side and a vice of deficiency state. on the other, and as aiming at the mean in the emotions and actions.

That is the reason why it is so hard to be virtuous; Difficulty for it is always hard work to find the mean in of the virtuous anything, e.g. it is not everybody, but only a man life. of science, who can find the mean or centre[1] of a circle. So too anybody can get angry—that is an easy matter—and anybody can give or spend money, but to give it to the right persons, to give the right amount of it and to give it at the right time and for the right cause and in the right way, this is not what anybody can do, nor is it easy. That is the reason

---

[1] Aristotle does not seem to be aware that the centre (τὸ μέσον) of a circle is not really comparable to the mean (τὸ μέσον) between the vices.

why it is rare and laudable and noble to do well. Accordingly one who aims at the mean must begin by departing from that extreme which is the more contrary to the mean; he must act in the spirit of Calypso's[1] advice,

"Far from this smoke and swell keep thou thy bark,"

for of the two extremes one is more sinful than the other. As it is difficult then to hit the mean exactly, we must take the second best course[2], as the saying is, and choose the lesser of two evils, and this we shall best do in the way that we have described, *i.e. by steering clear of the evil which is further from the mean.* We must also observe the things to which we are ourselves particularly prone, as different natures have different inclinations, and we may ascertain what these are by a consideration of our feelings of pleasure and pain. And then we must drag ourselves in the direction opposite to them ; for it is by removing ourselves as far as possible from what is wrong that we shall arrive at the mean, as we do when we pull a crooked stick straight.

But in all cases we must especially be on our guard against what is pleasant and against pleasure, as we are not impartial judges of pleasure. Hence our attitude towards pleasure must be like that of the elders of the people in the *Iliad* towards Helen, and we must never be afraid of applying the words

---

[1] *Odyssey* xii. 219, 220 ; but it is Odysseus who speaks there, and the advice has been given him not by Calypso but by Circe (*ibid.* 101—110).

[2] The Greek proverb means properly "we must take to the oars, if sailing is impossible."

they use[1]; for if we dismiss pleasure as they dismissed Helen, we shall be less likely to go wrong. It is by action of this kind, to put it summarily, that we shall best succeed in hitting the mean.

It may be admitted that this is a difficult task, especially in particular cases. It is not easy to determine e.g. the right manner, objects, occasions, and duration of anger. There are times when we ourselves praise people who are deficient in anger, and call them gentle, and there are other times when we speak of people who exhibit a savage temper as spirited. It is not however one who deviates a little from what is right, but one who deviates a great deal, whether on the side of excess or of deficiency, that is censured ; for he is sure to be found out. Again, it is not easy to decide theoretically how far and to what extent a man may go before he becomes censurable, but neither is it easy to define theoretically anything else within the region of perception ; such things fall under the head of particulars, and our judgment of them depends upon our perception.

So much then is plain, that the mean state is everywhere laudable, but that we ought to incline at one time towards the excess and at another towards the deficiency ; for this will be our easiest manner of hitting the mean, or in other words of attaining excellence.

[1] The lines are worth quoting :

οὐ νέμεσις Τρῶας καὶ ἐϋκνημῖδας Ἀχαιοὺς
τοιῇδ᾽ ἀμφὶ γυναικὶ πολὺν χρόνον ἄλγεα πάσχειν.
αἰνῶς ἀθανάτῃσι θεῇς εἰς ὦπα ἔοικεν,
ἀλλὰ καὶ ὣς τοίη περ ἐοῦσ᾽ ἐν νηυσὶ νεέσθω
μηδ᾽ ἡμῖν τεκέεσσί τ᾽ ὀπίσσω πῆμα λίποιτο.   Il. iii. 156—160.

BOOK III.

As virtue is concerned with emotions and actions, and such emotions and actions as are voluntary are the subjects of praise and blame, while such as are involuntary are the subjects of pardon and sometimes even of pity, it is necessary, I think, in an investigation of virtue to distinguish what is voluntary from what is involuntary. It will also be useful in legislation as bearing upon the honours and punishments which the legislator assigns.

It is generally admitted[1] that acts done under compulsion, or from ignorance, are involuntary. But an act is compulsory, if its origin is external *to the agent or patient,* i.e. if it is one in which the agent or the patient contributes nothing, as e.g. if the wind, or people who have us in their power, were to carry us in a certain direction. But if an action is done from fear of greater evils or for some noble end, e.g. if a tyrant, who had our parents and children in his power, were to order us to do some shameful act, on condition that, if we did it, their lives should be

---

[1] Such is the force of δοκεῖ in many passages of Aristotle.

spared, and, if not, they should be put to death, it is a question whether such action is voluntary or involuntary. The case of throwing goods overboard during a storm at sea is similar ; for although nobody would voluntarily make such a sacrifice in the abstract, yet every sensible person will make it for his own safety and the safety of his fellow passengers. Actions like this, although they are of a mixed character, are more like voluntary than involuntary actions, as they are chosen at the time of performing them, and the end *or character* of an action depends upon *the choice made at* the moment of performing it. When we speak then of an action as voluntary or involuntary, we must have regard to the time at which a person performs it. The person[1] *whose actions we are considering* acts voluntarily ; for in actions like his the original power which sets the instrumentality of his limbs in motion lies in himself, and when the origin of a thing lies in a person himself, it is in his power either to do it or not to do it. Such actions then are *practically* voluntary, although in the abstract they may be said perhaps to be involuntary, as nobody would choose any such action in itself.

Such actions are at times subjects of praise, when people submit to something that is shameful or painful for the sake of gaining what is great and noble ; or in the contrary case they are the subjects of censure, as it is only a bad man who would submit to what is utterly shameful, if his object were not noble at all, or were indifferent. There are also some

---

[1] i. e. the person who acts at the command of a tyrant or, when he is at sea, under stress of stormy weather.

actions which are pardonable, although not laudable, as when a person is induced to do what is wrong by such causes as are too strong for human nature and do not admit of resistance. Yet it is probable that there are some actions where compulsion is an impossibility; a person would rather suffer the most dreadful form of death than do them. Thus the reasons which constrained Alcmæon[1] in Euripides to murder his mother are clearly ridiculous.

It is sometimes difficult to determine what ought to be chosen or endured for the sake of obtaining or avoiding a certain result. But it is still more difficult to abide by our decisions; for it generally happens that, while the consequence which we expect is painful, the act which we are constrained to do is shameful, and therefore we receive censure or praise according as we yield or do not yield to the constraint.

Compulsory actions.

What class of actions then is it that may be rightly called compulsory? Actions it may be said are compulsory in the abstract, whenever the cause is external to the agent and he contributes nothing to it. But if an action, although involuntary in itself, is chosen at a particular time and for a particular end, and if its original cause lies in the agent himself, then, although such an action is involuntary in itself, it is voluntary at that time and for that end. Such an action however is more like a voluntary than an

---

[1] Alcmæon murdered his mother Eriphyle in revenge for the murder of his father; but as the play of Euripides is lost, it is impossible to say what "the reasons" alleged in it were.

involuntary action; for actions fall under the category of particulars, and *in the supposed case* the particular action is voluntary.

It is not easy to state what kind of actions are to be chosen for certain ends, as particular cases admit of many differences. It might be argued that whatever is pleasant or noble is compulsory, as pleasure and nobleness are external to ourselves and exercise a constraint upon us; but if that were so, every action would be compulsory, as these are the motives of all actions in us all. Again, if a person acts under compulsion and involuntarily, his action is painful to him; but if the motives of his action are pleasure and nobleness, it is pleasant. It is ridiculous to lay the blame of our wrong actions upon external causes, rather than upon the facility with which we ourselves are caught by such causes, and, while we take the credit of our noble actions to ourselves, to lay the blame of our shameful actions upon pleasure. It seems then that an action is compulsory if its origin is external to the agent, i.e. if the person who is the subject of compulsion is in no sense contributory to the action.

An action which is due to ignorance is always non-voluntary; but it is not involuntary, unless it is followed by pain and excites a feeling of regret. For if a person has performed an action, whatever it may be, from ignorance, and yet feels no distress at his action, it is true that he has not acted voluntarily, as he was not aware of what he was doing, but on the other hand, he has not acted involuntarily, so long as he feels no pain.

CHAP. II. Non-voluntary as distinguished from involuntary action.

If a person who has acted from ignorance regrets what he has done, it may be said that he is an involuntary agent; but, if he does not regret it, his case is different[1], and he may be called a non-voluntary agent, for, as there is this difference, it is better that he should have a special name.

Action from igno-rance and action in ignorance. It would seem, too, that there is a difference between acting from ignorance and doing a thing in ignorance. Thus, if a person is intoxicated or infuriated, he is not regarded as acting from ignorance, but as acting from intoxication or fury; yet he does not act consciously but in ignorance.

It[2] must be admitted then that every vicious person is ignorant of what he ought to do, and what he ought to abstain from doing, and that ignorance is the error which makes people unjust and generally wicked. But when we speak of an action as involuntary, we do not mean merely that a person is ignorant of his true interest. The ignorance which is the cause of involuntary action, as distinguished from that which is the cause of vice, is not such ignorance as affects the moral purpose, nor again is it ignorance of the universal ; for this is censurable. It is rather ignorance of particulars, i.e. ignorance of the particular circumstances and occasion of the action. Where this ignorance exists, there is room for pity and forgiveness, as one who is ignorant of any such particular is an involuntary agent.

---

[1] The comma should be placed after ἕτερος, not after ἔστω.

[2] The Socratic identification of virtue with knowledge lies at the root of this statement.

It will perhaps be as well then to define the nature and number of these particulars. They are

1. the agent,
2. the act,
3. the occasion or circumstances of the act.

Sometimes also

4. the instrument, e.g. a tool,
5. the object, e.g. safety,

and 6. the manner of doing an act, e.g. gently or violently.

Nobody but a madman can be ignorant of all these particulars. It is clear that nobody can be ignorant of the agent; for how can a person be ignorant of himself? But a person may be ignorant of what he is doing, as when people say that a word escaped them unawares or that they did not know a subject was forbidden, like Æschylus[1] *when he revealed* the mysteries, or that he only meant to show the working of a weapon when he discharged it, like the man who discharged the catapult. Again, a person may take his son for an enemy like Merope[2], or a pointed foil for a foil that has its button on, or a solid stone for a pumice stone, or he may kill somebody by a blow[3]

---

[1] The usual story, although it hardly suits the present passage, is that Æschylus was accused before the Areopagus of having revealed the Eleusinian mysteries and defended himself by alleging that he had never been initiated in them.

[2] Merope, wife of Cresphontes, was on the point of murdering her son Æpytus by mistake, as Aristotle himself relates *Poetic* ch. 14, p. 1454A$_{5-7}$. There was a play of Euripides called *Cresphontes*.

[3] I have kept, with some hesitation, the reading παίσας; but πίσας (from πιπίσκω) improves the sense and is adopted by Bernays and Bywater.

that was meant to save him, or he may deal a fatal blow while only intending, as in a sparring match, to give a lesson in the art of dealing a blow. As there may be ignorance in regard to all these particular circumstances of an action, it may be said that a person has acted involuntarily, if he was ignorant of any one of them, and especially of such particulars as seem to be most important, i.e. of the circumstances of the action, and of its natural result. But[1] if an action is to be called involuntary in respect of such ignorance, it is necessary that it should be painful to the agent and should excite in him a feeling of regret.

CHAP. III.
Voluntary action.

As an action is involuntary if done under compulsion or from ignorance, it would seem to follow that it is voluntary if the agent originates it with a knowledge of the particular circumstances of the action. For it is perhaps wrong to say that actions which are due to passion or desire are involuntary. For in the first place upon that hypothesis none of the lower animals can any more be said to act voluntarily, nor can children; and secondly is it to be argued that nothing which we do from desire or passion is voluntary? or are our noble actions done voluntarily, and our shameful actions involuntarily? Surely the latter view is ridiculous, if one and the same person is the author of both kinds of action. But it would seem irrational to assert that such things as ought to be the objects of desire are desired involuntarily; and there are certain things which ought to be the occasions of anger, and certain things

Actions due to passion or desire are voluntary.

---

[1] The δή should probably be δέ.

such as health and learning, which ought to be the
objects of desire. Again, it seems that what is involuntary is painful, but what is done from desire is
pleasant. Again, what difference is there, in respect of
involuntariness, between errors of reason and errors
of passion? It is our duty to avoid both; but the
irrational emotions seem to be as truly human *as the
reason itself and therefore we are as truly responsible
for our emotions as for our reasoning.* Such actions
then as proceed from passion and desire[1] are not less
the actions of the man than rational actions; it is
absurd therefore to regard these as involuntary.

Having thus distinguished voluntary from involun- CHAP. IV.
tary action, we naturally proceed to discuss moral pur- Moral purpose. For it would seem that the moral purpose is
most closely related to virtue, and is a better criterion
of character than actions themselves are.

It is clear that moral purpose is something volun- Moral pur-
tary. Still moral purpose and volition are not volition.
identical; volition is a term of wider range. For
while children and the lower animals participate in
volition, they do not participate in moral purpose.
Also we speak of actions done on the spur of the
moment as being voluntary, but not as being done
with moral purpose.

It would appear then that the definition of moral
purpose as desire, or passion, or wish, or opinion of
some sort is a mistake. For moral purpose is not
like desire and passion common to irrational creatures Nor desire.
as well as to Man. Again, an incontinent person acts

[1] I read with Mr Bywater ὥστε καὶ αἱ πράξεις, and insert αἱ
before ἀπὸ θυμοῦ.

W. N. E.   5

from desire but not from moral purpose. On the other hand a continent person acts from moral purpose but not from desire. Again, desire is contrary to moral purpose, but one desire is not contrary to another. Desire, too, is, but moral purpose is not, directed to pleasures and pains. Still less can moral purpose be the same thing as passion; for there are no actions which seem to be so little directed by moral purpose as those which are due to angry passion.

Nor passion.

Nor wish. Nor again is moral purpose the same thing as wish, although it is clear that it is nearly allied to it. For moral purpose does not apply to impossibilities, and anybody who should say that he had a purpose of achieving what is impossible would be thought a fool. But there is such a thing as wishing for the impossible, as e.g. for immortality. Again, while we may wish for things which could not possibly be affected by our own action, as e.g. for the victory of a certain actor or athlete, it can never be said that we purpose such things; we only purpose what may, as we think, be possibly effected by our own action. Again, the wish is directed rather to the end, but the moral purpose to the means. Thus we wish to be in good health, but we purpose or choose the means of being in good health. Or again we wish to be happy and admit the wish; but we cannot appropriately say that we purpose or choose to be happy. For it seems to be a general law that our moral purpose is confined to such things as lie within our own power. Nor again can moral purpose be opinion, for it seems that the sphere of opinion is universal; it embraces things

Nor opinion.

which are eternal or impossible as much as things which lie within our own power. Opinion too, unlike moral purpose, is distinguished by being true or false, not by being good or evil. Perhaps there is nobody who maintains that moral purpose is identical with opinion generally; but neither is it identical with opinion of a particular kind. For it is according as we purpose or choose what is good or evil, and not according as we hold particular opinions, that we possess a certain character. Again, we choose to accept or avoid a thing and so on, but we opine what a thing is, or for whom or in what way it is beneficial. We do not opine at all to accept or avoid a thing. Again, whereas moral purpose is praised rather as being directed to a proper end than as being correct, opinion is praised as being true. Again, we purpose or choose such things as we best know to be good; but we form an opinion of things of which we have no knowledge. Again, it is apparently not the same people who make the best choice and who form the best opinions. There are some people who form a better opinion than others, but are prevented by vice from making the right choice. It is possible that opinion may precede moral purpose or follow it, but that is not the point; for the question which we are considering is simply this, whether moral purpose is identical with opinion of a particular kind.

What then is the nature and character of moral purpose, since it is none of the things which have been mentioned? It is clearly voluntary, but there are things which are voluntary and yet are not chosen or purposed. It may be said, I think, that a thing is voluntary, if it is the result of previous deliberation, for moral purpose implies reason and thought. The very name (προαίρεσις)[1] seems to indicate previous deliberation, as it denotes something chosen in preference to other things.

CHAP. V.

Subjects of deliberation.

The question is, Do we deliberate upon everything? Is everything a matter for deliberation, or are there some things which are not subjects of deliberation?

We must presumably understand by "a matter of deliberation" not that about which a fool or a madman, but that about which a sensible person, would deliberate.

Nobody deliberates about things which are eternal, *i.e. immutable,* as e.g. the universe or the incommensurability of the diagonal and the side of a square; or about things which are in motion but always follow the same course, whether of necessity or by nature or for some other cause, as e.g. the solstices and sunrisings; or about things which are wholly irregular like droughts and showers; or about mere matters of chance such as the finding of a treasure. Nor again are all human affairs matters of deliberation; thus no Lacedaemonian will deliberate upon the best constitution for the Scythians. The reason why we do not deliberate about these things is that none of them can be effected by our action. The matters about which we deliberate are practical matters lying within our power. There is in fact no other class of matters left; for it would seem that the causes of things are nature, necessity, chance, and besides these

---

[1] The English translation will not represent the derivation of προαίρεσις (moral purpose) from πρὸ, αἱρεῖσθαι (to choose before).

only intelligence, and human agency in its various forms. But different classes of people deliberate about such practical matters as depend upon their several actions. Further, those sciences, which are exact and complete in themselves, do not admit of deliberation, as e.g. writing; for we are in no doubt as to the proper way of writing. But if a thing depends upon our own action and is not invariable, it is a matter of deliberation, as e.g. questions of medicine, of finance, or of navigation rather than of gymnastic, as being less exactly systematized, and similarly all other arts, and again, the arts more than the sciences, as we are more in doubt about them.

Deliberation occurs in cases which fall under a general rule, if it is uncertain what the issue will be, and in cases which do not admit of an absolute decision. We invite the help of other people in our deliberations upon matters of importance, when we distrust our own ability to decide them.

Again, we deliberate not about ends but about the means to ends. Thus a doctor does not deliberate whether he shall cure his patients, nor an orator whether he shall persuade his audience, nor a statesman whether he shall produce law and order, nor does any one else deliberate about his end. They all propose to themselves a certain end and then consider how and by what means it can be attained, and if it appears capable of attainment by several means, they consider what will be the easiest and best means of attaining it, and if there is only one means of attaining it, how it may be attained by this means, and by what means this means itself can be attained, until they come to the first cause, which in the order of discovery is last. For it seems that deliberation is a process of investigation and analysis such as this: it is like the analysis of a geometrical figure[1]. It appears[2] however that, while investigation is not always deliberation, mathematical investigations, e.g. not being so, deliberation is always investigation, and that that which is last in the order of analysis is first in the order of production.

If *in a deliberation* we come upon an impossibility, we abandon our task, as e.g. if money is required and it is impossible to provide the money; but if it appears to be possible, we set about doing it. By possibilities I mean such things as may be effected by our own actions ; for what is done by our friends may be said to be done by ourselves, as the origin of it lies in ourselves[3]. The question is sometimes what instruments are necessary, and at other times how they are to be used. Similarly in all other cases it is sometimes the means of doing a certain thing and at other times the manner or the agency that is in question.

p. 58.   It seems, as has been said, that a man originates his own actions. Deliberation touches such things as may be done by a man himself, and actions are done

---

[1] The point of the comparison is that, if it is desired to ascertain the construction of a geometrical figure, the best way is often to assume the figure as already constructed and then to work backwards to the conditions necessary for constructing it.

[2] Mr Bywater's plan of treating the words φαίνεται δ' ἡ μὲν ζήτησις...πᾶσα ζήτησις as parenthetical is an improvement in point of sense but grammatically so harsh that I have not felt justified in adopting it.

[3] The conception of a friend as "a second self" (ἕτερος αὐτός) is thoroughly Aristotelian.

for the sake of something which lies beyond themselves. Accordingly it is not the end, but the means to the end, that will be matter of deliberation. Nor again will particular questions be matters of deliberation, as e.g. the question whether a particular thing is a loaf or has been properly baked; that is rather a matter of perception, and, if we go on deliberating for ever, we shall never come to an end.

The objects of deliberation and of moral purpose are the same, except that the object of moral purpose is already determined; for it is that which is preferred after deliberation. For everybody gives up inquiring how he shall act when he has traced back the origin of his action to himself and to the dominant part of himself, i.e. to the part which exercises moral choice or purpose. There is an illustration of this principle in the ancient polities which Homer[1] represented, for in them the kings promulgated their purpose, whatever it might be, to the people.

But if the object of our moral purpose is that which, being in our power, is after deliberation the object of our desire, it follows that the moral purpose is a deliberative desire of something which is in our power; for we first deliberate upon a thing and, after passing judgment upon it, we desire it in accordance with our deliberation.

Let us now leave this rough sketch of the moral purpose. We have shown what are the matters with which it deals, and that it is directed to the means *rather than to the ends.*

---

[1] As the Homeric king issued his decree to the people without consulting them, so the moral purpose determines and declares what a man shall do.

CHAP. VI.   We have said that the wish is directed to the end;
Wish.
but there are some people who hold that the end is
the good, and others that it is what appears to be
Object of   good. If it is said that the object of wish is the
the wish.
good, it follows that where a person's moral purpose
or choice is wrong that which he wishes is not *in the
proper sense* an object of wish; for if it is an object of
wish it will also be a good, but it was perhaps an evil.
If on the other hand, it is said that it is what appears
to be good which is the object of wish, it follows that
there is no such thing as a natural object of wish, but
that it is in every man's case that which seems good
to him. But different, and it may be even opposite
things, seem good to different people.

If these conclusions are not satisfactory, it will
perhaps be best to say that in an absolute or true
sense it is the good which is the object of wish, but
that in reference to the individual it is that which
appears to be good. Hence it is the true good which
is good relatively to the virtuous man, and something
that need not be defined which is good relatively to
the vicious man. The case is much the same as in
the body; when people are in a good state of health
it is things which are truly wholesome that are wholesome to them, but when they are in a bad state of
health it is other things, and so with things that are
bitter, sweet, hot, heavy, and the rest. For the
virtuous man forms a right judgment of particular
cases, and in every case that which is true appears
true to him. For every moral state has its own
honours and pleasures, nor is there any point perhaps
so distinctive of the virtuous man as his power of
seeing the truth in all cases, because he is, as it were,

the standard and measure of things. It seems to be pleasure which most frequently deceives people, for pleasure appears to be good, although it is not, and the result is that they choose what is pleasant as if it were good, and avoid pain as if it were evil.

As it is the end which is the object of wish, and the means to the end which are the objects of deliberation and moral purpose, it follows that such actions as are concerned with the means will be determined by moral purpose and will be voluntary. But it is with the means that the activities of the virtues are concerned. *Chap. VII.*

Virtue and vice are both alike in our own power; for where it is in our power to act, it is also in our power to refrain from acting, and where it is in our power to refrain from acting, it is also in our power to act. Hence if it is in our power to act when action is noble, it will also be in our power to refrain from acting when inaction is shameful, and if it is in our power to refrain from acting when inaction is noble, it will also be in our power to act when action is shameful. But if it is in our power to do, and likewise not to do, what is noble and shameful, and if so to act or not to act is as we have seen to be good or bad, it follows that it is in our power to be virtuous or vicious. The saying *Virtue and vice voluntary.*

"None would be wicked, none would not be blessed[1],"

seems to be partly false and partly true; for while nobody is blessed against his will, vice is voluntary.

If this is not the case, it is necessary to dispute

---

[1] The line is of unknown authorship.

the statements which have just been made and to say
that a man is not the author or father of his actions
in the same sense as he is of his family. But if
these statements appear to be true and we cannot
refer our actions to any other original sources than
such as lie in our own power, then whatever it is
that has its sources in us must itself be in our own
power and must be voluntary. This view seems to be
supported by the testimony both of private individuals
and of legislators themselves; for legislators punish
and chastise evil-doers, unless the evil be done under
compulsion or from ignorance for which its authors
are not responsible; but they pay honour to people
who perform noble actions, their object being to
discourage the one class of actions and to stimulate
the others. Yet nobody stimulates us to do such
things as are not in our own power or voluntary. It
would be useless, e.g., to persuade us not to get hot,
or to feel pain or hunger, or anything of the kind, as
we should experience these sensations all the same. *I
say "ignorance for which a person is not responsible,"*
as we punish a person for mere ignorance, if it seems
that he is responsible for it. Thus the punishments
inflicted on drunken people who commit a crime are
double[1], as the origin of the crime lies in the person
himself, for it was in his power not to get drunk, and
the drunkenness was the cause of his ignorance.

Again, we punish people who are ignorant of any
legal point, if they ought to know it, and could easily

---

[1] Such was the effect of a law of Pittacus to which Aristotle
refers in the *Politics*, II. ch. 12, p. 1274B$_{18\,sqq}$.

know it. Similarly in other cases we punish people, whenever it seems that their ignorance was due to carelessness; for they had it in their power not to be ignorant, as they might have taken the trouble to inform themselves. It will perhaps be argued that a person is of such a character that he cannot take the trouble; but the answer is that people are themselves responsible for having acquired such a character by their dissolute life, and for being unjust or licentious, as their injustice is the consequence of doing wrong, and their licentiousness of spending their time in drinking and other such things. For a person's character depends upon the way in which he exercises his powers. The case of people who practise with a view to any competition or action is a proof of this law; for they are never weary of exercising.

Now a person must be utterly senseless, if he does not know that moral states are formed by the exercise of the powers in one way or another. Again, it is irrational to assert that one who acts unjustly does not wish to be unjust, or that one who acts licentiously does not wish to be licentious. If a person, not acting in ignorance, commits such actions as will make him unjust, he will be voluntarily unjust. But it does not follow that, if he wishes, he will cease to be unjust and will be just, any more than it follows that a sick man, *if he wishes*, will be well. It may happen that he is voluntarily ill through living an incontinent life, and disobeying his doctors. If so, it was once in his power not to be ill; but, as he has thrown the opportunity away, it is no longer in his power. Similarly, when a man has thrown a stone, it is no longer possible for him to recall it; still for all that it was in his power to throw or fling it, as the original act was in his power. So too the unjust or licentious person had it in his power in the first instance not to become such, and therefore he is voluntarily unjust or licentious; but when he has become such, it is no longer in his power not to be unjust or licentious.

But not only are the vices of the soul voluntary the vices of the body are also voluntary in some cases and in these cases are censured. For while nobody censures people who are born ugly, we censure people whose ugliness arises from negligence and want of exercise. It is the same with bodily infirmities and defects; nobody would find fault with a person who is born blind or whose blindness is the result of illness or of a blow; he would rather be an object of pity; but if his blindness were the result of intemperance or licentiousness of any kind, he would be universally censured.

Such bodily vices then as depend on ourselves are subjects of censure, and such as do not depend on ourselves are not. But if so, it follows that other than bodily vices, if they are objects of censure, must depend on ourselves.

It may be said however that we all aspire after what appears to be good, only we are not masters of the appearance. But the appearance which the end takes in the eyes of each of us depends upon his character. If each of us then is in a certain sense responsible for his moral state, he will be himself in a certain sense responsible for the appearance; but, if not, nobody will be responsible for his own evil doing, everybody will act as he does from ignorance of the end and under the impression that this will be the means of gaining the supreme good[1], the aspiration after the *true* end will not be a matter of our own choice, and it will be necessary for a man to be born with a sort of *moral* vision, enabling him to form a noble judgment and to choose that which is truly good. He who naturally possesses this noble judgment will be Nature's noble; for he will possess the greatest and noblest of all gifts, the gift which can never be received or learnt from anybody else, but must always be kept as Nature herself gave it, and to possess this natural gift in virtue and honour is to have a perfect and sincere nobility of nature.

If these considerations are true, why should virtue be voluntary rather than vice? For both alike, for the good and for the evil, the end is apparent and ordained by Nature, or in whatever way it may be, and it is to the end that men refer all their actions, however they may act. Whether the end then, whatever it be which any individual regards as the end, does not so appear to him by nature but depends in part on himself, or whether the end is naturally ordained, but virtue is voluntary, as the virtuous man does voluntarily all that he does to gain the end, in either case vice will be voluntary as much as virtue; for the personality of the bad man is as potent an influence as that of the good man in his actions, if not in his conception of the end.

If then, as is generally allowed, the virtues are

---

[1] The stop after ἔσεσθαι should be a comma.

voluntary (for we are ourselves, in a sense, partly responsible for our moral states, and it is because we possess a certain character that the end which we set before ourselves is of a certain kind), it follows that our vices too must be voluntary, as what is true of one is equally true of the other.

CHAP. VIII.   We have now described in outline the nature of the virtues generally. We have shown that they are means between two vices and that they are moral states. We have explained what are the causes producing them and that they naturally issue in the performance of the actions by which they are produced, that they are in our own power and voluntary, and that they are determined by the rule of right reason. But actions and moral states are not voluntary in the same sense. For while we are masters of our actions from beginning to end, inasmuch as we know the particulars, we are masters only of the beginning of our moral states; we do not perceive the particular steps by which they advance, as we do not perceive the particular steps in diseases. But as it was in our

Moral states voluntary. power to act in one way or another, our moral states are voluntary.

CHAP. IX. The several virtues. Let us then resume consideration of the several virtues and discuss their nature, the subjects with which they deal and the way in which they deal with them. In so doing we shall ascertain their number.

Courage.   We will begin with courage.

p. 49.   It has been already stated in this treatise that courage is a mean state in regard to sentiments of fear and confidence. It is clear too that the things which we fear are fearful; but fearful things may be broadly described as evil. Hence fear is sometime defined as an anticipation of evil.

Now, although we fear all evil things, e.g. ignominy, poverty, disease, friendlessness, and death, they do not all afford scope for a display of courage. There are some things which it is right and noble to fear, and which it is disgraceful not to fear, e.g. ignominy; for to fear ignominy is to be virtuous and modest, and not to fear it is to be shameless. A shameless person is sometimes called courageous by a figure of speech, as he possesses a certain similarity to a courageous person; for the courageous person is also fearless.

It is wrong perhaps to fear poverty or sickness or anything else that is not the consequence of vice or of one's own fault. Still fearlessness in regard to these things is not *necessarily* courage, although we speak of a person who is fearless in regard to them as courageous by analogy; for there are some people who are cowardly in military perils, and yet are liberal and confident in throwing money away. On the other hand a person is not a coward, if he fears insult offered to his children or his wife, or if he fears envy or any such thing, nor is he courageous, if he is brave in the prospect of a flogging.

We must inquire then what is the character of the fearful things in regard to which a courageous man exhibits his courage. It may be supposed that they will be the worst kind of fearful things; for nobody is better able to face dangers than the courageous man. But nothing is so fearful as death; for death is a limit, and when a man is dead, it seems that he is no more liable to good or evil. But it would seem not to be on all occasions that a man proves his courage by facing death itself; he does not prove it, e.g. by facing death at sea or from disease. What are these occasions then? Surely the noblest occasions, i.e. such occasions as present themselves in war; for that is the greatest and noblest of perils. It is in agreement with this view that special honours are paid, alike in free states and in monarchies, to citizens who have died on the field of battle.

Strictly speaking then, we may call a person courageous, if he is fearless in facing a noble death, and in all such sudden emergencies as bring death near, and therefore especially in facing the chances of war. Still the courageous man is fearless in disease and at sea too, although not in the same way as seamen; for while landsmen despair of safety and are distressed at the prospect of a watery grave, the experience which seamen possess makes them sanguine. It may be added that people display courage on occasions when prowess is possible or death is glorious; but in death at sea or from disease there is no room for courage or glory.

CHAP. X.
Fear.

People do not all feel the same things to be fearful. There are indeed things which we regard as exceeding the power of human endurance. Such things therefore excite fear in every intelligent person; but things which do not exceed the power of endurance are of various magnitudes and degrees, and the same is true of such things as inspire confidence. The courageous man is imperturbable so far as a man may be. Hence although he will fear such things he will face them in the right manner and in a rational spirit for the sake of what is noble, as this is the end of virtue.

But it is possible to fear these things too much or too little, and also to fear the things which are not fearful as if they were so. Mistakes occur because the fear is itself wrong, or because it is wrong in manner or time or so on, and it is the same with the things which inspire confidence.

Thus he who faces and fears the right things for the right motive and in the right way and at the right time, and whose confidence is similarly right, is courageous; for the courageous man in his emotions and actions has a sense of fitness and obeys the law of reason. But the end of every activity that a man displays is determined by the corresponding moral state. To the courageous man courage is noble; therefore the end or object of courage is also noble, for the character of everything is determined by its end. It is for the sake of what is noble then that the courageous man faces and does all that courage demands.

In regard to the excesses there is no name for a person whose fearlessness is excessive; it is one of the many qualities which, as has been already p. 49. remarked, have no names; but he would deserve to be called insane or insensible if there were nothing that he feared, not even an earthquake or a storm at sea, as is said to be the case with the Celts. One who is excessively confident in facing fearful things is called foolhardy. The foolhardy person may be re- Fool-garded as an impostor, and as one who affects a hardiness.

courage that he does not possess. Accordingly he wishes to appear to face fearful things in the spirit in which the courageous man really does face them; therefore he imitates him so far as he *safely* can. It follows that most foolhardy people are cowards at heart; for although they exhibit a foolhardy spirit where they safely can, they refuse to face *real* terrors. Cowardice. One whose fearfulness is excessive, on the other hand, is a coward; for he fears the wrong things and fears them in the wrong way, and so on. He is deficient too in confidence; but he reveals his character rather by his excess of fear in the presence of pain. The coward is a despondent sort of person, as being afraid of everything. It is the contrary with the courageous person; for it is natural to a confident person to be sanguine. Thus the coward, the foolhardy person, and the courageous person, while they have to do with the same things, assume different attitudes towards them. For while the two first go too far or not far enough, the third holds the intermediate position, which is right. Also, while the foolhardy are precipitate and eager before the hour of danger, they fail in its presence, but the courageous are keen in action, although they are quiet before the hour of action arrives.

Chap. XI.   Courage then, as has been said, is a mean state in Definition of courage. regard to the causes of confidence and fear, in such circumstances as have been described; and it chooses action or endures pain because this is the noble course or because the opposite course is disgraceful. Suicide.   But it is the act, not of a courageous person, but rather of a coward, to fly from poverty or love, or

anything that is painful, by death. For it is effeminacy to fly from troubles, nor does the suicide face
death because it is noble, but because it is a refuge
from evil.

Such then is, in general terms, the nature of Spurious
courage; but there are other alleged kinds of cour- kinds of
courage.
age which may be ranged under five different heads.

There is first political or civil courage. This is 1. Political
the most nearly akin to true courage; for it seems courage.
that citizens are induced to face dangers by the
penalties and censures which the laws inflict and by
the honours which they confer. This is the reason
why those are apparently the most courageous nations
in which cowards are held in contempt, and courageous people in honour. Homer represents persons
of this kind, such as Diomedes and Hector. *Thus
Hector says,*

"Polydamas will be the first to lay reproach on me[1],"

and Diomedes,

"Hector shall one day say among the Trojans
'Tydides by mine arm[2].'"

This courage bears the closest resemblance to the
courage which has been already described, as its
motive is virtue, or in other words a sense of honour,
and a longing for what is noble, i.e. for distinction,
and an avoidance of reproach as being disgraceful.
We may place in the same rank with it the courage of

[1] *Iliad* XXII. 100.
[2] *Iliad* VIII. 148, 149. The quotation would have been
clearer if the concluding words of the second line, φοβεύμενος
ἵκετο νῆας, had been given.

people who are compelled by superior authority to act in the same way; but they are inferior, as the motive of their conduct is not a sense of honour but fear, and an avoidance not of disgrace but of pain. For superiors employ compulsion, as when Hector says,

> "The man whom I find crouching far from fight
> Shall not avail to escape the hounds[1]."

It is the same with commanders who station their troops and flog them if they retreat, or who draw them up with trenches or such things at their back[2]. These are all cases in which compulsion is employed; but we ought to be courageous not because courage is compulsory, but because it is noble.

2. Experi- ence.

Secondly, it would seem that experience of particular things is a sort of courage. Hence it was that Socrates himself conceived courage to be knowledge. The people who possess this experience are different in different cases. In war they are the regular troops; for it seems that there are many false alarms in war, and regular troops are best able to compre- hend such alarms at a glance. The result is that they appear to be courageous because other people do not understand the nature of such alarms. Then their experience makes them most effective in attack and in defence, as they understand the use of their arms and possess such arms as will be most service-

---

[1] *Iliad* II. 391, 393, xv. 348. In neither passage are the words exactly as here; but in the former they are closely similar although it is Agamemnon who speaks them, and in the latter Hector is the speaker.

[2] So as to make escape difficult or impossible.

able alike in attack and in defence. Thus in battle they are like armed men contending against unarmed, and trained athletes against people who have had no special training; for even in athletic competitions it is not the most courageous men who are the best combatants, but the men who are strongest and whose bodies are in the best physical condition. But regular troops turn cowards when the danger is overpowering and they are inferior in number and appointment. At such a time they are the first to fly, while the citizens remain at their posts and die, as in fact happened at the temple of Hermes[1]. For while the citizens look upon flight as disgraceful, and prefer death to such a means of safety, the regulars who met the danger in the first instance under the conviction of their own superior strength, as soon as they discover the truth, take to flight, being more afraid of death than of disgrace. But that is not the character of true courage.

Again, a passionate spirit[2] is sometimes reckoned 3. Passion. as a kind of courage. It is supposed that people who under the influence of passion turn like wild beasts upon those who have wounded them are courageous, because courageous people are themselves spirited or passionate. For passion is preeminently eager to

[1] According to the Scholiast it happened in the sacred war that in an engagement which took place at the Ἑρμαῖον the Coronean citizens were killed to a man, but their Bœotian auxiliaries, who were regular soldiers, fled in a panic.

[2] The word θυμός may mean either "spirit" or "passion," and I have tried to preserve the balance of the two meanings.

encounter perils. Hence Homer says,

"He lent strength to his passion[1],"

and

"He roused his might and passion[2],"

and

"Fierce might breathed through his nostrils[3],"

and

"His blood boiled[4],"

all such being signs which seem to indicate the stir and impulse of passion. Now courageous people are moved to action by nobleness, although passion co-operates with them ; wild beasts, on the other hand, are moved by pain, i.e. they are moved by being shot or terrified ; for if they are in a forest or a marsh, they do not come near man. They do not deserve to be called courageous because they are goaded by pain and passion to rush upon peril without any foresight of the dangers which they incur. For if this were courage, asses themselves would be courageous when they are hungry, as blows cannot drive them away from their food. Adulterers too are often driven by their lust to do adventurous deeds. But to

[1] The nearest passage is *Iliad* XVI. 529; but μένος, not σθένος, is read there.

[2] Apparently *Iliad* V. 470; but the words are ὤτρυνε μένος καὶ θυμὸν ἑκάστου.

[3] Apparently *Odyssey* XXIV. 318,

$$\text{ἀνὰ ῥῖνας δέ οἱ ἤδη}$$
$$\text{δριμὺ μένος προῦτυψε.}$$

[4] Not in Homer.

It may be permitted me to observe here how very lax is the idea of a quotation in all ancient literature, sacred and profane.

be goaded by pain or passion into facing perils is not to be courageous. Yet it seems that the courage arising from passion is the most natural kind of courage, and that if a right purpose and motive are added to it, it becomes *true* courage.

Men feel pain in anger and pleasure in revenge ; but if their motive in fighting is to gain pleasure and escape pain, they are not courageous, however well they may fight, as their motive is not nobleness, nor their principle reason, but emotion. Still there is a certain resemblance between them and courageous people.

Nor again are sanguine people courageous, as it 4. San-
guineness. is only their numerous victories over a number of enemies that inspire them with confidence in the face of danger. Still they resemble courageous people, inasmuch as both are confident ; but while the confidence of the courageous arises from such causes as have been already defined, that of the sanguine arises from a belief in their own superiority, and in their probable immunity from suffering[1]. (It may be observed that intoxicated people behave in this sort of way, for intoxication renders them sanguine[2].) But when the result does not correspond with their expectation, these people turn tail, whereas a courageous person, as we know, is one who faces such things as inspire and are seen to inspire fear in a man, because it is noble to face them and disgraceful not to face them. Hence it seems more courageous to be fearless and cool amidst sudden alarms than amid

[1] Reading μηθὲν ἂν παθεῖν.
[2] An incidental remark, in the nature of a footnote.

such as have been foreseen; for fearlessness of the former kind is more the outcome of a moral state or at least is less the outcome of premeditation. For while the resolution to meet such perils as are foreseen may be the result of calculation and reasoning, the resolution to meet sudden perils depends upon the moral state.

5. Ignor-
ance.

Lastly, people who are ignorant of their danger appear courageous, nor indeed are they very different from sanguine people, although they are inferior to them, as having no self-esteem. It is self-esteem which makes the sanguine hold their ground for a certain time; but the ignorant, being the victims of deception, if they discover or suspect that the case is not as they supposed, turn to flight, as happened to the Argives[1] when they fell in with the Lacedaemonians, whom they took to be Sicyonians.

We have now described the character of courageous people, and of people who are sometimes thought to be courageous.

Chap. XII.
Relation of
courage to
pleasure
and pain.

Although courage is concerned with sentiments of confidence and fear, it is not equally concerned with both, but chiefly with the causes of fear. For he who is cool in the circumstances, and shows a proper spirit on the occasions, which excite fear is more truly courageous than he who shows a proper spirit on the occasions which inspire confidence.

p. 79.

It is endurance of painful things, as has been said, that entitles people to be called courageous. Hence it is that courage is painful, and is justly a subject of praise; for it is more difficult to endure pains than

[1] The story is told by Xenophon, *Hellenica* IV. ch. 10.

to abstain from pleasures. At the same time it would seem that the end which courage proposes to itself is pleasant, but that it is obscured by attendant circumstances, as happens also in gymnastic contests. For while the end or object which boxers have in view, viz. the crown and the honour, is pleasant, the blows which they receive, and all their exertions, are painful and grievous to flesh and blood, and, as these are numerous, while the object *or prize* itself is small, it appears not to afford any pleasure.

If then the case in regard to courage is similar to this, death and wounds will be painful to the courageous man and involuntary ; but he will endure them because endurance is honourable and avoidance disgraceful. Nay, in proportion as he possesses virtue in its fulness, and is happy, will be his pain at the prospect of death ; for to such an one life is pre-eminently valuable, and he will be consciously deprived at death of the greatest blessings. But painful as such deprivation is, he is none the less courageous, nay perhaps he is even more courageous, as he willingly sacrifices these blessings for noble conduct on the field of battle.

It is not the case then that all the virtues imply a pleasurable activity, except in so far as one attains to the end. Still, it is true perhaps, after all, that people who enjoy a happy life are not such good soldiers as people who are less courageous but have nothing to lose, as these last are ready to face any danger, and will sell their lives for a small sum of money.

This may be taken as a sufficient account of

courage ; its nature may be easily comprehended, at least in outline, from what has been said.

CHAP.XIII.
Temperance.

We will proceed to consider temperance, as it seems that courage and temperance are the virtues of the irrational parts of human nature.

p. 49.

We have already said that temperance is a mean state in respect of pleasures ; for it is not in the same degree or manner concerned with pains. Pleasure is also the sphere in which licentiousness displays itself.

Let us therefore define now the character of these pleasures. We will accept the distinction which is commonly made between bodily and psychical or mental pleasures, such as ambition and the love of learning ; for he who is ambitious or fond of learning takes pleasure in the object of which he is fond, although it is not his body which is affected but his mind. But where pleasures of this kind are in question people are not called either temperate or licentious. It is the same with all such other pleasures as are not bodily. Thus people who are fond of talking and of telling stories, and who spend their days in trifling pursuits we call gossips, but we do not call them licentious, nor do we call people licentious who feel pain at the loss of money or friends.

Temperance then will apply to bodily pleasures only, but not to all even of these. For if people take pleasure in gratifications of the sight, e.g. in colours, forms, and painting, they are not called either temperate or licentious. Yet it would seem possible to take a right pleasure or an excessive or insufficient pleasure in these things as well as in others. It is the same with gratifications of the ear. Nobody speaks of such people as take an excessive pleasure in music or acting as licentious, or of people who take a right pleasure as temperate. Nor again do we speak of people who enjoy gratifications of the smell as licentious or temperate, except accidentally. Thus we do not call people licentious if they take pleasure in the smell of apples or roses or incense, but rather if they take pleasure in the smell of unguents and relishes ; for it is in these that a licentious person takes pleasure, as they remind him of the objects of his desire. It is true that we may see other people, when they are hungry, taking pleasure in the smell of food ; but it is only a licentious person who *habitually* takes pleasure in such things, as they are the objects of his desire.

The lower animals again, are not, in general, capable of the pleasures of these senses, except accidentally. Dogs, e.g. do not take pleasure in scenting hares' flesh but only in eating it, although the smell gives them the sensation of eating. Again, a lion takes pleasure not in hearing an ox's lowing[1], but in devouring the ox, although, as it is the lowing by which he perceived that the ox is near, he appears to take pleasure in the lowing. Similarly it is not the sight or discovery of a stag or wild goat that gives him pleasure, but the prospect of a meal.

Temperance and licentiousness then have to do Licentiousness. with pleasures of such a kind as the lower animals generally are capable of, and it is hence that these pleasures appear slavish and brutish. They are the

---

[1] φονῇ is a misprint for φωνῇ.

pleasures of the touch and the taste. It appears that the taste comes little, if at all, into question ; for it is the taste which judges of flavours, as when people test wines or season dishes, but it is in no sense this judgment of flavours which gives pleasure, at least to such people as are licentious, but rather the actual enjoyment of them, and the medium of enjoyment is invariably the sense of touch, whether in meats or in drinks or in what are called the pleasures of love. This was the reason why a certain gourmand prayed that his throat might become longer than a crane's, showing that his pleasure was derived from the sense of touch. Thus the sense of which incontinence is predicable is the most universal of the senses. It would seem too that incontinence is justly censurable, as it is a characteristic not of our human, but of our animal, nature. To take delight and supreme satisfaction in such things is brutish; for the most liberal or refined of the pleasures of the touch, such as the pleasures of rubbing and of taking a hot bath in the gymnasium, are denied to the profligate, as the sense of touch which an incontinent man cultivates belongs, not to the whole body, but only to certain parts of it.

Desires universal and individual. It seems that some desires are universal and others are individual and acquired. Thus the desire of food is a natural desire. Everybody who feels want desires meat or drink or perhaps both. A young man, too, in the prime of life, says Homer[1], desires the love of a woman. But it is not equally true that everybody desires a particular form of gratification, or the same

---

[1] The reference seems to be to *Iliad* xxiv. 129, the words addressed by Thetis to Achilles.

forms. Hence the particular desire is peculiar to ourselves *or individual.* Nevertheless, there is something natural in it ; for although different people are
pleased by different things, yet there are some things
which are pleasanter to all people than others.

Now in respect of such desires as are natural
there are but few people who make a mistake, and
their mistake is always on one side, viz. that of
excess. For to eat or drink anything to the point of
surfeit is to exceed the natural limit of quantity, as
the natural desire does not go beyond the satisfaction
of our want. Accordingly such persons are called
gluttons because they go beyond what is right in
satisfying their want. It is only exceedingly slavish
people who behave in this way.

In regard to such pleasures as are individual there
are many people who go wrong, and they go wrong
in many different ways. For if people are said to be
unduly fond of particular things, either as taking
pleasure in wrong things or as taking more pleasure
than ordinary people[1] or as taking pleasure in a
wrong way, the excess of which the licentious are
guilty may assume all these forms. For they take
pleasure in some things which are detestable and
therefore wrong, and if these are things in which it is
right to take pleasure ; they take a greater pleasure
in them than is right or than most people take[2].

It is clear then that excess in respect of pleasures
is licentiousness, and that it properly is a subject of

[1] The ὡς may probably be retained, but the text should be
ἢ τῷ μᾶλλον ἢ ὡς οἱ πολλοί, without the comma after μᾶλλον.
[2] Omitting the comma after δεῖ.

censure. But in respect of pains there is this difference between temperance and courage. A person is not called temperate if he bears pains bravely, and incontinent if he does not; but the incontinent person is so called because he feels more pain than is right at not obtaining pleasures, his pleasure being the cause of his pain, and the temperate man is so called because he is not pained at the absence *of pleasure* and at his abstinence from it.

CHAP. XIV. The licentious man then desires all pleasures, or the greatest pleasures, and is led by his desire to prefer these to anything else. He feels a double pain therefore, viz. the pain of failing to obtain them and the pain of desiring them, as all desire is attended by pain. Yet it seems paradoxical to assert that his pleasure is the cause of his pain.

We never find people whose love of pleasures is deficient and whose delight in them is less than it ought to be. Such insensibility to pleasures is not human; for even the lower animals distinguish different kinds of food, liking some and disliking others. A being who should not take pleasure in anything, nor make any difference between one thing and another, would be far from being a man. But there is no name for such a being, as he never exists.

Character of the temperate man. The temperate man holds a mean position in respect of pleasures. He takes no pleasure in the things in which the licentious man takes most pleasure; he rather dislikes them; nor does he take pleasure at all in wrong things nor an excessive pleasure in anything that is pleasant, nor is he pained at the absence of such things, nor does he desire them,

except perhaps in moderation, nor does he desire
them more than is right, or at the wrong time, and so
on. But he will be eager in a moderate and right
spirit for all such things as are pleasant and at the
same time conducive to health or to a sound bodily
condition, and for all other pleasures, so long as they
are not prejudicial to these or inconsistent with noble
conduct or extravagant beyond his means. For unless
a person limits himself in this way, he affects such
pleasures more than is right, whereas the temperate
man follows the guidance of right reason.

Licentiousness seems to have more the character
of voluntary action than cowardice, as the former is
due to pleasure, and the latter to pain ; and whereas
pleasure is something that we choose, pain is something that we avoid.   Also, while pain distracts and
destroys the nature of one who suffers it, pleasure
has no such effect, but rather leaves the will free.
Hence licentiousness deserves more severe reproach
than cowardice ; for it is easier to train oneself to
meet its temptations as they frequently occur in life,
nor does the training involve any danger, whereas the
contrary is the case in meeting alarms.

CHAP. XV.
Licentious-
ness vo-
luntary
more than
cowardice.

It would seem too that cowardice as a moral state
is not voluntary in the same degree as particular acts
of cowardice.   For cowardice in itself is painless, but
particular acts of cowardice occur because people are
so utterly driven out of their wits by pain that they
throw away their arms and disgrace themselves
generally, and this is the reason why such acts have
the appearance of being compulsory.   In the case of
the licentious man on the other hand, the particular

acts are voluntary, as he eagerly desires them, but licentiousness as a whole is not so voluntary, as nobody desires to be licentious.

We apply the term "licentiousness" (ἀκολασία), to the faults of children as well as to those of grown-up people, as there is a certain similarity between them. It does not matter to my present purpose which of the two kinds of faults is named after the other; but it is clear that the later is named after the earlier[1].

The metaphor[2] (in the word ἀκολασία) is not, it seems, a bad one. For that which is prone to disgraceful things, and capable of rapid growth, stands in need of pruning or chastisement (κεκολάσθαι δεῖ), but such proneness and such growth are preeminently characteristic of desire or of childhood; for children, like licentious people, live by desire and not by reason, and the longing for pleasure is nowhere so strong as in them. If then this disposition is not obedient and subject to authority, it will greatly develope. For the longing for pleasure which a foolish person has is insatiable and universal, and the active exercise of the desire augments its native strength, until the desires, if they are strong or vehement, actually expel the reasoning power. They ought therefore to be moderate and few, and in no way contrary to reason. But we speak of such a

---

[1] If the word "licentious" were used of a child in English, it would, I think, be used with a certain reservation.

[2] The observation, which cannot be translated into English, depends upon the etymological connexion between ἀκολασία "licentiousness" and κόλασις "chastisement."

disposition as obedient and chastened ; for as a child ought to live according to the direction of his tutor[1] so ought the concupiscent element in man to live according to the reason.   In the temperate man then the concupiscent element ought to live in harmony with the reason, as nobleness is the object of them both, and the temperate man desires what is right, and desires it in the right way, and at the right time, i.e. according to the law of reason.   We may now bring our discussion of temperance to a close.

[1] It will be understood that the παιδαγωγός was not so much a "tutor" in the modern sense as the confidential servant who took charge of a child.

BOOK IV.

THE next virtue to be considered is liberality. Liberality seems to be a mean state in regard to property. For the liberal man wins praise, not in war, nor in the same sphere as the temperate man, nor again in respect of his judgments, but in regard to the giving and taking of property and particularly in giving it. By property we understand all such things as have their value measured by money. Prodigality and illiberality are excesses and deficiencies in regard to property. We invariably apply the term "illiberality" to people whose hearts are set more than is right upon property, but we sometimes employ the term "prodigality" in a complex sense, speaking of people who are incontinent and who spend money in licentious living as "prodigals." Prodigals therefore are held to be utterly worthless people as combining in themselves a number of vices. But this is not a proper application of the term "prodigal," it strictly means a person who has one particular vice, viz. that of wasting his substance, for a prodigal[1] is

[1] The statement that the prodigal (ἄσωτος) ruins himself depends upon the derivation of ἄσωτος from ἀ, σώζειν.

me who is ruining himself, and to waste one's sub-
tance seems in a way to be ruining oneself, as this is
he only means of life. It is in this sense then that
ve understand the term "prodigality."

Things which admit of use[1] may be used either
vell or badly. But riches are a useful thing. Again,
he person who makes the best use of anything is the
person who possesses the virtue appropriate to that
hing. Accordingly he will make the best use of
iches who possesses the virtue which is appropriate
o property, i.e. the liberal man. Further it seems
hat the use of property consists in spending and
;iving; the taking and keeping of property should
ather be described as acquisition. Hence it is more
ruly distinctive of the liberal man to give to the
ight people than to take from the right quarter and
lot to take from the wrong quarter. For it is more
ruly distinctive of virtue to be the author than to be
he recipient of benefactions, and to do what is noble
han to abstain from doing what is shameful. But it
s clear that, while giving implies doing well and
,cting nobly, taking implies only being well treated
»r not behaving in a shameful manner. Gratitude
oo is the due of one who gives, not of one who does
lot take, and praise is his due in a higher degree.
Also, it is easier to abstain from taking than to give,
or people are less ready to throw away what is their
»wn than to abstain from taking what belongs to
.omebody else. Again, people who give are called

---

[1] χρεία, χρῆσθαι, χρήσιμος, χρήματα, all words occurring in this
»assage, are etymologically connected.

liberal, people who abstain from taking are not praised for liberality so much as for justice, but people who take are not praised at all. Of all virtuous people none are so much beloved as the liberal; for they are benefactors, and their benefaction consists in their giving.

CHAP. II.
Characteristics of liberality.
Virtuous actions are noble and have a noble motive. The liberal man, being virtuous, then will give from a noble motive and in a right spirit; for he will give the right amount, and will give it to the right persons and at the right time, and will satisfy all the other conditions of right giving. He will do all this too with pleasure or without pain; for a virtuous action is pleasant or painless, and it is certainly anything but painful. But he who gives to the wrong people, or who gives not from a noble motive but for some other cause, will not be called liberal, but by some other name; nor will he be so called, if giving is painful to him, as in that case he would prefer the wealth to the noble action, and this preference is illiberal. Nor will the liberal man take from wrong sources; for such taking, again, is unlike the character of one who is no admirer of property. Nor, again, will he be inclined to ask favours; for one who is in the habit of conferring benefits will not be ready at any moment to receive them. When he does take, it will be from right sources, e.g. from his own possessions, and he will take not as if taking were noble, but because it is necessary, if he is to have the means of giving. He will not neglect his own property since he wishes to employ it in relieving other people. He will refrain from giving indiscriminately that he may have the

means of giving to the right people, and at the times and in the places where giving is noble.

If a man is excessively liberal, he will actually go too far in his giving, the result being that he will reserve too little for himself; for disregard of self is a characteristic of liberality. But in estimating liberality we must take account of a person's fortune; for liberality consists, not in the amount of the money given, but in the moral state of the giver[1], and the moral state proportions the gift to the fortune of the giver. It is quite possible then that one who gives less than another may be more liberal, if his means are smaller. It seems that people who have not made their own fortune, but have inherited it, are more liberal, as they have never known what want is, and people are always fondest of their own productions, e.g. parents of their children, and poets of their poems.

It is difficult for a liberal man to be rich, as he is not fond of getting or of saving money, but rather of spending it, and values wealth not for its own sake, but as affording an opportunity of giving. Hence it is a reproach often levelled against fortune that the people who deserve riches most have often the least. But the fact is easily explained; for it is impossible to have wealth or anything else without taking the trouble to have it. At the same time the liberal man will not give to the wrong people, or on any wrong occasion, and so on; for to do so would be to cease to act in a liberal spirit, and if he were to spend

---

[1] As in the parable of the widow's two mites.

money upon these objects, he would not have the
means of spending it upon the right objects. For the
liberal man, as has been said, is one who spends in
proportion to his substance, and who spends upon
the right objects. But one who spends in excess of
his fortune is a prodigal. Hence it is that we do not
call despots prodigals, as it does not seem easy for
them to exceed the amount of their property by their
gifts and expenses.

As liberality is a mean state in regard to the
giving and taking of property, the liberal man will
both give and spend on the right objects and to the
right amount, whether in small matters or in great,
and will feel pleasure in doing so. He will also take
from the right sources and to the right amount. For
as the virtue is a mean state in regard both to giving
and to taking, he will do both in the right manner.
For honourable taking is consistent with honourable
giving ; but such taking as is not honourable is
incompatible with it. Thus the giving and taking
which are consistent are found to exist together in
the same person, but the giving and taking which are
incompatible are clearly not so found.

If it happens that the liberal man spends more or
less than is right and noble, he will feel pain, but it
will be a moderate and right pain ; for virtue
naturally feels pleasure and pain on the right occasions and in the right manner.

Again, the liberal man is easy to deal with in
money matters. He is one who can easily be cheated,
as he does not care for money, and is more distressed
at not having spent what is right than pained at

having spent what is not right ; in fact he is a person who does not approve of Simonides[1].

The prodigal on the other hand goes wrong in these respects as in others ; for he does not feel pleasure or pain at the right causes or in the right manner, as we shall see more clearly when we proceed.

We have said that prodigality and illiberality are excesses and deficiencies, and that they are so in two respects, viz. in giving and taking, for we reckon spending as a form of giving. Prodigality then exceeds in giving and not taking, but is deficient in taking. Illiberality is deficient in giving and exceeds in taking, but is deficient and exceeds in giving and taking on a small scale.

Now the two characteristics of prodigality *viz.* *giving and not taking*, are seldom combined in the same person. It is not easy for a person, if he has no source of revenue, to give to everybody ; for private persons, if they give in this way, soon find that their property runs short, and it is private persons who are commonly called prodigals. A prodigal of this kind however, if he existed, would seem to be far superior to an illiberal person ; for his faults are easily cured by age and lack of property, and he is capable of attaining to the mean or intermediate state. In fact he possesses the characteristics of a liberal man, as he gives and does not take, although

---

[1] There are several *dicta* of Simonides, such as those which Sir A. Grant quotes, showing his appreciation of wealth. Cp. *Rhetoric* II. ch. 16, p. 1391 A_{8-12}.

in neither respect is his action right or good. If he were to be trained aright or otherwise reformed, he would be liberal; for then he would give to the right people, and would not take from the wrong sources. It seems then that his character is not a bad one ; for it is not a vicious or ignoble nature, but a foolish one, which exceeds in giving and in abstinence from taking. A prodigal of this kind seems to be far superior to an illiberal person, not only for the reasons which have been given but because the former does good to many people while the latter does good to nobody, not even to himself. But most prodigals, as has been said, not only give to the wrong people but take from the wrong sources, and are so far illiberal. They become grasping because they are eager to spend, and are not able to do so easily, as their means soon run short ; they are therefore obliged to get the means from other sources. At the same time as nobleness is a matter of indifference to them, they are reckless and indiscriminate in their taking ; for they are eager to give but they do not care at all how they give or how they get the means of giving. The result is that their very gifts are not liberal, as they are not noble in themselves or in their object or made in the right manner. These prodigals sometimes enrich people who ought to be poor, and, while they will not give a penny to persons of respectable character, they heap presents upon their flatterers or the ministers of their various pleasures. Thus they are generally licentious ; for as they are fond of spending, they squander money on licentious living among other things, and as nobleness is not the rule of their lives, they sink into being mere pleasure seekers. A prodigal then, if left destitute of guidance, commits these vagaries, but by careful training he may come to the mean or right state of life.

Illiberality on the other hand is incurable; for it seems that old age and impotence of any kind makes men illiberal. Also it runs in human nature more than prodigality; for most people are fonder of money than of giving money away. It is of wide extent too, and assumes numerous forms; there seem to be many aspects of illiberality. For as it consists in two things, viz. deficiency of giving and excess of taking, it is not always found in its entirety. It sometimes happens that the two parts are separated, and while some people go too far in taking, others do not go far enough in giving. The people who are described by such names as "niggards," "misers," and "curmudgeons," are all deficient in giving, but they do not covet or wish to take other people's property. They are influenced in some cases by a sense of equity, and a desire of avoiding disgrace; for there are some people who seem, or pretend, to hoard their money with the view of securing themselves against ever being compelled to do what is disgraceful. This is the class of skinflints, and all such people whose names are derived from an excessive unwillingness to give to anybody. Others again are induced to abstain from taking other people's property by fear, feeling that it is difficult for them to take other people's property without having their own property taken by other people; hence they choose neither to take nor to give. Others again go

Illiberality.

too far in taking by taking anything from anybody, e.g. such people as pursue illiberal[1] or degraded occupations, keepers of brothels and the like, and usurers who lend small sums of money at extortionate rates of interest. All these are people who take money from wrong sources, and take more than is right. It appears that a sordid love of gain is the common characteristic of them all, as they all consent to bear an evil name for the sake of gain, and this a trifling gain ; for if people take large sums from improper sources or of an improper kind, we do not call them illiberal. Thus we do not so speak of despots when they sack cities and plunder temples; we rather speak of them as wicked, impious, and unjust. But cardsharpers, cutpurses[2] and robbers are illiberal people, as making gain by sordid or disgraceful means; for it is the love of gain which makes both cardsharpers and robbers ply their business and consent to bear an evil name. It is for profit that robbers face the greatest dangers, and cardsharpers make gain from their friends, to whom they ought to give. Both classes, as wishing to make gain from improper sources, may be said to have a sordid or disgraceful love of gain, and all such forms of taking are illiberal.

It is reasonable to regard illiberality as the opposite of liberality ; for it is a greater evil than

---

[1] The Greek word ἐλεύθερος, like the English "liberal," may mean either "generous" or "honourable," and Aristotle hardly seems to be aware that he confuses the meanings.

[2] The Greek word means one who steals the clothes of somebody while he is bathing.

prodigality, and men are more likely to err on the side of illiberality than in the direction of prodigality as we have described it. This must suffice then, as our account of liberality and of the vices which are opposed to it.

It would seem natural to discuss magnificence next, as magnificence[1] seems also to be a virtue which has to do with property. But it does not extend, like liberality, to all the uses of property ; it touches only such as involve a large expenditure, and here it exceeds liberality in scale ; for as the name[2] itself suggests, magnificence is suitable expenditure upon a great scale. But the greatness is relative to the occasion ; for a person who fits out a trireme does not incur the same expense as one who is the head of a sacred legation. What is suitable then is relative to the person, occasion and circumstances. If a person spends money duly upon small or unimportant occasions, if he can say, e.g. *in the poet's words,*

"Oft to a vagrant gave I[3],"

he is not called magnificent, but only if he makes such an expenditure upon great occasions ; for although the magnificent person is liberal, it does not follow that the liberal person is magnificent.

The deficiency of such a moral state is called meanness ; its excess vulgarity, bad taste, and the like, implying not so much an excessive expenditure

Margin notes: Chap. IV. Magnificence. Meanness. Vulgarity.

---

[1] Reading αὕτη.
[2] μεγαλοπρέπεια.
[3] *Odyssey* XVII. 420. It is Odysseus who speaks.

on right circumstances as an ostentatious expenditure
on wrong occasions and in a wrong manner. But of
this we will speak later.

The magnificent man is like a connoisseur in art;
he has the faculty of perceiving what is suitable, and
of spending large sums of money with good taste.
For as we said at the outset, a moral state is determined by its activities and its objects. The expenses
of the magnificent man then are large and suitable[1];
so too are his results; for this is the only way in
which a large expenditure can at the same time be
suitable to its result. It follows that the result ought
to be worthy of the expenditure, and the expenditure
worthy of the result, or of an even greater result.
The motive of the magnificent man in incurring this
expense will be nobleness; for nobleness is a characteristic of all the virtues. He will spend his money
too in a cheerful and lavish spirit, as a minute
calculation of expense is a mark of meanness. He
will consider how a work can be made most beautiful
and most suitable, rather than how much it will cost,
and how it can be done in the cheapest way. The
magnificent man will necessarily be liberal as well;
for the liberal man too will spend the right amount
of money and will spend it in the right manner.
But here the greatness, i.e. the great scale, of the
magnificent man, will appear, although liberality has
the same field as magnificence; with equal expenditure he will make the result more magnificent. For
the virtue or excellence of a possession is not the

[1] Again the argument turns upon the etymological meaning
of μεγαλοπρέπεια.

p. 44.

same as that of a result or a work of art; for it is the possession which is worth most that is the greatest prize or honour, as e.g. gold, but a work of art is prized for its greatness and nobleness. For the contemplation of such a work excites admiration, and what is magnificent is always admirable. In a word, magnificence is excellence of work on a great scale.

There is a kind of expenditure which we call honourable, such as expenditure upon the Gods, votive offerings, temples, and sacrifices, and similarly all that appertains to divine worship, or upon the favourite objects of patriotic rivalry, as when people consider it their duty to supply a chorus or fit out a trireme or even to give a public dinner in a handsome style.

CHAP. V. Conditions of magnificence.

But in all these matters, as has been said, there must be a regard paid to the agent and his resources. The expenditure ought to be worthy of him and his resources, and to be suitable not only to the result but to its author. It follows that a poor man cannot be magnificent, as he does not possess the means of spending large sums of money suitably. He is foolish if he makes the attempt, as his expenditure will be neither proportionate to his means nor proper in itself, but unless a thing is done in a right way, it cannot be virtuous. But magnificence is suitable to people who are in possession of the necessary means, whether they have acquired them by their own efforts or have inherited them from their ancestors or connexions, and to persons of rank and reputation and the like, as all these advantages confer importance and dignity.

p. 101.

Such may be said to be, in general, the character

of the magnificent man, and such, as has been said, the expenditure in which his magnificence displays itself; for this is the greatest and most honourable kind of expenditure. It displays itself also on such private occasions as occur once in a lifetime, e.g. marriage and the like, or on any occasion of peculiar interest to the state or the upper classes, or in receiving foreigners and taking leave of them or in making an interchange of presents; for the magnificent man spends money not on himself but upon public objects, and gifts have a certain similarity to religious offerings. Again, a magnificent man will erect a house in a manner suitable to his wealth; for even a private house may be an ornament to the city. He will prefer to spend his money upon such works as are permanent, for none are so noble as these, and in all these cases he will observe the law of propriety ; for the same things are not appropriate to gods and to men, or in building a temple and in making a tomb. In his expenditure too, everything will be great of its kind; there is nothing so magnificent as great expenditure on a great occasion, but, *when that is impossible*, the next thing is such greatness as the particular occasion allows.

There is a difference between greatness in the result and greatness in the expenditure. Thus the most beautiful of balls or bottles has a certain magnificence as a present for a child, although its price is trifling and paltry. It is characteristic then of the magnificent man, whatever be the class of work that he produces, to produce it in a magnificent way ; for the result so produced cannot easily be surpassed, and it is proportionate to the expenditure made upon it.

Such then being the character of the magnificent man, the man who is guilty of excess, or the vulgar man, exceeds in spending more than is right, as has been said ; for he spends large sums upon trifles and makes a display which is offensive to good taste, as e.g. by entertaining members of his club at a breakfast which is as sumptuous as a wedding-breakfast, or if he provides a comic chorus, by bringing the members of it on to the stage in purple dresses, after the manner of the Megarians.   And all this he will do, not from a noble motive, but merely to exhibit his wealth, and because he thinks that it will win him admiration.   Where he ought to spend a great deal, he will spend little, and where he ought to spend little, he will spend a great deal. Chap. VI.
Vulgarity.

The mean man, on the other hand, will be deficient on all occasions, and after an enormous expenditure, will ruin the beauty of his work for a trifle, never doing anything without hesitating about it, and considering how he can reduce his expenditure to a *minimum*, and grieving over it and always imagining he is doing things on a larger scale than is necessary. Meanness.

Thus these moral states, viz. *vulgarity and meanness*, are vices, although they do not bring reproach upon us, as they are not injurious to others nor particularly indecorous.

Highmindedness[1], as its very name suggests, Chap. VII.
Highmind-
edness.

[1] One cannot help regretting that "magnanimity," which is the precise English equivalent of μεγαλοψυχία, has come by usage to bear a limited sense.

seems to be occupied with high things. Let us begin
then by ascertaining the character of those things. It
makes no difference whether we consider the moral
state or the person in whom the moral state is seen.

A highminded person seems to be one who regards himself as worthy of high things, and who is
worthy of them. For he who does so without being
worthy is foolish, and no virtuous person is foolish or
absurd.

Such then is the highminded person. One who is
worthy of small things, and who regards himself as
worthy of them, is temperate *or sensible,* but he is
not highminded; for highmindedness can only exist
on a large scale as beauty can only exist in a tall
person. Small people may be elegant and well pro-
portioned, but not beautiful.

He who regards himself as worthy of high things
and is unworthy of them is conceited, although it is
not everyone who takes an exaggerated view of his
own worth that is a conceited person.

He who takes too low a view of his own worth is
mean-minded[1], whether it be high things, or moderate,
or even small things that he is worthy of, so long as
he underrates his deserts. This would seem to be
especially a fault in one who is worthy of high
things; for what would he do, it may be asked, if his
deserts were less than they are?

The highminded man, while he holds an extreme
position by the greatness of his deserts, holds an

[1] It would be desirable to use "lowmindedness" as the
opposite of "highmindedness," but the word has received an
inappropriate shade of meaning.

ntermediate or mean position by the propriety of his
:onduct, as he estimates his own deserts aright, while
ıthers rate their deserts too high or too low.

But if then he regards himself as worthy of high
hings, and is worthy of them, and especially if he is
ıorthy of the highest things, there will be one
ıarticular object of his interest. Desert is a term
ısed in reference to external goods, but we should
ıaturally esteem that to be the greatest of external
;oods which we attribute to the gods, or which
ıersons of high reputation most desire, or which is
he prize awarded to the noblest actions. But honour
ınswers to this description, as being the highest of
xternal goods.

The highminded man, then, bears himself in a
ight spirit towards honours and dishonours. It
ıeeds no proof that highminded people are concerned
ıith honour ; for it is honour more than anything else
ıf which the great regard themselves, and deservedly
egard themselves, as worthy. The mean-minded man _{Mean-}
ınderestimates himself both in respect of his own _{minded-
ness.}
leserts and in comparison with the acknowledged
leserts of the highminded man. The conceited man _{Conceit.}
ıverestimates his own deserts, but he does not estimate
ıis own deserts more highly than the highminded man.

The highminded man, as being worthy of the
ıighest things, will be in the highest degree good, for
he better man is always worthy of the highest things,
ınd the best man of the highest things. It follows
hen that the truly highminded man must be good.

It would seem too that the highminded man
ıossesses such greatness as belongs to every virtue.

It would be wholly inconsistent with the character of the highminded man to run away in hot haste, or to commit a crime ; for what should be his object in doing a disgraceful action, if nothing is great in his eyes? If one examines the several points of character, it will appear quite ridiculous to say that the highminded man need not be good. Were he vicious, he would not be worthy of honour at all ; for honour is the prize of virtue, and is paid to none but the good.

It seems then that highmindedness is, as it were, the crown of the virtues, as it enhances them, and cannot exist apart from them. Hence it is difficult to be truly highminded, as it is impossible without the perfection of good breeding.

A highminded man then is especially concerned with honours and dishonours. He will be only moderately pleased at great honours conferred upon him by virtuous people, as feeling that he obtains what is naturally his due or even less than his due ; for it would be impossible to devise an honour that should be proportionate to perfect virtue[1]. Nevertheless he will accept honours, as people have nothing greater to confer upon him. But such honour as is paid by ordinary people and on trivial grounds, he will utterly despise, as he deserves something better than this. He will equally despise dishonour, feeling that it cannot justly attach to him.

While the highminded man, then, as has been said, is principally concerned with honours, he will, at

---

[1] This sentence as showing Aristotle's exalted conception of "highmindedness," throws light upon several remarks before and after.

he same time, take a moderate view of wealth, political power, and good or ill fortune of all kinds, however it may occur. He will not be excessively elated by good, or excessively depressed by ill fortune; or he is not affected in this way by honour itself, as if honour were the greatest thing in the world. For it is honour which makes political power and wealth to be objects of desire; at all events the possessors of power and wealth are eager to make use of them as means of gaining honour. He therefore who regards honour as insignificant will regard everything else in the same light.

This is the reason why highminded people seem CHAP. VIII. to be supercilious. It seems too that the gifts of fortune contribute to highmindedness; for people of high birth or great political power or wealth are considered to be worthy of honour, as they are in a position of superiority, and that which is superior in any good is always held in higher honour. It is thus that such gifts of fortune enhance a person's highmindedness, as *in consequence of them* he receives honour from certain quarters. But in truth it is only the good man who deserves honour, although if a man possesses gifts of fortune as well as goodness he is considered to be in a higher sense worthy of honour. People who possess goods of this kind, without virtue, are not justified in considering themselves to be worthy of great things, nor is it right to call them highminded, as neither greatness nor highmindedness is possible without complete virtue. The possessors of such goods belong to the class of people who are apt to become supercilious and insolent; for without

8—2

virtue it is not easy to bear the gifts of fortune in good taste. Not being able to bear them, and imagining themselves to be superior to everybody else, such people treat others with contempt, and act according to their own sweet will; for they imitate the highminded man without being like him, but they imitate him only so far as they have the power; in other words they do not perform virtuous actions, but they treat other people with contempt. The highminded man is justified in his contempt for others, as he forms a true estimate of them, but ordinary people have no such justification. Again, the highminded man is not fond of encountering small dangers, nor is he fond of encountering dangers at all, as there are few things which he values *enough to endanger himself for them*. But he is ready to encounter great dangers, and in the hour of danger is reckless of his life, because he feels that life is not worth living without honour. He is capable of conferring benefits but ashamed of receiving them, as in the one case he feels his superiority, and in the other his inferiority. He will try to return a benefit which has been conferred upon him with interest, as then the original benefactor will actually become his debtor, and will have been the recipient of a benefit. It seems too that a highminded person remembers those upon whom he has conferred a benefit, but not those from whom he has received it; for the recipient of a benefaction is inferior to the benefactor, and the highminded man always aspires to superiority. Again, he is glad to be told of the benefits which he has conferred, but he cannot bear being told of those which he has received. That is the reason (he thinks) why Thetis[1] does not recount to Zeus the services which she has done him, and why the Lacedaemonians[2] in negotiating with the Athenians recounted not their services but their obligations. It is characteristic too of the highminded man that he never, or hardly ever, asks a favour, that he is ready to do anybody a service, and that, although his bearing is stately towards persons of dignity and affluence, it is unassuming towards the middle class ; for while it is a difficult and dignified thing to be superior to the former, it is easy enough to be superior to the latter, and while a dignified demeanour in dealing with the former is a mark of nobility, it is a mark of vulgarity in dealing with the latter, as it is like a display of physical strength at the expense of an invalid. Such a person too will not be eager to win honours or to dispute the supremacy of other people. He will not bestir himself or be in a hurry to act, except where there is some great honour to be won, or some great result to be achieved. His performances will be rare, but they will be great and will win him a great name. He will, of course, be open in his hatreds and his friendships, as secrecy is an indication of fear. He will care for reality more than for reputation, he will be open in word and deed, as his superciliousness will lead him to speak his mind boldly. Accordingly

---

[1] *Iliad* I. 503, 504.. It is where Themis invokes the aid of Zeus on behalf of Achilles.

[2] The occasion is said to have been one when the Thebans invaded Laconia. It may be assumed that the Lacedaemonians were seeking Athenian support.

he will tell the truth too, except where he is ironical, although he will use irony in dealing with ordinary people. He will be incapable of ordering his life so as to please anybody else, unless it be a friend, as such dependence would be servility. That is the reason why all toadies have the spirit of menials, and persons of a mean spirit are toadies. Nor again will he be given to admiration, as there is nothing which strikes him as great. Nor will he bear grudges ; for no one who is highminded will dwell upon the past, least of all upon past injuries ; he will prefer to over-look them. He will not be a gossip, he will not talk much about himself or about anybody else ; for he does not care to be praised himself or to get other people censured. On the other hand he will not be fond of praising other people. And not being a gossip, he will not speak evil of others, even of his enemies, except for the express purpose of insulting them. He will be the last person to set up a wailing or cry out for help when something happens which is inevitable or insignificant, as to do so is to attach great importance to it. He is the kind of person who would rather possess what is noble, although it does not bring in profit, than what is profitable but not noble, as such a preference argues self-sufficiency.

It seems too that the highminded man will be slow in his movements, his voice will be deep and his manner of speaking sedate ; for it is not likely that a man will be in a hurry, if there are not many things that he cares for, or that he will be emphatic, if he does not regard anything as important, and these are the causes which make people speak in shrill tones and use rapid movements.

Such then being the character of the highminded man, *whose character is the mean*, he who is deficient is called meanminded, and he who exceeds is called conceited.

It does not follow that these persons are them- Mean-minded-selves bad ; they are not evil doers, they are only ness. misguided ; for the meanminded man is one who, being worthy of good things, deprives himself of the things of which he is worthy, and seems to prejudice his own position by self-depreciation and self-ignorance, as otherwise he would try to get what he deserves, assuming it to be good. Not that people of this kind seem to be foolish, they are rather timorous. But it seems that their way of thinking deteriorates the character, as our aims always depend upon our estimate of our own deserts, and these people abandon the hope of noble actions and pursuits as well as of external goods from a feeling that they do not deserve them.

Conceited people on the other hand, are foolish Conceit. and ignorant of themselves, and make themselves conspicuous by being so ; for they try to obtain positions of honour under an impression of their own deserts, and then if they obtain them, prove failures. They get themselves up in fine dresses, and pose for effect, and so on, and wish their good fortune to be known to all the world, and talk about themselves, as if that were the road to honour.

Meanmindedness, rather than conceit, is opposed to highmindedness ; for it is a more common and a worse defect.

Highmindedness then has to do with honour on a

Virtuous state respecting honour on a small scale. p. 50.

large scale, as has been said. But there is apparently another virtue which has to do with honour, as was remarked at the outset. It would seem to be related to highmindedness, as liberality is related to magnifi-. cence ; for neither this virtue nor liberality is concerned with great things, but they both produce in us a right disposition in regard to things of moderate or small importance.

As in the taking and giving of property there is a mean state, an excess, and a deficiency, so it is with the desire of honour. It is possible to desire honour too much or too little, or to desire to obtain it from

Ambition.

the right sources and in the right manner. We censure the ambitious man for desiring honour more than is right and for desiring to obtain it from wrong sources, and the unambitious man for not choosing to be honoured even for his noble deeds. But there are occasions when we praise the ambitious man as a man of spirit and a lover of nobleness, or praise the unambitious man for his moderation and self-restraint

p. 50.

as we said at the beginning.

It is clear then that there are various senses in which a person is said to be fond of a thing. We do not always understand the word "ambitious" or "fond of honour," in the same sense; when we use it as a term of praise we mean "ambitious more than ordinary people," and when as a term of censure we mean "ambitious more than is right."

There is no name for the mean state, and it seems that both extremes lay claim to it, as if it were unoccupied ground. But where there is excess and deficiency, there is also a mean. People desire honour both more and less than is right; therefore they sometimes desire it also[1] in a right spirit. At least this moral state is a subject of praise, as being a mean state in respect of honour, although it has no recognized name. As compared with ambition, it appears to be lack of ambition, as compared with lack of ambition, it appears to be ambition, as compared with both, it appears to be a sort of combination of the two. It seems that this is the case with other virtues as well; but in this case it is the extremes which appear to be opposed to each other *rather than to the mean*, there being no name for the intermediate or mean state.

Gentleness[2] or good temper is a mean state in respect of angry feelings; but there is no recognized name for the mean or indeed, it may be said, for the extremes. We apply the term "good temper" to the mean, although it inclines in sense to the deficiency which has no name.

The excess may be described as a sort of angriness or irascibility, for the emotion is anger, although the causes which produce it are many and various.

A person is praised if he grows angry on the right occasion and with the right people, and also in the right manner, at the right times and for the right length of time; such a person will be good-tempered

CHAP. XI.
Gentleness
or good
temper.

Irasci-
bility.

---

[1] Reading ἔστι δὴ καὶ ὡς δεῖ.

[2] There is no satisfactory English equivalent for πραότης; "gentleness" and "mildness" are not specially limited to anger, and "placability," although it refers to it, denotes only one condition or aspect of the angry feelings. Perhaps "good temper" represents the Greek word as nearly as possible.

therefore, as good temper is a term of praise. For a good-tempered person is in effect one who will be cool and not carried away by his emotion but will wax wroth in such a manner, on such occasions, and for so long a time, as reason may prescribe. But it seems that he will err rather on the side of deficiency; for a good-tempered or gentle person is inclined to forgiveness rather than to revenge.

The deficiency, whether it be called a phlegmatic disposition or anything else, is a subject of censure, for people look foolish, if they do not grow angry on the right occasions or in the right way. For it seems that they have no feeling or no feeling of pain, and that, if they do not grow angry, they are incapable of defending themselves. But it is only a slavish nature which will submit to be insulted, or will let a friend be insulted, without protest.

The excess may take any one of all these forms. We may be angry with the wrong people, or on the wrong occasions, or more than is right, or sooner, or for a longer time. I do not mean that all these faults are found in the same person; that would be impossible, as evil is self-destructive, and, if it exists in its entirety, becomes intolerable.

Irascible people then soon grow angry, and grow angry with the wrong person, or on the wrong occasions, or more than is right. But they soon cease being angry; indeed, this is the best point in their character. The reason is that they do not control their anger; they are so quick-tempered that they retaliate in an open way and then have done.

Quick temper. Choleric people again are excessively quick-tempered, and get angry at every provocation and on every occasion; hence their name[1].

Sullen people are slow to make friends again and, Sullenness. as they keep their temper down, their anger lasts a long time. Retaliation brings a feeling of relief; for the revenge makes a person cease from his anger, by producing a state of pleasure instead of pain. But if this does not take place, the burden remains; for as he does not reveal his anger, nobody helps to reason him out of it, and it takes time for a person to digest his anger in his own soul. Sullen people are the greatest possible nuisance to themselves and to their best friends.

We call people stern if they wax wroth on the Sternness. wrong occasions, and more than is right, and for a longer time, and if they will not make friends again without revenge or punishment. Such people are more difficult to live with than others[2]. We generally regard the excess, viz. the irascible rather than the phlegmatic disposition, as the opposite of good temper, as it is more frequent; for it is more natural to men to take vengeance *than to forgive*.

This account of anger proves what has been p. 57. already said; it is not easy to define the right manner, objects, occasion, and duration of anger, or how far it may rightly go, and where it begins to be wrong; for we do not censure a person who deviates a little from the right, whether on the side of excess or of deficiency. Sometimes we praise people who

---

[1] ἀκρόχολος, connected with χόλος.

[2] I have ventured to transpose this clause, as it clearly refers to "sternness."

are deficient and call them good-tempered; sometimes we speak of people who exhibit a stern character
as manly, believing them to be capable of rule. How
far and in what way a person must deviate *from the
mean* in order to be censurable is a question which it
is not easy to decide theoretically; for the judgment
depends upon particular circumstances and is an
affair of the perception. So much however is clear, that
the mean moral state is laudable, i.e. the state in
which we grow angry with the right persons and on
the right occasions, and in the right manner and so
on, whereas the excesses and deficiencies are censurable, slightly censurable, if they go but a little way,
censurable in a higher degree, if they go further, and
exceedingly censurable, if they go a long way. It is
clear then that we must cling to the mean moral
state.

CHAP. XII.   This must be a sufficient account of the moral
states which have to do with anger.

In human society, with its common life and association in words and deeds, there are some people
who seem to be obsequious. They are people who
try to please us by praising all that we do and never
thwarting us, and who think they ought to avoid
causing annoyance to anybody who comes in their
way. There are others who take the contrary line of
always thwarting us and never give a thought to the
pain which they cause; these are called surly and
contentious people.

Obse-
quious-
ness.

Surliness.

It is clear enough then that the moral states thus
described are censurable, and that the intermediate
or mean state, in virtue of which a person will assent

and similarly will object to the right things in the right spirit, is laudable. No special name is assigned to this mean state, but it most nearly resembles friendliness; for the person in whom it exists answers to our idea of a virtuous friend, except that friendliness implies affection as well. It differs from friendliness in being destitute of emotion or affection for the people with whom one associates, as it is not friendship or hatred that makes such a person assent to things in a right spirit but his own character. For he will so act alike to strangers and acquaintances, and to people with whom he is or is not intimate; only in each case his action will be suitable; for it is not natural to pay the same regard to strangers as to intimate friends, or to be equally scrupulous about causing them pain.

Friendliness.

While it is thus stated in general terms that such a person will associate with other people in a right spirit, it must be added that, in his endeavour to avoid causing pain or to cooperate in giving pleasure, he will never lose sight of what is noble and expedient. For it seems that he has to do with such pleasures and pains as occur in human society. Whenever then it is not honourable for him or is injurious to cooperate in giving pleasure, he will object to giving it, and will prefer to cause pain; or if a thing brings discredit and considerable discredit or injury upon its author, while opposition to it causes him only slight pain, he will not accept it but will raise an objection to it.

He will not associate in the same spirit with people of high position and with ordinary people, or

with people whom he knows well and whom he knows
only slightly, and so on as other differences may
occur; but he will render to each class its proper due.
Again, while he chooses the promotion of pleasure in
itself, and shrinks from the infliction of pain, he will
be guided by a consideration of consequences, if they
are greater than the immediate pleasure or pain, i.e.
of nobleness and expediency; in other words he will
inflict slight pains for the sake of great subsequent
pleasure.

Such is then the intermediate or mean character,
although it has no proper name. But if a person
tries to promote the pleasure of others, he may either
aim at being pleasant without having an ulterior
object, and then he will be called complaisant, or it
may be his object to get some personal advantage in
the way of money or of the good things which money
Flattery.   brings with it, and then he will be called a flatterer.
If a person on the other hand is disagreeable to
everybody, he is a surly and contentious fellow, as
p. 124.   has been said.

The extreme states here appear to be opposed to
one another *rather than to the mean state*, because
the mean state has no name.

Chap.XIII.   The mean state of which boastfulness is an extreme has very much the same sphere, and it[1] also is
nameless. But it will be worth while to examine
these states; for we shall better understand the facts
of character after discussing the moral characters
severally, and shall be convinced that the virtues are
mean states, by finding this to be the universal rule.

[1] Reading αὔτη.

The people who in the converse and intercourse
of life make it their object to give pleasure or
pain have been already described. Let us now speak
of such people as are truthful and false, whether in
word or in deed or in their pretensions.

It seems that the boaster is one who is fond of Boastful-ness.
pretending to possess the qualities which the world
esteems, although he does not possess them, or does
not possess them to the extent that he pretends.
The ironical[1] person on the contrary disclaims or Irony.
disparages what he possesses, the intermediate person,
who is a sort of "plain dealer," is truthful both in
life and in speech; he admits the fact of his possessions, he neither exaggerates nor disparages them.

It is possible to be both boastful and ironical
either with or without an ulterior object. But every
man speaks, acts and lives in accordance with his
character, unless he has an ulterior object in view.

Falsehood in itself is base and censurable, truth is
noble and laudable; so too the truthful person, as
holding a mean or intermediate position, is laudable,
the untruthful people are both censurable, but especially the boaster.

Let us speak of them both, beginning with the Truthful-ness.
truthful person. We are not speaking of one who is
truthful in legal covenants, or in all such matters as
lie within the domain of justice or injustice (for these
would be matters belonging to a different virtue), but
where without any such important issue at stake a

---

[1] "Irony" is not an exact equivalent of the Greek εἰρωνεία,
which denotes the character of one who depreciates himself;
"dissimulator opis propriæ" in Horace's words.

person is truthful both in word and in life, because his moral state is truthful. Such a person would seem to be virtuous; for he who is a lover of truth and truthful where truth is of no importance will be equally true where it is of greater importance. He will avoid falsehood in important matters as involving disgrace; for he avoided it in itself apart from its consequences; but so to avoid it is laudable. He inclines by preference to an understatement of the truth, as it appears to be in better taste than an overstatement, for all excesses are offensive.

Preten-
tiousness.

A person who pretends to greater things than he possesses, if he has no ulterior object in doing so, seems to be a person of low character, as otherwise he would not take pleasure in a falsehood; but he looks more like a fool than a knave. Supposing he has an object, if the object be glory or honour, the pretentious person, like the boaster[1], is not highly censurable; but if it be money or the means of getting money, his

Boastful-
ness.

conduct is more discreditable. It is not a particular faculty, but a particular moral purpose, which constitutes the boaster; for it is for virtue of his moral state and his character that he is a boaster, as a person is a liar, if he takes pleasure in falsehood for its own sake, or as a means of winning reputation or gain. Thus it is that boastful people, if their object is reputation, pretend to such qualities as win praise or congratulation, but if their object is gain, they pretend to such qualities as may be beneficial to their

[1] The words ὡς ὁ ἀλαζών are probably spurious, as Mr Bywater has seen; they make good sense, but it would seem that the sense requires rather ὡς οὐδὲ ὁ ἀλαζών.

neighbours, and cannot be proved not to exist, e.g. to kill in prophesying or medicine. This is the reason why the great majority of boasters pretend to such qualities as these, and make a boast of them as they are beneficial and it is difficult to disprove them.

Ironical people, on the other hand, in depreciating themselves, show a more refined character, for it seems that their object is not to make gain but to avoid pomposity. They are particularly fond of disclaiming the same qualities as the boaster affects, viz. the qualities which the world esteems, as was the way, e.g. of Socrates. *Irony.*

People, whose pretensions apply to such things as are trivial and obvious, are called humbugs; they deserve nothing but contempt. *Humbug.*

Sometimes irony itself appears to be boastfulness, as in the dress of the Lacedaemonians; for exaggerated deficiency is a form of boastfulness as well as excess. But people who employ irony with moderation, and upon such occasions as are not too obvious and palpable, present an appearance of refinement.

The boaster appears to be the opposite of the truthful man, as being worse than the ironical man.

As relaxation enters into life no less than business, and one element of relaxation is playful diversion, it seems that here too there is a manner of intercourse which is in good taste; there are right things to say and a right way of saying them, and the same is true of listening. But the right way of speaking or listening will differ according to the class of people to whom one speaks or listens. *Chap. XIV.*

It is clear that in this matter as in others it is

possible to go beyond, or to fall short of, the mean.

Buf-
foonery.

Now they who exceed the proper limit in ridicule seem to be buffoons and vulgar people, as their heart is set upon exciting ridicule at any cost, and they aim rather at raising a laugh than at using decorous

Boorish-
ness.

language and not giving pain to their butt. On the other hand they who will never themselves speak a word that is ridiculous, and who are indignant with everybody who speaks so, may be said to be boorish and rude.

Wittiness.

People whose fun is in good taste are called witty (εὐτράπελοι), a name which implies the happy turns[1] of their art, as these happy turns may be described as movements of the character; for characters, like bodies, are judged by their movements. But as it is never necessary to look far for subjects of ridicule and as an excessive fondness for fun and mockery is pretty universal, it happens that not only true wits but buffoons are described as witty, because they are amusing. But it is clear from what has been said that there is a difference, and indeed a wide difference, between the two.

Tact.

The characteristic of the mean state is tact. A person of tact is one who will use and listen to such language only as is suitable to an honourable gentleman; for there is such language as an honourable gentleman may fitly use and listen to in the way of fun, and the fun of a gentleman is different from that of a slavish person, and again, the fun of a cultivated person from that of one who is uncultivated. We

---

[1] εὐτραπελία is connected with τρέπειν "to turn."

ay see this to be so at once by a comparison of the
d and the new comedy; in the former it was
)scenity of language which raised a laugh, but in
ιe latter it is rather innuendo, and this makes a
·eat difference from the point of view of decorum.

Is it then to be the definition of a good jester that
) uses such language as befits a gentleman, or that
) does not give pain, or actually gives pleasure, to
s listener? It is probably impossible to determine
ιis point, as different things are detestable or agree-
)le to different people. But the language to which
person listens will correspond to the language which
) uses; for it seems that he will make such jests as
) can bear to listen to. There will be some kinds of
st then that he will not make, for mockery is a
ιecies of reviling, and there are some kinds of re-
ling which legislators prohibit; they ought perhaps
have prohibited certain kinds of jesting as well.

This will be therefore the moral state of the
fined gentleman; he will be, so to say, a law unto
mself.

Such is then the mean, or intermediate character,
hether it be called tact or wittiness.

But the buffoon is the slave of his own sense of
ımour; he will spare neither himself nor anybody
зе, if he can raise a laugh, and he will use such
nguage as no person of refinement would use or
metimes even listen to.

The boor is one who is useless for such social
ırposes; he contributes nothing, and takes offence
everything. Yet it seems that relaxation and fun
e indispensable elements in life.

The mean states then in life which have been described, are three, viz. *friendliness, truthfulness* *and wittiness*. They are all concerned with the association of people in certain words and deeds They are different in that one is concerned with truth and the others with pleasure, and, of the two which are concerned with pleasure, one finds its sphere in amusements, the other in the general intercourse of life.

It would not be right to speak of a sense of shame as a virtue, for it is more like an emotion than a moral state; at least it may be defined as a kind of fear of ignominy, and in its effects it is analogous to the fear of dangers, for people blush when they are ashamed, and turn pale when they are afraid of death. It is clear then that both affections are in a sense corporeal, and this seems to be a mark of an emotion rather than of a moral state.

The emotion is one which is appropriate not to all ages but to youth. We consider that the young ought to show a sense of shame, as their life being directed by emotion is full of mistakes, and it is shame which holds them in check. Again, while we praise young men for exhibiting a sense of shame nobody would praise an old man for shamefacedness as we hold that he ought not to do anything which occasions shame. Neither will a virtuous person feel shame, as shame is occasioned by misconduct; for he ought not to misconduct himself. It makes no difference if there are some things which are really disgraceful, and others which are regarded as disgraceful; people ought not to do either, and therefore

ght not to be ashamed. It is only a man of low
aracter who will be capable of doing anything that
disgraceful.

The idea of a person living in such a moral state
at, if he were to do anything of the kind, he would
: ashamed, and of his therefore imagining himself to
: virtuous, is absurd; for shame is occasioned by
luntary actions alone, and the virtuous man will
:ver voluntarily do what is base. Still shame can be
rtuous only hypothetically. It implies that, if a
:rson should act in a particular way, he would be
hamed; but there is nothing hypothetical in the
rtuous. Again, granting that it is base to be shame-
ss and to feel no shame at doing disgraceful deeds,
: need not conclude that it is virtuous to do them
ld to be ashamed of doing them.

Similarly, continence[1] is not a virtue, but a sort of
ixed state as will be shown in the sequel[2]. But let
: now proceed to consider justice.

[1] The point of similarity is that continence (ἐγκράτεια) implies
: presence of a wrong desire as shame (αἰδώς) implies the
rformance of a wrong action.
[2] In Book vii.

BOOK V.

CHAP. I.
Justice.

WE come now to investigate justice and injustic We have to consider what is the character of tl actions with which they deal, what is the sense i which justice is a mean state, and what are tl extremes between which the just is a mean. In ou investigation we will follow the same plan as in tl virtues already described.

We see that everybody who uses the term "justice means by it the moral state which makes peop capable of doing what is just, and which makes the just in action and in intention. In the same wɛ injustice is the moral state which makes them unju in action and in intention. Let us begin then I assuming this rough definition of justice and injustic *We regard justice as one moral state and injusti*

Difference
between
moral
states and
sciences or
faculties.

as another. For the moral states are different in or respect from the sciences and faculties. Whereas seems that the same faculty or science applies contraries, one of two contrary moral *or physic* states[1] does not apply to its contraries; thus heali

---

[1] ἕξις is a "state," in Latin *habitus*, generally, but n necessarily, a "moral state."

loes not produce results which are contrary to health
ut only results which are healthy; for we speak of
, person as walking healthily when he walks as a
iealthy person would walk.

Now it is often possible to ascertain one of two
:ontrary moral states from the other, or to ascertain
noral states from their phenomena, *i.e. from their
auses and consequences.* For if it is evident what is
, good state of health, it becomes evident at once
vhat is a bad state; or again, a good state of health
s evident from the conditions which produce good
iealth, and the conditions which produce good health
rom the good state of health; for if a good state of
iealth is a state in which the flesh is plump, it
iecessarily follows that a bad state of health is a
tate in which the flesh is lean, and that that which
)roduces plumpness of flesh is that which produces
;ood health.

Again, it follows as a general rule that, if one of
;wo opposite terms be used in a plurality of senses, so
s the other, e.g. if the word "just" has several senses,
o has the word "unjust."

It seems that the words "justice" and "injustice" Chap. II.
ire used in a plurality of senses, but as the various
ienses are closely allied, their homonymy[1] or ambi-
;uity escapes notice, and is not so evident, as it is
vhen the various senses are wholly distinct; for the
lifference is striking when it is one of external ap-
)earance, e.g. the ambiguous use of the word κλείς

---

[1] A "homonym" in Aristotelian phraseology is a word having
;wo or more distinct senses, such as " bull," "bill " or " ball."

for the clavicle of animals, and for the key which is
used in locking doors.

Different
senses of
"justice"
and "in-
justice."

It is necessary therefore to ascertain all the various
senses in which a person may be called unjust. He
is said to be unjust, if he breaks the law of the land;
he is also said to be unjust, if he takes more than his
share of anything[1]. It is clear then that the just
man will be (1) one who keeps the law, (2) one who
is fair. Accordingly what is just is (1) what is lawful,
(2) what is fair; what is unjust is (1) what is unlaw-
ful, (2) what is unfair.

Sphere of
justice and
injustice.

Now, as the unjust man in the second of these two
senses is one who takes more than his share, he will
have to do with goods, not indeed with all goods, but
with all the goods of fortune, which are always good

Goods
absolute
and
relative.

in an absolute sense, but not always good relatively
to the individual. These are indeed the objects of
men's prayers and pursuits; but they ought rather to
pray that such things as are absolutely good may be
good also relatively to themselves, and to choose such
things as are good for themselves.

The unjust man does not always choose what is
more than his share; on the contrary he chooses
what is less than his share of such things as are
absolutely evil. But as it seems that the less of two
evils may, in a sense, be called a good, and to take
more than one's share means to take more than one's
share of what is good, he is regarded as taking more

---

[1] I agree with Dr Jackson in omitting the words καὶ ὁ ἄνισος
and in thinking they were inserted by a copyist who did not see
that " unfairness " was implied in ὁ πλεονέκτης.

than his share. Such a person may be called unfair; for unfairness is a general and comprehensive term.

The law-breaker being, as we saw, unjust and the law-abiding person just, it is clear that whatever is lawful is in some sense just; for such things as are prescribed by legislative authority are lawful, and all such things we call just. Laws pronounce upon all subjects with a view to the interest of the community as a whole, or of those who are its best or leading citizens whether in virtue or in any similar sense. Thus there is one sense in which we use the term "just" of all that tends to create and to conserve happiness and the elements of happiness in the body politic. The law commands us to perform the actions of the courageous person, i.e. not to leave the ranks, or run away, or throw down our arms; the actions of the temperate person, i.e. to abstain from adultery and outrage, or the actions of the gentle person, i.e. to abstain from assault and abuse, and so with all the other virtues and vices, prescribing some actions and prohibiting others, and doing all this in a right spirit, if it be a right law, but in a spirit which is not equally right, if it be a law passed on the spur of the moment.

Justice then, as so defined, is complete virtue although not complete in an absolute sense, but in relation to one's neighbours. Hence it is that justice is often regarded as the supreme virtue, "more glorious than the star of eve or dawn"[1]; or as the proverb runs

"Justice is the summary of all Virtue[2]."

CHAP. III.

Justice and virtue.

[1] It looks as if the expression were a poetical quotation.
[2] A line attributed to Theognis, Phocylides and other poets.

It is in the highest sense complete virtue, as being an exercise of complete virtue[1]. It is complete too, because he who possesses it can employ his virtue in relation to his neighbours and not merely by himself; for there are many people who are capable of exhibiting virtue at home, but incapable of exhibiting it in relation to their neighbours. Accordingly there seems to be good sense in the saying of Bias that "office will reveal a man," for one who is in office is at once brought into relation and association with others. It is this same reason which makes justice alone of the virtues seem to be the good of others, as it implies a relation to others, for it promotes the interests of somebody else, whether he be a ruler or a simple fellow-citizen.

As then the worst of men is he who exhibits his depravity both in his own life and in relation to his friends, the best of men is he who exhibits his virtue not in his own life only but in relation to others; for this is a difficult task.

Justice therefore in this sense of the word, is not a part of virtue but the whole of virtue; its opposite, injustice, not a part of vice but the whole of vice. If it be asked what is the difference between virtue and justice in this sense, it is clear from what has been already said; they are the same, but the underlying conception of them is different; the moral state which, if regarded relatively to others, is justice, if regarded absolutely as a moral state, is virtue.

CHAP. IV. But we are investigating the justice which is a
Justice as
a part part of virtue; for there is such a justice, as we hold.
of virtue.   [1] Reading τῆς τελείας ἀρετῆς χρῆσις.

Similarly there is a particular injustice which requires Injustice as a part of vice. investigation. We may infer the existence *of this particular injustice* from the following fact: a person who exhibits any other form of wickedness in action, although he acts unjustly[1], does not take more than properly belongs to him, e.g. if he throws away his shield out of cowardice, or makes use of abusive language from bad temper, or from illiberality refuses pecuniary help; but when he takes more than his share, it often happens that he acts not from any one of these forms of vice, and certainly not from all, but from a species of vice (*as is plain* because his action is censurable), or in other words from injustice. There is then another injustice which is, as it were, a part of injustice as a whole, and a sense of the word "unjust" in which it is a part of the whole field of injustice or illegality.

Again, if one man commits adultery for the sake of gain, and makes money by it, while another incurs expenditure and loss for the sake of gratifying his passion, the latter would seem to be licentious rather than grasping, but the former to be unjust and not licentious, the reason being clearly that his object was not the gratification of his passion but gain. Again, while it is possible to refer all other unjust actions or crimes to some particular vice, e.g. to incontinence in the case of adultery, to cowardice in the case of desertion from the ranks, and to anger in the

---

[1] The English words "unjust" and "injustice" have properly a more restricted meaning than ἄδικος and ἀδικεῖν as here used. A person who should throw away his shield in battle would not be said to act "unjustly."

case of assault, where it is a case of *unjust* gain, there is no vice to which it can be referred except injustice.

It is evident then that, besides injustice as a whole, there is another particular injustice which has the same name[1], as its definition falls under the same genus, for both take effect in relation to other people; but the one is concerned with honour or property or safety or whatever comprehensive name we may have for all such things, and is due to the pleasure of making gain, the other is concerned with the whole sphere of virtuous action.

CHAP. V.
Two kinds of virtue and injustice.

It is clear then that there are various kinds of justice, and that there is a kind which is different from complete virtue. We must therefore ascertain its nature and character.

The unjust has been defined in two distinct senses, viz. as what is illegal or what is unfair. Similarly, the just as what is legal or what is fair. Now the injustice already described corresponds to or *is coextensive with* illegality. But as what is unfair and what is illegal are not the same thing, but stand to each other in the relation of part to whole, what is unfair being always illegal but what is illegal not being always unfair, it follows that the words "unjust" and "injustice," *when used in the limited sense*, have

---

[1] At the beginning of the *Categories*, Aristotle distinguishes ὁμώνυμα, ὧν ὄνομα μόνον κοινόν, ὁ δὲ κατὰ τοὔνομα λόγος τῆς οὐσίας ἕτερος from συνώνυμα, ὧν τό τε ὄνομα κοινὸν καὶ ὁ κατὰ τοὔνομα λόγος τῆς οὐσίας ὁ αὐτός. The distinction is not here important: cp. p. 80, l. 24. As general and particular injustice are specifically different, they are homonymous ; as they fall under the same general head, they are synonymous.

a different meaning from the same words when used in the large sense, standing to them in the relation of parts to wholes; for this injustice is a part of universal injustice, and similarly this justice a part of universal justice. It is necessary therefore to speak of particular justice and particular injustice, and similarly of the just and the unjust in a particular sense.

We may set aside then the justice and injustice *Universal justice.* which correspond to complete virtue *and vice,* the former being the exercise of complete virtue, and the latter of complete vice, in relation to others. It is evident too how the just and the unjust corresponding to universal justice and injustice are to be determined. The majority of such actions as the law prescribes are actions issuing from complete virtue; for the law bids us live in the practice of every virtue, and forbids us to live in the practice of any vice. But the causes which are productive of complete virtue are all such legislative enactments as have been passed in regard to education for the duties of citizenship. As to the education of the individual which makes him *not a good citizen but* a good man in an absolute sense, it will be necessary to determine hereafter[1] whether it is a branch of the political art or of some other; for it is possibly not the same thing in all cases to be a good man and to be a good citizen.

There are two kinds of particular justice and of *Particular justice. Its two kinds.*

---

[1] The promise is not fulfilled in the *Ethics,* but the question here raised is considered in the *Politics* III. ch. 4. It must not be forgotten that Aristotle looks upon Ethics as a branch of Politics.

the just action which corresponds to particular justice, one consisting in the distributions of honour or wealth or any other things which are divided among the members of the community, as it is here that one citizen may have a share which is equal or unequal to another's, the other kind which is corrective *of wrong* in private transactions. This latter again has two subdivisions, private transactions being (1) voluntary, (2) involuntary. Voluntary transactions are such as selling, buying, lending at interest, giving security, lending without interest, depositing money, hiring; and they are said to be voluntary because the origin of these transactions is voluntary, *i.e. people enter upon them of their own free will.* Involuntary transactions again are either (1) secret, as e.g. theft, adultery, poisoning, pandering, enticing slaves away from their masters, assassination, and false witness, or (2) violent, as assault, imprisonment, murder, rape, mutilation, slander, and contumelious treatment.

Chap. VI.
Distributive justice.

As the person who is unjust is unfair, and the thing which is unjust is unfair, it is clear[1] that there is a certain mean in respect of unfairness, or inequality. This mean is that which is fair or equal; for whatever be the nature of an action that admits of excess or defect, it admits also of fairness or equality.

If then that which is unjust is unfair, that which is just is fair, as indeed every one sees without argument.

But since that which is fair or equal is a mean between two extremes, that which is just will in a certain sense be a mean. But fairness or equality

---

[1] Because τὸ ἄνισον implies τὸ πλεονεκτεῖν.

implies two persons or things at least[1]. It follows therefore that that which is just is a mean, that it is fair[2] or equal and that it is relative to certain persons. It follows also that, inasmuch as it is a mean, it is a mean between certain extremes, viz. excess and defect, and that inasmuch as it is just, it is relative to certain persons. But, if so, then that which is just must imply four terms at least; for the persons relatively to whom it is just are two, and the things in which it consists[3] are two likewise. Also, if the persons are equal, the things will be equal; for as one thing is to the other thing, so is one person to the other person. For if the persons are not equal, they will not have equal shares; in fact the source of battles and complaints is either that people who are equal have unequal shares, or that people who are not equal have equal shares, distributed to them. The same truth is clearly seen from the principle of merit; for everybody admits that justice in distributions is determined by merit of some sort; only people do not all understand the same thing by merit. The democrats understand freedom, the oligarchs wealth or nobility, and the aristocrats virtue.

Justice then is a sort of proportion; for proportion is not peculiar to abstract quantity[4], but belongs Justice proportionate.

[1] τὸ ἴσον is either "the fair" or "the equal" but fairness in distribution cannot exist, unless there are two recipients, nor equality unless there is a division of goods.

[2] Omitting the words καὶ πρός τι.

[3] It seems desirable, with Dr Jackson, to omit τὰ πράγματα; but if the words are retained, they do not alter the sense.

[4] "Abstract quantity" is, Sir A. Grant says, "number expressed in ciphers." It is e.g. the number 2, not two horses or two carts etc.

to quantity generally, proportion being equality of ratios and implying four terms at least.

Now it is plain that discrete proportion implies four terms; but the same is true of continuous proportion; for in continuous proportion one of the terms is used as two, and is repeated. Thus as A is to B, so is B to C[1]; here B is repeated; consequently if B be set down twice, the terms of the proportion will be four.

That which is just then requires four terms at least, and an equality of ratio between them, the persons and the things being similarly divided[2]. As then the term A is to the term B, so will C be to D, and consequently *alternando* as A is to C, so will B be to D. The whole therefore will bear the same ratio to the whole i.e. $A + C$ *will be to* $B + D$ *as A is to B or C to D*[3]; but this is the combination which the distribution effects, and, if the terms be thus united, it is a just combination.

CHAP. VII.   The conjunction therefore of A with C and of B with D is what is just in distribution, and this justice is a mean between the violations of proportion; for that which is proportionate is a mean, and that which is just is proportionate. Mathematicians call this kind of proportion geometrical; for in geometrical

---

[1] If $A : B :: B : C$ be taken as the example of continuous proportion, $A : B :: C : D$ will be an example of discrete proportion.

[2] i.e. so that person should be to person, as thing to thing.

[3] In the supposed instance A and B are persons, C and D are things, and the combination consists in adding C (thing) to A (person) and D (thing) to B (person).

roportion the whole is to the whole as each of the eparate terms is to each[1]. But this proportion is ot continuous, as no one arithmetical term can stand oth for person and for thing.

That which is just then in this sense is that which ι proportionate, and that which is unjust is that hich is disproportionate. It follows that this dispro- ortion may take the form either of excess or defect; nd this is actually the case, for the author of the ijustice has too much, and the victim has too little, f the good. In regard to evil the contrary is the ase; for the lesser evil in comparison with the greater ounts as a good, as the lesser evil is more desirable han the greater, and that which is desirable is a good, nd that which is more desirable is a greater good.

This then, is one form of justice *i.e. of particular ιstice.*

The remaining form of justice is the corrective, hich occurs in private transactions whether volun- ιry or involuntary.

Corrective justice.

This justice is different in kind from the former. ΐor distributive justice in dealing with the public ιnds invariably follows the proportion which has εen described, *i.e. geometrical proportion,* as even if ιe distribution be made *to two or more people* out f the public funds, it will be in accordance with the ιtio of the contributions which they have severally ιade[2]. Also the injustice which is opposite to this

[1] i.e. $A + C : B + D :: A : B$ or $:: C : D$.
[2] The meaning is that, if A pays a larger income-tax than B, ε will receive a larger share of such public property as may be stributed.

form of justice is the violation of *geometrical* proportion. But the justice which exists in private transactions, although in a sense it is fair or equal, and the
corresponding injustice is unfair or unequal, follows
not geometrical but arithmetical proportion[1]. For it
makes no difference here whether it be a virtuous
man who defrauded a bad man, or a bad man who
defrauded a virtuous man, or whether it be a virtuous
or a bad man who committed adultery; the law looks
only to the degree of the injury, it treats the parties as
equal, and asks only if one is the author and the other
the victim of injustice or if the one inflicted and the
other has sustained an injury. Injustice then in this
sense is unfair or unequal, and the endeavour of the
judge[2] is to equalize it; for even when one person
deals a blow and the other receives it, or one person
kills and the other is killed, the suffering and the
action are divided into unequal parts, and it is the
effort of the judge to restore equality by the penalty
which he inflicts, as the penalty is so much subtracted
from the profit. For the term "profit" is applied
generally to such cases, although it is sometimes not
strictly appropriate; thus we speak of the "profit" of
one who inflicts a blow, or the "loss" of one who
suffers it, but it is when the suffering is assessed *in a*

[1] If in geometrical proportion 2 : 4 :: 3 : 6, in arithmetical
proportion 2 : 4 :: 4 : 6, 4 being the arithmetical mean between 2
and 6.

[2] As the Athenian δικαστής was partly judge and partly juror
it is necessary, in every case of translating it, to use the English
word which best represents the particular functions denoted by
the Greek.

ourt of law that the prosecutor gets profit, and
ne guilty person loss. That which is fair or equal
nen is the mean between excess and defect. But
rofit and loss are excess and defect, although in
pposite senses, the excess of good and the defect of
vil being profit, and the excess of evil and the defect
f good being loss. The mean between them, is, as
e said, the equal, which we call just. Hence correc-
ve justice will be the mean between profit and loss.

This is the reason why, when people dispute, they
ave recourse to a judge (δικαστής) and to go to a
idge is to go to what is just; for the judge professes
o be a sort of personification of justice[1].

Again, people look for the mean in a judge, and
ometimes give judges the name of " mediators,"[2]
'hich implies that, if they attain the mean, they will
ttain what is just. That which is just then is, in a
ense, a mean, as the judge is a mean.

It is the judge's function to redress inequality.
t is as if a line were divided into unequal segments,
nd he were to cut off the amount by which the larger
f the two segments exceeds the half and to add it to
ne smaller segment. It is when the whole is equally
ivided into two segments that people are said to
ave what belongs to them, as having received an
qual amount. This equal amount is an arithmetical
ean between the greater and the smaller lines.
his is in fact the reason why it is called "just"

---

[1] The English words "judge," "just," "justice" may fairly
present the connexion of δικαστής with τὸ δίκαιον.

[2] μεσίδιος is connected with μέσος, as δικαστής with δίκαιος.

(δίκαιον), because the division is just an equal one[1] (δίχα).

For when a part is cut off from one of two equals, and added to the other, the second exceeds the first by twice the part so added to it. For if the part had been cut off from the one, and not added to the other the second would have exceeded the first by once this part only. Therefore *the line to which the addition is made* exceeds the mean by once this part, and the mean exceeds the line by which the part was cut off by once this part. This then will be our means of ascertaining what it is necessary to subtract from that which has too much, and what to add to that which has too little. We must add to that which has too little the amount by which the mean exceeds it, and subtract from the greatest the amount by which it exceeds the mean. Let the lines AA', BB', CC', be equal to one another; let the segment AE be subtracted from AA' and the segment CD added to CC'; then the whole line DCC exceeds EA' by CD and CZ, and therefore exceeds BB' by CD^2.

---

[1] The argument rests upon a false etymology; for δίκαιος i totally distinct from δίχα. The next sentence, which is omitte as being incapable of translation, means "It is equivalent t calling τὸ δίκαιον, δίχαιον, and the δικαστής, διχαστής."

[2] This sentence may be illustrated by a figure

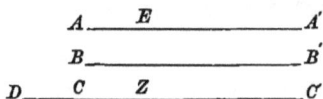

A———E————————A'
B————————————B'
D——C———Z—————————C'

It is assumed, although not stated, that AE, DC and CZ are a equal.

¹The terms "profit" and "loss" are derived from
oluntary exchange. For *in such exchange*, if a
ierson has more than what belongs to him, he is said
o be making profit, and if he has less than he had to
tart with, he is said to be suffering loss; it is so
.g. in buying and selling, and in all other transactions
vhich the law freely allows². But when people get
ıs the result of exchange³ exactly what they had at
he beginning, neither more nor less, they are said to
ıave what belongs to them and to be neither losers
ıor gainers.

That which is just then *in corrective justice* is a
ıean between profit and loss of a particular kind in
ınvoluntary cases⁴. It implies that the parties to a
ıransaction have the same amount after it as before.

There are some people who hold that retaliation⁵ CHAP.VIII.
Retalia-
tion.

¹ There can be no doubt that the sentence ἔστι δὲ τοῦτο καὶ ἐπὶ
ὧν ἄλλων τεχνῶν . . . . τοσοῦτον καὶ τοιοῦτον, which Bekker, follow-
ıg Trendelenburg, transfers to p. 89, l. 7, is out of place here.

² It is better to place a colon, instead of a full stop, after νόμος
ınd a full stop, instead of a colon, after κερδαίνειν.

³ It seems to me that the true reading is αὐτὰ δι' αὐτῶν
ἔνηται and that it means " by using their original properties in
ıxchange come to possess those properties again or their exact
ȧlues, neither less nor more." At all events αὐτά is = τὰ ἐξ
ρχῆς.

⁴ The transactions in which profit and loss occur, although
hey may be voluntary in their origin, are so far involuntary in
heir result as the loser is not a consenting party to his loss ;
ıence the words τῶν παρὰ τὸ ἑκούσιον may stand and may bear
heir natural meaning.

⁵ The word "retaliation," which is the nearest English equiva-
ınt of τὸ ἀντιπεπονθός, must not be understood as meaning only
equital of *evil*.

is absolutely just. This was the doctrine of the Pythagoreans, who defined justice absolutely as retaliation on one's neighbour.

But retaliation does not accord with the conception of either distributive or corrective justice, although corrective justice is certainly what is intended by the Rhadamanthine[1] rule:

> "As a man's action, such his fate;
> Then justice shall be true and straight[2]."

The law of retaliation and the law of corrective justice in many cases do not agree. For instance, if a person who strikes another is a magistrate, he ought not to be struck in return, and if a person strikes a magistrate, he ought not only to be struck but to be punished. Again, it makes a great difference whether what is done to a person is done with his consent or against it, *and the law of retaliation takes no account of this difference.* Still in such associations as depend upon exchange it is this kind of justice, viz. retaliation, which is the bond of union; but it is proportionate, and not equal retaliation[3]; for it is proportionate requital which holds a state together.

People seek to requite either evil or good. It looks like slavery not to requite evil; and if they do not requite good, no interchange *of services* takes place, and it is this interchange which holds society together. It is thus that men build a temple of the Graces in their streets to ensure reciprocity, as being

---

[1] Rhadamanthus was one of the judges of the lower world.

[2] A line ascribed to Hesiod.

[3] What Aristotle calls "equal retaliation" is the law of "An eye for an eye, and a tooth for a tooth."

he peculiar characteristic of grace[1]; for it is our
.uty to return the service of one who has been
racious to us, and to take the initiative in showing
race ourselves.

Now, proportionate requital is produced by cross-
onjunction[2]. Thus let A represent a builder, B a
obbler, C a house, and D a shoe. Then the builder
ught to receive from the cobbler some part of his
rork, and to give him his own work in return. If
hen there is proportionate equality in the first in-
tance, and retaliation *or reciprocity* follows, the
esult of which we are speaking will be attained[3].
)therwise the exchange will not be equal or perma-
ent. For there is no reason why the work of the
ne should not be superior to that of the other, and

Propor-
tionate
requital.

---

[1] The connexion of χάρις with the χάριτες suggests the pro-
riety of adopting the English word "grace" in translating
iis passage ; but χάρις is more strictly "favour" or "kindness"
ian "grace."

[2] "Cross-conjunction" is a technical term which may be
κplained thus. Suppose that in
ie figure, A is the builder, B
ie cobbler, C the house and D
ie shoes, suppose too that A is
)mbined with D and B with C,
ien the proportion

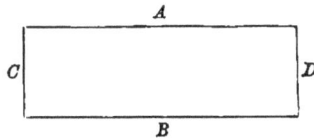

$$A+D : B+C :: A : B,$$

ι the result of "cross-conjunction."

[3] I think it is clear that the case here supposed is one in
·hich two persons desiring to make an exchange of goods have
oods of equal value to exchange ; then the simple exchange of
ne good for the other satisfies the law of retaliation or reci-
rocity.

therefore they ought to be equalized. (¹This is equally the case with all the arts; they would be destroyed, if the effect upon the patient were not, in kind, quantity and quality, the same as the effort of the agent.) For association is formed, not by two doctors, but by a doctor and a husbandman, and generally by people who are different, and not equal, and who need to be equalized. It follows that such things as are the subjects of exchange must in some sense be comparable. This is the reason for the invention of money. Money is a sort of medium or mean; for it measures everything and consequently measures among other things excess or defect, e.g. the number of shoes which are equivalent to a house or a meal. As a builder then is to a cobbler, so must so many shoes be to a house or a meal; for otherwise there would be no exchange or association. But this will be impossible, unless the shoes and the house or meal are in some sense equalized. Hence arises the necessity of a single universal standard of measurement, as was said before. This standard is in truth the demand for mutual services, which holds society together; for if people had no wants, or their wants were dissimilar², there would be either no exchange, or it would not be the same as it is now.

Money.

¹ The sentence transposed from p. 87, l. 31 is most conveniently placed here, but at the best it is an interruption of the argument. It seems to mean that in such an art or science as e.g. medicine a person by using certain means must be sure of producing certain effects.

² I understand by "dissimilar wants" wants which cannot be at once supplied by mutual service.

Money (νόμισμα) is a sort of recognized represen-
tative of this demand. That is the reason why it is
called money (νόμισμα), because it has not a natural
but a conventional (νόμῳ) existence, and because it is
in our power to change it, and make it useless.

Retaliation or reciprocity will take place, when
the terms have been so equated that, as a husbandman is to a cobbler, so is the cobbler's ware to the
husbandman's[1]. But we must bring the terms to a
figure of proportion not[2] after the exchange has
taken place—or one of the two extremes will have
both advantages *i.e. will have its superiority counted
twice over*—but when both parties still retain their
own wares; they will then be equal and capable of
association, because it is possible to establish the
proper equality between them. Thus let A be a
husbandman, C food, B a cobbler, and D his wares,

[1] Suppose the husbandman to offer in exchange a quarter of
corn and the cobbler a certain number of pairs of boots ; it is
necessary to decide how many pairs of boots are equal in value to
a quarter of corn before reciprocity (τὸ ἀντιπεπονθός) can take
place.

[2] The οὐ should be retained ; but it is desirable to treat the
words εἰ δὲ μὴ .... ἄκρον as parenthetical, and to place a comma
after ἄκρον and a colon after τὰ αὑτῶν.

If I understand this difficult sentence, it means that the
husbandman (in the case supposed above) having received in
exchange a number of pairs of boots calculated upon an estimate
of his commercial superiority to the cobbler must not claim to
have that superiority calculated again, when the exchange has
already been effected. But τὸ ἕτερον ἄκρον is an incorrect phrase
as the two parties of the exchange are not the two ἄκρα in the
"figure of proportion." See note on p. 151 of this translation.
I incline to think that ἄκρον should be omitted.

which are equated *to the food.* But if this kind of reciprocity were impossible, there would be no association.

The fact that it is demand which is like a principle of unity binding society together is evident because, if there is no mutual demand on the part of two persons, if neither of them or one only needs the services of the other, they do not effect an exchange, whereas, if somebody wants what somebody else has, e.g. wine, they effect an exchange, giving the wine e.g. in return for the right of importing corn. Here then the wine and the corn must be equated.

Money is serviceable with a view to future exchange; it is a sort of security which we possess that, if we do not want a thing now, we shall be able to get it when we do want it; for if a person brings money, it must be in his power to get what he wants.

It is true that money is subject to the same laws as other things; its value is not always the same; still it tends to have a more constant value than any thing else. All things, then, must have a pecuniary value, as this will always facilitate exchange, and so will facilitate association.

Money therefore is like a measure that equates things, by making them commensurable; for association would be impossible without exchange, exchange without equality, and equality without commensurability.

Although it is in reality impossible that things which are so widely different should become commensurable, they may become sufficiently so for practical purposes. There must be some single standard

hen, and that a standard upon which the world
ıgrees; hence it is called money ($\nu\acute{o}\mu\iota\sigma\mu\alpha$)[1], for it is
his which makes all things commensurable, as money
s the universal standard of measurement. Let A be
ı house, B ten minae, C a couch. Now A is half B,
f the house is worth, or is equal to, five minae. Again,
he couch C is the tenth part of B. It is clear then
hat the number of couches which are equal to a
ıouse is five. It is clear too that this was the method
ıf exchange before the invention of money; for it
nakes no difference whether it is five couches or the
ʼalue of five couches that we give in exchange for a
ıouse.

The nature of the just and the unjust has now CHAP. IX.
ıeen described. The definitions which have been
ʑiven make it clear that just conduct is a mean be-
ween committing and suffering injustice; for to
ʒommit injustice is to have too much, and to suffer it
s to have too little. But justice is a mean state, not Justice a
n the same sense as the virtues already described, mean state
but not in
ıut rather as aiming at the mean, while injustice the same
sense as
ʌims at the extremes[2]. It is justice which entitles other vir-
he just man to be regarded as capable of deliberately tues.
ʒffecting what is just, and of making a distribution
ʋhether between himself and somebody else, or be-
ʼween two other people, not in such a way as to give
ıimself too large, and his neighbour too small a share

---

[1] Again, the point lies in the connexion of $\nu\acute{o}\mu\iota\sigma\mu\alpha$ "money"
ʋith $\nu\acute{o}\mu o\varsigma$ "convention" or "agreement."

[2] Justice then is distinguished from the other virtues, inasmuch
ɑs the extremes of which it is the mean fall under the same,
ınstead of under different vices.

of what is desirable, and conversely to give himself too small and his neighbour too large a share of what is injurious, but to give both himself and his neighbour such a share as is proportionately equal, and to do the same when the distribution is between other people. Injustice on the contrary aims at that which is unjust; but that which is unjust is disproportionate excess and defect of what is profitable or injurious. Hence injustice is excess and defect, inasmuch as it aims at excess and defect, viz. excess of what is absolutely profitable, and defect of what is injurious in one's own case, while in the cases of other people, although they are generally similar, the violation of proportion may take the form either of excess or of defect. But the defect of unjust action is to suffer injustice, the excess is to inflict it.

This then may be taken as a sufficient account of the nature of justice and injustice respectively, and similarly of that which is just or unjust in general.

CHAP. X.
Unjust action not the same thing as injustice.

But a person may do injustice without being necessarily unjust. What then, is the nature of such unjust actions that, if a person commits them, he is proved at once to be in some particular respect unjust, e.g. to be a thief, an adulterer, or a robber? I think the answer is that there is no such distinct class of actions[1], for a person may commit adultery with a woman, knowing who she is, although he commits it not from any original defect of moral purpose, but from the passion *of the moment*. Such

---

[1] It is not the action but the moral purpose, which makes a man ἄδικος : cp. p. 95, l. 10 ὅταν δ' ἐκ προαιρέσεως, ἄδικος καὶ μοχθηρός.

a person then, although he commits an act of injustice, is not unjust; thus he is not a thief, although he committed a theft, nor an adulterer, although he commit adultery, and so on[1].

The relation of retaliation to justice has been already described. But we must not forget that the object of our inquiry is at once justice in an absolute sense, and political justice[2] i.e. such justice as exists among people who are associated in a common life with a view to independence, and who enjoy freedom and equality whether proportionate or arithmetical[3]. It follows that, where this condition does not exist, people are not capable of mutual political justice, but only of a certain justice which is analogous to it. For justice, *strictly so called*, can exist only where the relations[4] of people are determined by law, and the existence of law implies injustice, as the *administration of* justice is the determination of what is just and

Political justice.

---

[1] Dr Jackson transfers the first two sentences of ch. 10, p. 91, ll. 18—26 to p. 95, l. 9, and the transference is clearly an improvement especially as the third sentence resumes the subject of retaliation and of justice generally. There is no such reason, I think, for disturbing the position of the words πῶς μὲν οὖν ἔχει ... εἴρηται πρότερον ll. 26, 27.

[2] I apprehend that "political justice" is not the same as "justice in an absolute sense" but is, as Dr Jackson says, "the most perfect representation of it." See p. 92, ll. 15, sqq. Aristotle is led to a special consideration of "political justice" by the political view which he always took of Ethics.

[3] In an aristocracy or oligarchy the "equality" is, in Aristotle's language, "proportionate," in a democracy it is "arithmetical." The condition of "freedom" excludes the slave population from participation in "political justice."

[4] πρὸς αὑτοὺς is better than πρὸς αὐτούς.

unjust. But injustice implies unjust action, although unjust action does not always imply injustice, and unjust action consists in assigning to oneself an unduly large share of such things as are good in an absolute sense, and an unduly small share of such things as are bad in an absolute sense. Hence we submit to the authority, not of an individual, but of the statute book, because an individual is apt to exercise his authority in his own interests, and to make himself despot.

The magistrate is a guardian of justice, and, if of justice, then of equality. It seems that he gains no advantage *from his office*, as he is assumed to be just; for he does not assign to himself a larger share of what is absolutely good, unless indeed it be proportionate to his own merit. Hence he labours[1] in the interest of others; which is the reason why justice is called the good of others, as we said before. Some reward therefore must be given him in the shape of honour or privilege; and it is when a magistrate is not content with these rewards that he makes himself despot.

p. 138.

Justice of masters and slaves, fathers and children. Justice, as between masters and slaves, or between fathers and children, is not the same as political justice, *i.e. justice between citizen and citizen*, although it resembles it, for a man cannot commit injustice in an absolute *or strict* sense against what is his own; but his property[2] and his children, until they reach a

---

[1] Reading πονεῖ.

[2] It must be remembered that a slave was as much a κτῆμα of his master as any other chattel.

certain age and become independent[1], are, as it were, parts of himself, and nobody deliberately chooses to hurt himself; hence injustice to oneself is an impossibility. It follows that political justice and injustice are also impossible *in the relation of a master to slaves or of a father to children;* for they depend, as we said, upon law, and exist only where law has a p. 157. natural existence i.e. among people who, as we saw, enjoy equality of rule and subjection. There is more scope then for justice in relation to a wife than in relation to children and property, for this, *i.e. justice in the relation of husband and wife,* Justice of husband is domestic justice, although this again is different and wife. from political justice.

Political justice is partly natural and partly con-Political ventional. justice.

The part which is natural is that which has the (1) natural, same authority everywhere, and is independent of opinion; that which is conventional is such that it (2) conventional. does not matter in the first instance whether it takes one form or another, it only matters when it has been laid down, e.g. that the ransom of a prisoner should be a mina, or that a goat, and not two sheep, should be offered in sacrifice, and all legislative enactments which are made in particular cases, as the sacrifice in honour of Brasidas[2] at Amphipolis, and the provisions of an Act of Parliament.

It is the opinion of some people that all the rules of justice are conventional, because that which is

---

[1] The MSS. authority is in favour of omitting μὴ before χωρισθῇ.

[2] See Thucydides v. ch. 11.

natural is immutable and has the same authority everywhere, as fire burns equally here and in Persia, but they see the rules of justice continually altering.

But this is not altogether true, although it is true to some extent. Among the gods indeed it is probably not true at all; but in this world, although there is such a thing as natural justice, still all justice is variable. Nevertheless there is a justice which is, as well as a justice which is not, natural.

Within the sphere of the contingent it is easy to see what kind of thing it is that is natural, and what kind that is not natural but legal and conventional, both kinds being similarly variable. The same distinction will apply to other cases; thus the right hand is naturally stronger than the left, although there is nobody[1] who may not acquire the power of using both hands alike.

Such rules of justice as depend on convention and convenience may be compared to standard measures; for the measures of wine and corn are not everywhere equal, but are larger where people buy and smaller where they sell[2]. Similarly, such rules of justice as exist not by nature, but by the will of Man, are not everywhere the same, as polities themselves are not everywhere the same, although there is everywhere only one naturally perfect polity.

But every rule of justice or law stands *to indivi-*

---

[1] Reading πάντας with the MSS.

[2] The buyers and sellers are, I conceive, the same people, viz. merchants who make wholesale purchases and sell them by retail. So Dr Jackson, who translates " being larger in wholesale, and smaller in retail, markets."

ual actions in the relation of the universal to par-
iculars; for while actions are numerous, every such
ule is one, as being universal.

There is a difference between an act of injustice
nd that which is unjust, between an act of justice
nd that which is just. A thing is unjust by nature,
r by ordinance; but this very[1] thing, when it is done,
i an act of injustice, although, before it is done, it is
nly unjust. The same is true of an act of justice[2].
!ut the several kinds of acts of justice, or injustice,
heir number, and their sphere, will form subjects of
ivestigation hereafter.

Such being the things which are just and unjust,
person may be said to act justly or unjustly when
e does them voluntarily. When he does them in-
oluntarily, he does not act justly or unjustly, except
i an accidental sense, i.e. he does what is accidentally
ist or unjust.

The definition of an act of justice or injustice Voluntary character of just and unjust action.
epends upon its voluntary or involuntary character;
ir when it is voluntary, it is open to censure, and it
i then also an act of injustice. It will be unjust then
i a sense, but will not amount to an act of injustice,
? it lacks voluntariness.

By a voluntary action I mean, as has been already Voluntary action. p. 64.
aid, such an action as is in a person's power, and is

---

[1] The best MSS. give αὐτὸ δὲ τοῦτο.

[2] After this sentence Aristotle remarks that the word for an
act of justice" is generally δικαιοπράγημα, δικαίωμα being re-
ricted in meaning to the " correction of an act of injustice" but
ie remark, as it turns upon the correct use of the Greek words,
untranslateable.

performed by him knowingly, and not in ignorance o
the person to whom he does it, or of the instrumen
with which he does it, or of the result, e.g. of th
person whom he strikes, and the instrument witl
which he strikes, and the effect of his blow; and no
only so, but he must not perform it accidentally o
under compulsion; for if a person e.g. were to seiz
his hand and strike somebody else with it, it would no
be a voluntary action, as not being in his own powei
Again, it is possible that the person struck may be hi
father, and that he may know him to be a man o
some one who is present, but may not know him t
be his father. The same sort of distinction must b
made in regard to the effect and to the action gene
rally. If an action is done in ignorance, or, althougl
not done in ignorance, is not in a person's power, o
if he is compelled to do it, it is involuntary; for ther
are many things in the course of nature which w
both do and suffer with full knowledge but which ar
not either voluntary or involuntary, as e.g. growin
old or dying.

The accidental character may belong equally t
just and unjust actions. Thus a person may restor
a deposit involuntarily and from motives of fear
but in that case it is not right to say that he doe
what is just or that his conduct is just, except acci
dentally. Similarly, if a person under compulsion an
involuntarily refuses to restore a deposit, he mus
be said to be unjust and to do what is unjust acci
dentally.

Voluntary actions we perform either with or with
out deliberate purpose—with it, if we perform then

fter previous deliberation, and without it, if without
uch deliberation.

There are three ways in which people may hurt
ach other in society. An action done in ignorance
; called a mistake, when the person affected, or the Mistake.
hing done, or the instrument, or the effect, is not
uch as the agent supposed. For instance, he sup-
osed that he would not hit or would not hit with
he particular instrument or would not hit the par-
icular person, or that the blow would not have the
articular effect; but the effect proved different from
is expectation, e.g. it was his intention to prick a
erson, and not to wound him, or the person was
ifferent, or the instrument[1].

Now when the hurt done is contrary to expecta- Mishap.
ion, it is a mishap; but when, although it is not
ontrary to expectation, it does not imply malice, it
; a mistake; for a person makes a mistake, when the
riginal culpability lies in himself, but he meets with
 mishap, when it lies outside himself[2]. When a
erson acts with knowledge, but without deliberation,
; is an act of injustice, as in all human actions which Act of
rise from anger and other necessary or natural injustice.
motions; for in doing such hurt, and making such
nistakes we are unjust, and they are acts of injustice,
ut it does not follow that we are at once unjust or
icious, as the hurt is not the consequence of vice.

But when the action is the result of deliberate Injustice.

---

[1] Reading ᾧ for ὡς.

[2] The distinction seems tolerably clear: a person may do
omething with knowledge, but without malice, then it is ἁμάρ-
ημα; or he may do it quite unintentionally, then it is ἀτύχημα.

purpose, the agent is unjust and wicked. Hence it is
rightly held that such actions as arise from anger are
not done of malice prepense; for it is not he who acts
in anger, but he who provoked the anger, that begins
the quarrel.

Again, *in cases of anger* it is not whether the deed
was done or not but whether it was just that is the
question in dispute; for anger arises at the appearance of injustice. It is not as in contracts, where two
parties dispute about the fact, and one of them must
be a rascal, unless they are acting in forgetfulness
Here they agree as to the fact, but they dispute as to
the side on which justice lies. The case of a deliberate aggressor is different; he knows on which side
justice lies[1]. Hence the person who acts in anger
thinks he is injured, the deliberate aggressor does no
think so.

If a person hurts another from deliberate mora
purpose, he acts unjustly. Such acts of injustice
necessarily prove a man who acts unjustly to be
unjust, when they are violations of proportion o
equality. Similarly a person is just, if he acts justly
from deliberate moral purpose[2]; but he acts justly i
he merely acts voluntarily, *although, it may be, no
deliberately.*

Involuntary actions are either venial, or not. The
are venial, if they are mistakes committed not only in
ignorance but from ignorance; but if they are no
committed from ignorance but in ignorance, and from

---

[1] There should, I think, be a full stop after ἀγνοεῖ.

[2] The full stop after δικαιοπραγῇ should be a colon or
comma.

in emotion which is neither natural nor human, they
are not venial.

It may be doubted if we have adequately defined
what is meant by suffering and committing injustice.
In the first place is it the case, as Euripides puts it in
his strange way,

CHAP. XI.
Possibility
of suffering
injustice
volun-
tarily.

"I killed my mother, that 's the tale in brief.
Were you both willing or unwilling both[1]?"

In other words, is it really possible for a person to
suffer injustice voluntarily? or is the suffering of injustice always involuntary, as the committing of it is
always voluntary? Again, is the suffering of injustice
always voluntary or always involuntary, as the committing of it is always voluntary; or is it sometimes
voluntary and sometimes involuntary?

The same question may be raised in regard to just
treatment; for as all just action *and all unjust action*
is voluntary, it is reasonable to suppose that the
voluntariness or involuntariness of being justly and
unjustly treated should similarly correspond to the
voluntariness or involuntariness of acting justly and
unjustly. But it would seem absurd to say that
everybody who is justly treated is so treated voluntarily, as there are some people who are justly treated
involuntarily. There is in fact the further question

---

[1] The quotation is said to come from the *Bellerophon*; but it
more probably comes from the *Alcmæon*. For Alcmæon the son
of Amphiaraus slew his mother Eriphyle who had betrayed his
father to death.

I adopt Dindorf's reading

μητέρα κατέκταν τὴν ἐμήν, βραχὺς λόγος.
ἑκὼν ἑκοῦσαν ἢ οὐ θέλουσαν οὐχ ἑκών;

which may be raised, Is every one who suffers what is
unjust unjustly treated, or is it true of suffering
injustice as well as of committing it, *that it depends
upon a certain moral purpose?* It is possible that
the justice, whether in acting justly or in being
treated justly, may come in only incidentally, and the
same is clearly true of injustice. For it is not the
same thing to do what is unjust as to commit injustice,
nor to suffer what is unjust as to suffer injustice; and
this is equally true of acting justly and being justly
treated; for it is impossible to be treated justly or
unjustly, unless there is somebody who acts justly or
unjustly.

If then to do injustice means simply to hurt somebody voluntarily, and voluntariness implies knowledge
of the person, the instrument, and the manner, then
an incontinent person, if he hurts himself voluntarily,
will voluntarily suffer injustice, and it will be possible
to commit injustice to oneself. (The possibility of
committing injustice to oneself is another difficult
question[1].) Again, a person may through incontinence
be voluntarily hurt by another person acting voluntarily, and if so, it is possible to suffer injustice
voluntarily.

But perhaps this definition is incorrect, and we
must add to the words "hurting with knowledge of
the person, the instrument, and the manner," the
words "contrary to the person's wish." Thus a person
may be hurt, and may suffer what is unjust, volun-

---

[1] The sentence in brackets is a sort of note, which may or may
not be in its true place here. It naturally connects itself with
ch. 12.

tarily, but he cannot be the voluntary victim of injustice. For nobody, not even the incontinent person, wishes to be hurt; but the incontinent person acts contrary to his wish[1]. For nobody wishes what he does not think to be good, and the incontinent person does not do what he thinks it his duty to do. But he who gives his own property, as Glaucus gives Diomedes in Homer

"Gold gifts for bronze, a hundred beeves for nine[2],"

suffers no injustice, for it is in his own power to give, but it is not in his own power to suffer injustice, as injustice presupposes an unjust agent. It is clear then that the suffering of injustice is not voluntary.

It still remains to discuss two of the questions CHAP. XII. which we proposed viz. (1.) Is it he who assigns to somebody else more than he deserves, or he who enjoys it, that commits injustice? (2.) Can a person do injustice to himself?

For if the first supposition is possible, i.e. if it is the distributor, and not the recipient of the excessive share, who commits the injustice, then, if a person knowingly and voluntarily assigns more to another than to himself, he does injustice to himself. This is what moderate people are thought to do; for the virtuous or equitable man is inclined to take less than

---

[1] The suffering of injustice, in Aristotle's view, may possess the characteristic of voluntariness but not of wish; in other words a person may voluntarily do himself hurt but cannot voluntarily do himself injustice. But, if so, his language is not free from obscurity.

[2] *Iliad* vi. 236.

his due. Perhaps however the case is not so simple as it seems; for it may happen that *in assigning more of some good to another than to himself* a person aspired to gain an excessive share of some other good, e.g. reputation or absolute nobleness. Or the question may be answered by reference to the definition of committing injustice; for in the supposed case the distributor suffers nothing contrary to his own wish, consequently he is not unjustly treated, at least on this account, but at most is only hurt. It is evident too, that it is the distributor who commits the injustice, and in all cases not the recipient of the excessive share. For it does not follow, if a person possesses what is unjust, that he commits injustice, but only if he voluntarily does it, and this is the case with the person who originates the action, i.e. with the distributor, and not with the recipient.

Again, there are various senses of the word "do." There is a sense in which inanimate things may be said to commit murder, or in which the hand, or a servant at his master's bidding, may be said to commit it. But these do not commit injustice, although they may do what is unjust.

Again, if the distributor gave his judgment in ignorance, he does not commit injustice in the eye of the law, nor is his judgment unjust, except in a particular sense, as there is a difference between legal justice and primordial justice[1]; but if he knowingly

---

[1] " Primordial justice " (τὸ πρῶτον δίκαιον) is abstract or universal justice, independent of such legislative or judicial enactments as exist in particular states.

pronounced an unjust judgment, he is aiming at a larger share of popularity or revenge than he ought to have. And if he is induced by such motives as these to pronounce an unjust judgment, he is an unfair gainer as truly as if he were to participate in the unjust award; for even in that case he who adjudged a plot of land *unjustly* would receive not land but money.

People suppose it is in their own power to commit Chap.XIII. injustice, and therefore suppose it is easy to be just. Difficulty of justice. But that is not the case. For it may be easy and in our own power to commit adultery with our neighbour's wife, or to strike somebody else, or to give away money; but it is not easy, nor is it in our own power, to do these things from a certain moral state.

- Similarly, people suppose it requires no special wisdom to understand what is unjust, as it is not difficult to comprehend the actions prescribed by law; but these actions are not just actions except accidentally, they are just only if the action or distribution assumes a particular form. It is a harder task to understand just actions as so defined than to understand the means of health, although that too is anything but easy. For here it is easy to understand the nature of honey, wine, hellebore, cautery, and the knife; but to know how and to whom, and on what occasions they must be applied, to produce health, is as difficult a task as to be a doctor.

The same idea leads people to suppose that it is not less characteristic of the just man to act unjustly than to act justly; for the just man will be not less but actually better able than anybody else to perform

such actions as committing adultery, or dealing a
blow, and the brave man to throw away his shield,
turn tail, and run in any direction. But cowardice
and injustice consist not in doing what is cowardly
and unjust except accidentally, but in doing it from a
certain moral state, just as the art of medicine or
healing consists not in using or not using the knife,
nor in giving or not giving drugs, but in a particular
science of doing so.

The rules of justice apply to people who participate in such things as are absolutely good, although
it is possible to have too much or too little of them;
for to some beings, e.g. perhaps to the gods, there is
no possibility of having too much of these goods,
while to others, the incurably wicked, there is no such
thing as a beneficial share of them *however small it
may be*, but, whatever their share may be, it will be
hurtful. To most men, however, they are beneficial
up to a certain point; hence justice is *essentially
human, i.e. it affects the mutual relations of men as
men.*

CHAP. XIV.
Equity.

We have next to discuss equity, and the equitable,
i.e. the relation of equity to justice, and of that which
is equitable to that which is just. For it appears
upon investigation that they are not absolutely the
same, nor generically different. Sometimes too we
praise that which is equitable, and the equitable man,
and actually apply the word metaphorically as a term
of praise to other objects, using it as an equivalent[1]

---

[1] The Greek word ἐπιεικής means "virtuous" as well as
" equitable."

for good, and meaning, that the more equitable of
two things is the better. But there are other times
when, as we pursue our reflexions, we feel it to be a
paradox that the equitable, if it be different from the
just, should be laudable; for we argue that, if that is
so, either the just is not good, or the equitable is not
good[1], if it be different, or, if both be good, they are
identical.

These are, I think, the considerations which give
rise to the difficulty respecting the equitable. But
they are all in a manner correct, and not inconsistent;
for that which is equitable, although it is better than
that which is just in one aspect of the word "justice,"
is yet itself just, and is not better than what is just in
the sense of being generically distinct from it. It
follows that the just and the equitable are the same
thing, and that, while both are good, the equitable is
better.

The difficulty arises from the fact that, while that
which is equitable is just, it is not just in the eye of
the law, but is a rectification of legal justice. And
the reason is that all law is couched in general terms,
but there are some cases upon which it is impossible
to pronounce correctly in general terms. Accordingly,
where a general statement is necessary, but such a
statement cannot be correct, the law embraces the
majority of cases, although it does not ignore the
element of error. Nor is it the less correct on this
account; for the error lies not in the law, nor in the
legislature, but in the nature of the case. For it is

---

[1] Omitting οὐ δίκαιον.

plainly impossible to pronounce with complete accuracy upon such a subject-matter as human action[1].

Whenever then the terms of the law are general, but the particular case is an exception to the general law, it is right, where the legislator's rule is inadequate or erroneous in virtue of its generality, to rectify the defect which the legislator himself, if he were present, would admit, and had he known it, would have rectified in legislating.

That which is equitable then is just, and better than one kind of justice, not indeed better than absolute justice, but better than the error of justice which arises from legal generality. This is in fact the nature of the equitable; it is a rectification of law where it fails through generality. For the reason why things are not all determined by law is that there are some things about which it is impossible to lay down a law and for which a special decree is therefore necessary. For where the thing to be measured is indefinite the rule must be indefinite, like the leaden rule[2] that is used in Lesbian architecture; for as the rule is not rigid but adapts itself to the shape of the stone, so does the decree to the circumstances of the case.

We see then what is the nature of equity, and

---

[1] In the sentence I have ventured to expand the sense of τοιαύτη which sums up, as often in Plato and Aristotle, the general idea of the context.

[2] What the "leaden rule" was is clear from the passage itself, but there is some reason to think that the polygonal masonry used in Lesbian buildings required a flexible or self-adapting rule.

that it is just, and what is the justice to which it is superior.

From this it is easy to see the nature of the equitable man; for one who in his moral purpose and action aims at doing what is equitable, who does not insist upon his rights to the damage of his neighbours, but is content to take less than is his due, although he has the law on his side, is equitable, and his moral state is equity which is a kind of justice, and not a different moral state.

The foregoing considerations[1] clear up the ques- CHAP. XV. tion whether it is possible for a person to act unjustly to himself or not. For justice, in one of its senses, includes such exercise of the several virtues as are prescribed by law. Thus the law does not allow suicide, and whatever it does not allow it forbids. Suicide. Again, when a person voluntarily hurts another in defiance of the law, not by way of retaliation, he commits injustice voluntarily, "voluntarily" meaning "with knowledge of the person and the instrument." But a man, who cuts his throat in a fit of anger, does so voluntarily in defiance of right reason, and this the law does not allow; accordingly he may be said to act unjustly. But unjustly to whom? Surely to the state, and not to himself; for he suffers voluntarily, but no one is voluntarily treated with injustice. That is the reason why it is the state which inflicts a penalty, i.e. attaches a certain

---

[1] It cannot be said that the passage which begins here follows naturally upon the consideration of equity. Dr Jackson would place it at p. 98, l. 2.

ignominy to the suicide as acting unjustly to the state.

Again, in the sense in which a man is said to be unjust, if he merely commits injustice and is not entirely vicious[1] it is impossible for him to act unjustly to himself. (This is a different case from the last; for the unjust man here may be said to be wicked in the same sense as the coward, not as possessing an entirely wicked character nor as exhibiting such a character in his injustice, but as wicked in a particular and limited sense[2].) Otherwise it would be possible for the same thing to be subtracted from and added to the same person. But this is an impossibility; the words "just" and "unjust" necessarily imply more persons than one.

Again, an act of injustice is not only voluntary and deliberate but prior in time to the injury received. (A person who retaliates because of wrong done to him, and retaliates on the same scale, is not regarded as acting unjustly[3].) But if a person can act unjustly to himself, he will be simultaneously the author and victim of the same injustice. Again, if a person could act unjustly to himself, it would be possible for him to suffer injustice involuntarily.

Further, nobody commits injustice without committing some particular act of injustice; but nobody commits adultery with his own wife, or breaks into his own house, or steals his own property.

---

[1] i.e. when his action, but not his moral purpose, is unjust.

[2] The sentence is bracketed, as being parenthetical; it merely explains the difference between general and particular injustice.

[3] Again I conceive the sentence to be parenthetical.

But the whole question whether a person can act unjustly to himself is settled by the answer which we gave to the question whether a person can be voluntarily treated with injustice.

[1]It is evident that it is bad to suffer injustice and bad to commit it; for the one is to have less and the other to have more than the mean, and the mean corresponds to what is healthful in medicine and productive of a good condition in gymnastic. Still it is worse to commit injustice than to suffer it; for the committing of injustice is censurable and implies vice, whether complete and absolute vice or an approximation to it (for it is not every voluntary unjust action which implies injustice) but the suffering of injustice does not imply vice or injustice. The suffering then is in itself the less evil, although it may well prove accidentally the greater. Science however does not concern itself with such a possibility as this; it calls pleurisy a more serious mischief than a stumble, although the latter may be accidentally worse than pleurisy, e.g. if a man should happen to stumble, and so to fall, and in consequence of his fall should be taken prisoner by the enemy and put to death.

Speaking metaphorically, or by analogy, we may say that there is a justice, not indeed between a man and himself, but between certain parts of himself, I do not mean justice in all its senses, but such justice as occurs in the relation of master and slave or of the

Injustice to oneself.

---

[1] The loose structure of this chapter is shown by the passage which occurs here p. 101, ll. 8—22, interrupting, as it does, the discussion of self-injury or injustice to oneself.

different members of a family, for in these discussions the rational and the irrational parts of the soul are kept distinct. It is this distinction of parts that people have in view when they hold that a person is capable of injustice to himself, because these parts are liable to suffer something contrary to their inclinations; hence there exists some such justice between them as the justice between ruler and subject.

This then may be taken as a sufficient description of justice, and the other moral virtues.

BOOK VI.

WE have already stated that it is right to choose the mean rather than the excess or deficiency, and that the mean is such as right reason prescribes. It is time then to explain this definition of the mean.

In all the moral states which we have described, as well as in others, there is some object which the rational man keeps in view in intensifying or relaxing his activity; in other words, there is a certain criterion of the mean states which lie, as we hold, between the excess and the deficiency, and are in accordance with right reason.

But this statement, although it is true, is not explicit. For in all such studies as admit of scientific treatment, it is true enough that we ought not to take too much or too little trouble or ease, but to observe "the mean as right reason prescribes"; but if we tell a person only this, he will not be any wiser than before; he will not know e.g. what sort of remedies ought to be applied to the body, if he be told merely that they are all such as medicine or a medical man prescribes. Similarly therefore in

W. N. E.   12

regard to the moral states of the soul it is necessary not only that the rule laid down should be a true one but also that the nature of right reason, and of the criterion which it supplies, should be determined.

CHAP. II.
p. 33.
Intellectual virtues.
We distinguished the virtues of the soul as being either virtues of the character or virtues of the mind. We have discussed[1] the moral virtues and we may now consider the others; but there is a preliminary remark to be made upon the soul itself.

p. 31.
Rational and irrational parts of the soul.
It was laid down before that there are two parts of the soul, the rational and the irrational. We must now make a similar division of the rational part.

Division of the rational part of the soul into
Let it be assumed then that the rational elements are two, viz. (1) that with which we contemplate such existences[2] as have invariable principles and (2) that with which we contemplate such as are variable. For, when things are generically different, there must be generically different parts of the soul which are naturally correspondent to each of them, as the knowledge which these parts possess of such things is due to a certain similarity and affinity between the parts themselves and the things.

(1) the scientific,
(2) the ratiocinative part.
Let one of these parts be called the scientific and the other the ratiocinative part. For deliberation and ratiocination are identical; but nobody deliberates upon such things as are invariable. The ratiocinative then is one part of the rational part of the soul.

It is necessary therefore to ascertain what is the

---

[1] In Books II—V.

[2] The difference between the two kinds of existences is the difference between necessary and contingent truths.

perfect state of each of these parts of the soul; for the perfect state will be the virtue of each. But its virtue will be relative to its proper function.

There are three faculties in the soul which deter- *Deter-mination of action and truth.* mine action and truth, viz. sensation, reason[1], and appetite or desire.

Of these, sensation cannot originate any action, as *Sensation.* is plain from the fact that the brutes possess sensation but are incapable of *moral*[2] action.

If we pass to the other faculties, we see that pursuit and avoidance in the appetite or desire cor- *Appetite or desire. Reason.* respond to affirmation and denial in the intellect; hence as moral virtue is a state of deliberate moral purpose, and moral purpose is deliberative desire, it follows that the reason must be true and the desire must be right, if the moral purpose is good, and that what the reason affirms the desire must pursue.

Now intellect and truth as so defined are practical *Apprehension of truth the function of the intellect whether moral or speculative.* or *moral.* But the good and evil of the speculative intellect, which is neither practical nor productive, are *simply abstract* truth and falsehood. For the function of the intellect generally is the apprehension of truth; but the function of the practical intellect is the apprehension of truth in conformity with right desire.

Moral purpose then is the origin of action, i.e. the *Moral purpose the original motive of action.* original motive, but not the final cause; and the origin of moral purpose is desire or reason directed

[1] It would not be right to limit νοῦς in this passage to *intuitive* reason.

[2] The word "moral" must be inserted to give the force of the Aristotelian, or rather Eudemian, πρᾶξις.

to a certain end. Moral purpose then implies reason or intellect on the one hand, and a certain moral state on the other; for right action and its opposite in action are impossible without both intellect and character.

The mere intellect has no motive power; it must be intellect directed to a certain end, in other words it must be practical. For the practical intellect governs the productive, as every producer has an object in producing, and the thing produced is not an end in itself, but is relative or conducive to something else. But action is an end in itself; for right action is an end, and this is the object of desire.

The moral purpose then may be defined as desiderative reason or intellectual desire *i.e. as reason qualified by desire or desire qualified by intelligence* and it is this originative faculty which makes a man.

The past not an object of moral purpose.

Nothing that is past can be an object of the moral purpose. Nobody for instance proposes to have sacked Ilium; for we deliberate not upon what is past but upon what is future or contingent; but the past cannot be undone. Thus Agathon says rightly enough

"God himself lacks this power alone
To make what has been done undone."

It appears then that the apprehension of truth is the function of both the intellectual parts of the soul. We may conclude therefore that the state which will best enable each of these parts to arrive at the truth will be its excellence or virtue.

CHAP. III. Let us go back then and resume the discussion of these virtues.

We may take it that the means by which the soul Means of arrives at truth in affirmation or denial are five in arriving at truth. number, viz. art, science, prudence, wisdom, and intuitive reason; for conception and opinion admit the possibility of falsehood.

The nature of "science" is clear from the follow- (1) Science. ing considerations, if we must use exact language and not be led away by analogies[1].

We all conceive that that which we know, *i.e. that which is an object of science,* is invariable. As to things which are not invariable, they are no sooner out of our sight than we cannot tell whether they do or do not exist. It follows that the object of science is necessary. It is therefore eternal; for all such things as are necessary in themselves are eternal, and that which is eternal admits neither of generation nor of corruption, *i.e. it has neither beginning nor end.*

Again, it may be said that all science is capable of being taught, and that that which is an object of science is capable of being learnt. But all teaching depends upon pre-existing knowledge, as we say e.g. in the *Analytics*[2]. It proceeds either by induction or by syllogism. Now induction is a first principle and leads to the universal, but syllogisms start from universals. There are first principles then from which syllogisms start, but they are not arrived at by syllo-

---

[1] i.e. by analogical or metaphorical, and therefore incorrect, uses of the term " science."

[2] Cp. the first sentence of *Post. Analyt.* πᾶσα διδασκαλία καὶ πᾶσα μάθησις διανοητικὴ ἐκ προυπαρχούσης γίνεται γνώσεως.

gisms; they must therefore be arrived at by induction[1].

Definition
of science.

Science then may be defined as a demonstrative state of mind, *i.e. a state in which the mind exercises its faculty of demonstration*, with all such further qualifications as we add to the definition in the *Analytics*[2]. For it is only when a person has a certain belief, and is sure of the principles on which his belief rests that he can be said to possess scientific knowledge, as, if he is not more sure *of his principles or premisses* than of his conclusion, his scientific knowledge, if he possesses it, will be only accidental.

So much then for the definition of Science.

CHAP. IV.
(2) Art.

That which is variable includes the objects both of production and of action. But production is different from action. This is a point on which we may trust the popular or exoteric view.

The rationally practical state of mind then is different from the rationally productive state. Accordingly neither of them is included in the other; for action is not production, and production is not action. But as architecture e.g. is an art, and as it may be defined to be a rationally productive state of mind, and there is no art which is not a rationally productive state of mind, nor any such state of mind which is not an art, it follows that art must be the same thing as a productive state of mind under the guidance of true reason.

Again, all art has to do with creation, i.e. it has to

---

[1] The words ἐπαγωγὴ ἄρα should be retained in the text.
[2] *Post. Analyt.* I. ch. 2.

contrive and[1] consider how to create some one or other of the things whose existence is contingent rather than necessary, and whose original cause lies in the producer, and not in the production itself. For art does not apply to things which exist or come into existence by necessity or by nature, as the original cause of these things lies in themselves.

Production and action being different, it necessarily follows that the end of art is production and not action. There is a sense too in which chance and art have the same sphere, as Agathon says

"Art fosters Fortune, Fortune fosters Art."

Art then, as has been said, is a certain productive state of mind under the guidance of true reason, and its opposite, viz. the absence of art, is a productive state of mind under the guidance of false reason, and both are concerned with the variable or contingent. *Definition of art.*

We may ascertain the nature of prudence by considering who are the people whom we call prudent. *CHAP. V. (3) Prudence.*

It seems to be characteristic of the prudent man to be capable of deliberating well upon what is good or expedient for himself, and that not in a particular sense, e.g. upon the means of health or strength, but generally upon the means of living well. This view derives support from the fact that we go so far as to speak of people who deliberate well in some particular line as "prudent," when their calculations are successfully directed to some good end, if it is such as does not fall within the scope of art. It may be said

---

[1] Retaining καὶ before θεωρεῖν.

generally then that a person who is successful in
deliberation is prudent.

But nobody deliberates upon such matters as
are incapable of alteration, or upon such as lie beyond his own power of action.

Now science implies demonstration, and demonstration is impossible in matters where the first principles are variable *and not necessary;* for all the
results of such principles are variable [1]. On the other
hand such things as are necessary do not admit of
deliberation. It follows then that prudence cannot
be a science or an art—not a science, because the
sphere of action is variable and not an art, because
all art is productive and action is generally different
from production. It remains therefore that prudence
should be a true rational and practical state of mind
in the field of human good and evil; for while the
end of production is different from the production
itself, it is not so with action, as right action is itself
an end. It is in this view that we consider Pericles
and people like him to be prudent, as having the
capacity of observing what is good for themselves and
for mankind; and this is our conception of such
persons as are successful in administering a household or a State. This too is the reason why we call
temperance by its name (σωφροσύνη) [2], as being preservative of prudence. It is prudential opinion that
temperance preserves, for pleasure and pain do not

---

[1] The words πάντα γὰρ ἐνδέχεται καὶ ἄλλως ἔχειν, but only these
words, are parenthetical in the Greek.

[2] σωφροσύνη, as derived in Eudemus' view from σῶς (σώζειν)
and φρόνησις.

destroy or distort every opinion; they do not e.g. destroy or distort the opinion that the angles of a triangle are, or are not, equal to two right angles, but only such opinions as relate to practice. For the first principles of actions are the ends for which actions are done; but no sooner is a person corrupted by pleasure or pain than he loses sight of the principle, he forgets that this ought to be the object or motive of all his choice and action, as vice is destructive of principle. We conclude then that prudence Definition must be a true rational state of mind which is active dence. in the field of human goods.

It must be added that, while art admits of excellence, prudence does not, and that, while in art voluntary error is preferable to involuntary, in the case of prudence, as of the virtues generally, it is worse. It is clear then that prudence is a virtue or excellence and not an art.

As there are two parts of the soul in rational beings, prudence will be the virtue of one of them, viz. of the part which opines; for the sphere of prudence as of opinion is that which is variable. At the same time it is something more than a rational state of mind, as may be inferred from the fact that, while such a state may be lost by forgetfulness, prudence can not be so lost[1].

Science is a mode of conceiving universal and CHAP. VI. necessary truths. But demonstrable truth or science in general implies first principles, as science is impos-

[1] It is the moral element in prudence which gives it permanence, as compared with the merely intellectual virtues. See p. 15, ll. 31 sqq.

sible without reasoning. It follows that the first principles of scientific truth cannot be themselves the subjects of science or art or prudence; for scientific truth is matter of demonstration, and art and prudence deal only with contingencies. Nor again are they the subjects of wisdom, as upon some matters the wise man proceeds demonstratively *i.e. proceeds from premisses which are not themselves demonstrable.* If then the means, by which we apprehend truth and always apprehend it in the sphere of such things as are necessary or contingent, are science, prudence, wisdom, and intuitive reason[1], and if it can be no one of the first three, i.e. prudence, science and wisdom, *which is the means or instrument of apprehending first principles,* the only possible conclusion is that these principles are apprehended by intuitive reason.

(4) Wisdom.

(5) Intuitive reason.

We apply the term "wisdom" $(\sigma o\phi \acute{\iota}a)$[2] in art to the greatest masters of the several arts. Thus we apply it to Phidias as a sculptor, and to Polyclitus as a statuary, meaning no more by it than artistic excellence. But there are some people whom we conceive to be wise generally, and not in a particular sense or any other such sense, as Homer intends, when he says in the *Margites*

Chap. VII.
Wisdom.

> "Him the Gods made not wise to delve or plough
> Nor in aught else."

It is clear then that *this general* wisdom will be the most consummate of the sciences.

---

[1] Aristotle here omits "art." Cp. p. 104, l. 10.

[2] The English word "wisdom" is hardly capable of this extended signification.

If this is so, it follows that the wise man ought not only to know the inferences from the first principles; he should know also the truth about these principles. Wisdom therefore will be the union of intuitive reason and science; it may be defined as the capital science of the most honourable matters. For it would be absurd to suppose that statesmanship or prudence is the most excellent science, unless man is the best thing in the universe.

If then some words have the same meaning always and others have different meanings, if e.g. the words "wholesome" and "good" mean one thing for man and another thing for fishes, but the words "white" and "straight" have always the same meaning, it will be universally admitted that the word "wise" has always the same meaning, while the word "prudent" is capable of different meanings. For whatever is keenly observant of its own interests would be called "prudent," and would be entrusted with the control of those interests; hence we actually speak of certain beasts as "prudent," if they are seen to possess a faculty of forethought in regard to their own life.

It is clear too that wisdom and statesmanship cannot be identical. For if we mean by "wisdom" such wisdom only as has regard to our personal interests, there will be many kinds of wisdom; there will not even be one wisdom having regard to the good of all animals, but different kinds of wisdom having regard to the good of different animals; in a word there will no more be one wisdom than there is one art of medicine for all existing things. Nor will it make any difference, if it be said that Man is superior to all other animals; for there are many other things of far diviner nature than Man, such as to take the most obvious example—the constituent elements of the universe.

From these facts it is clear that wisdom is the union of science and intuitive reason in the sphere of things of the most honourable nature. Hence people call Anaxagoras, Thales, and such men "wise," but not "prudent," seeing how ignorant they are of their own interests, and speak of their knowledge as extraordinary, surprising, difficult, and superhuman, but still useless, inasmuch as they have no human good in view.

CHAP. VIII.
Prudence.

Prudence, on the other hand, deals with such things as are of human interest and admit of deliberation. For wise deliberation is, as we conceive, the principal function of the prudent man; but nobody deliberates on such things as are invariable, or as have no definite end or object, or whose end is not some practicable good. And he who is absolutely wise in deliberation is he who aims, by a reasonable process, at that which is best for a man in practical life.

Again, prudence does not deal in universals only, but equally demands the knowledge of particular facts; for prudence is a practical virtue, and in practice we have to do with particulars. Hence it is that some people, without *scientific* knowledge, are more practical than other people with it, especially if they possess experience; for if a person knows that light meats are digestible and wholesome, but does not know what kinds of meat are light, he will not cure people so well as one who knows only that fowls are wholesome[1].

But prudence is a practical virtue. We need therefore the knowledge both of universals and of particulars, but especially the latter. But there must be an architectonic *or supreme* form of prudence; *viz. statesmanship.*

Statesmanship and prudence are identical as states of mind, but they are not essentially the same.

Prudence and statesmanship.

In statesmanship, the architectonic prudence, as it may be called, is legislation *i.e. the framing of codes of laws;* but the prudence which deals with particular cases is called by the general name of "statesmanship." This second form of prudence is practical and deliberative; for an act of parliament relates to practice, like the minor premiss in the syllogism[2]. Accordingly it is people who exhibit this form of prudence that alone are said to be statesmen, for they alone are men of action in the same sense as artisans are.

But prudence, in the strict sense, is generally taken to relate to one's own individual interests. It is this which has the general name of "prudence," the other forms of prudence being domestic economy, legislation, and statesmanship, *i.e. statesmanship in the narrower sense,* which is subdivided into deliberation and judicial procedure.

One species of knowledge then is the knowledge Chap. IX.

---

[1] Omitting κοῦφα καὶ.

[2] Sir A. Grant seems right in taking τὸ ἔσχατον to denote the minor premiss of a syllogism which, as it applies a general rule to a particular case, may be said to be practical or to relate to practice.

of one's own interests, although it has many varieties.
A person who understands and studies his own interests is generally looked upon as prudent, while
politicians are looked upon as busybodies. Hence
Euripides[1] says

"I *prudent?* when I might have lived untroubled
  A unit in a multitude of units;
  For busy, restless, and aspiring souls..."

For people generally seek their own good, and
think they are doing their duty in seeking it. It is
this opinion then which has originated the idea that
such people are prudent. Yet it is perhaps impossible
for a person to seek his own good successfully, without domestic economy or statesmanship, *i.e. unless he
takes part in the administration of a household or of
the State.* Moreover the right manner of administering one's own affairs is an obscure subject and needs
consideration, as may be inferred from the fact that,
while the young become geometricians and mathematicians, and wise in matters of that sort, they do not
seem to become prudent. The reason is that prudence
applies to particular cases, and these cases become
known by experience. But it is impossible for a
youth to be experienced, as experience is the ripe
fruit of years. It may indeed be asked why it is that
a boy can become a mathematician but not a philosopher or a physicist; and the answer is probably
that mathematics is an abstract science, but the first
principles of philosophy and physics are derived from
experience, and thus the young do not believe, al-

[1] In the *Philoctetes.*

though they may repeat, philosophical or physical truths, but they easily comprehend the meaning of mathematical truths.

Again, error in deliberation may affect either the universal or the particular judgment; it may be an error e.g. to hold either that water of a high specific gravity is bad, or that some particular water is of a high specific gravity. But it is evident that prudence is not science, as it deals with the minor premiss, *i.e.* with the particular, as has been said; for action is p. 189. always particular.

Prudence is the antithesis of intuitive reason. Prudence and in- For while the intuitive reason deals with terms which tuitive are incapable of logical demonstration, prudence deals reason. with particular facts which are not matters of scientific knowledge but of perception, not indeed of the perception of the special senses, but of a sense analogous to that by which we perceive that the ultimate *or simplest* figure in mathematics is a triangle. For there must be a limit to scientific demonstration in matters of the sense as well as in matters of the intellect. But this *apprehension of particular facts* is rather perception than prudence; prudence is something specifically distinct.

There is a difference between investigation and CHAP. X. deliberation, for deliberation is a particular form of Delibera- tion. investigation. But it is necessary to ascertain what is the nature of wise deliberation, whether it is a kind of science or opinion or happy conjecture, or something generically distinct from all.

It is clearly then not science; for if we are sure of things, we do not investigate them. But wise deliberation is a species of deliberation, and to deliberate is to investigate and calculate.

Nor again is it happy conjecture; for happy conjecture is an irrational and hasty process, but deliberation takes a long time, and it is a common saying that one should be quick in execution but slow in deliberation.

Sagacity too is distinct from wise deliberation, sagacity being a species of happy conjecture.

Nor again is wise deliberation opinion of any kind. But as to deliberate ill is to commit an error, and to deliberate well is to deliberate correctly, it is clear that wise deliberation is a sort of correctness, but not a correctness of science or of opinion; for science does not admit of correctness any more than of error, and correctness of opinion is truth, *but not wise deliberation*, and whatever is a matter of opinion is something *not future but* already decided.

At the same time wise deliberation necessarily implies the exercise of reason. It remains therefore that it must be correctness of thought, as thought *or reasoning* does not amount to assertion; for while opinion is not investigation, but actual assertion of some kind, deliberation, whether it be good or bad, is a species of investigation and calculation.

But as wise deliberation is a certain correctness of deliberation, it is necessary to investigate first the nature and subject-matter of deliberation.

Now correctness is of various kinds. It is clear then that there are some kinds of correct deliberation which are not wise deliberation; for the incontinent or wicked man may arrive by a process of reasoning at the goal which he sets before himself, and it may be said therefore that he has deliberated correctly, although what he has gained is a serious evil. But it is considered a good thing to have deliberated well; for it is only such correctness of deliberation as arrives at what is good that deserves to be called wise deliberation. But it is possible to arrive at what is good by a false syllogism, i.e. to arrive at what ought to be done, but not to arrive at it by right means. The middle term of the syllogism may be false[1]; but again it does not amount to a case of wise deliberation, when one arrives at the right conclusion, but does not arrive at it by the right means.

Again, one person may arrive at the right conclusion by long deliberation, another person in a moment. Wise deliberation then implies something more than has yet been said. It is correctness in matters of expediency, correctness of object, manner, and time.

Lastly, it may be said that a person has deliberated well either absolutely or relatively to a certain end. Wise deliberation in an absolute sense is such as leads correctly to the absolute end. Wise deliberation of a particular kind is such as leads correctly to a particular end.

If then it is characteristic of the prudent to de-

---

[1] The "falsity" of the "middle term" or, to speak correctly, of the "minor premiss" may be exemplified by supposing such a syllogism as this :

Quinine is good for a fever;
This medicine is quinine;
Therefore this medicine is good for my fever,

where the medicine may not be quinine but may still be good for the fever.

liberate wisely, wise deliberation will be correctness in matters of expediency with reference to a particular end, of which prudence is a true conception.

CHAP. XI.
Intelli-
gence.

Again, intelligence and its opposite, in virtue of which we speak of people as intelligent or unintelligent, are not in general the same as science or opinion. For if intelligence and opinion were the same thing, everybody would be intelligent. Nor is it any one of the particular sciences, such as medicine which deals with matters of health, or geometry with magnitudes; for intelligence is not concerned with such things as are eternal and immutable, nor with everything and anything that occurs, but only with the natural subjects of human doubt and· deliberation. Hence intelligence has the same sphere as prudence, although intelligence and prudence are not identical. ·Prudence is imperative, *i.e. it issues commands;* for its end or object is what ought or ought not to be done. Intelligence on the other hand is merely critical, *i.e. it makes distinctions;* for there is no difference between intelligence and wise intelligence, or between people of intelligence and people of wise intelligence.

Intelligence is neither the possession nor the acquisition of prudence; but as a learner is said to be intelligent, when he turns his scientific knowledge to some use, so a prudent man is said to show his intelligence in making use of his opinion to form a judgment and a sound judgment upon matters of prudence which he learns from somebody else; for a wise judgment is the same thing as a sound judgment. It is from this intelligence in learning that the word

"intelligence," in virtue of which people are called
intelligent, is derived, for we often speak of learning
as intelligence.

Judgment[1] or consideration, as it is called, in Judgment
or Con-
virtue of which we say that some people are con- sideration.
siderate or show consideration, is a correct determination of what is equitable. It is a proof of this
definition that we regard the equitable man as especially disposed to exercise kind consideration or
forgiveness, and speak of kind consideration or
forgiveness in certain cases as being equitable. But
forgiveness is correct judgment or consideration in
determining what is equitable, a correct judgment
being a judgment of the truth.

All the states of mind which have been enume- Chap. XII.
rated may be regarded as having the same tendency.
We apply the terms "judgment," "intelligence,"
"prudence," and "intuitive reason" to the same
people. We say that they have come to possess
judgment and intuitive reason, and that they are
prudent and intelligent; for all these faculties are
concerned with ultimate[2] and particular truths, and

---

[1] γνώμη in this passage varies between "judgment" and
"consideration," as the first sentence shows ; and it cannot be
translated by one English word.

[2] There appears to be some confusion of thought in this passage. The "intuitive reason" (νοῦς) apprehends "first principles"
(ἀρχαί) which are "ultimates" (ἔσχατα) as being the primary or
fundamental concepts upon which all knowledge or action
depends ; "prudence" (φρόνησις) on the other hand apprehends
particular facts or duties which are also "ultimates" as being the
last steps in the process of reasoning from "first principles" to
knowledge or action; but the "ultimates" are essentially different

it is the capacity for judging of prudential matters that entitles a person to be considered a person of intelligence, and of sound or considerate judgment; for equity is the common characteristic of all that is good in our relation to our neighbours.

Another proof that these faculties have the same tendency is that matters of action are always particular and ultimate; for it is the business of the prudent man to understand them, and intelligence and judgment are also concerned with matters of action, *i.e.* with ultimate truths.

Intuitive reason.

The intuitive reason, too, deals with ultimate truths at both ends of the mental process; for both the first and last terms, *i.e. both first principles and particular facts*, are intuitively, and not logically, apprehended, and while on the one hand in demonstrative reasonings it apprehends the immutable first terms, on the other in matters of conduct it apprehends the ultimate or contingent term which forms the minor premiss of the syllogism; for it is truths of the latter sort which are the first principles or original sources of the idea of the end or object of human life. *As the universal law then is derived from particular facts*, these facts must be apprehended by perception, or in other words, by intuitive reason.

This is why it is thought that these faculties are natural, and that while nobody is naturally wise, men are naturally gifted with judgment, intelligence, and intuitive reason. It is an argument in favour of this

in the two cases. It is clear from p. 112, l. 26 that Eudemus does not use νοῦς here in its strict sense, but cp. p. 110, ll. 10—13.

view that we regard these faculties as accompanying
the different periods of life, and that intuitive reason
and judgment belong to a particular period ; which
implies that they are the gifts of Nature.

The intuitive reason then is at once beginning and
end. It is from the truths of intuitive reason that
demonstration starts, and with them that it is concerned. It is right therefore to pay no less attention
to the undemonstrated assertions and opinions of
such persons as are experienced and advanced in
years or prudent than to their demonstrations; for
their experienced eye gives them the power of correct
vision[1].

Thus the nature of prudence and of wisdom, the
subjects with which they are severally concerned and
the fact that each is a virtue of a different part of the
soul, have now been explained.

But it is still possible to raise the question in CHAP.XIII.
regard to them, What is their utility? For wisdom Utility of
wisdom
pays no regard to any thing which makes a man and prudence.
happy, as it is wholly unproductive. Prudence on
the other hand does regard happiness; but what is
the good of it? For let it be granted that it is
prudence which deals with all that is just and noble
and good for a man, and that these are the things
which a good man naturally does; still the mere

---

[1] At the close of this difficult chapter it may be observed that
Eudemus (so far as he expresses himself clearly) regards the
"intuitive reason" ($\nu o \hat{v} s$) as having the power of apprehending
(1) the universal axiomatic truths which deductive reasoning
presupposes, (2) the particular facts in life which form the
materials of induction.

knowledge of them no more augments our capacity of
action, if the virtues are, as they are, moral states,
than the knowledge of what is healthy or vigorous,
i.e. healthy or vigorous in the sense not of producing
health or vigour but of issuing from a healthy or
vigorous state; for mere knowledge of medicine or
gymnastics does not augment our capacity of action.

If again it be assumed that a man is to be
prudent, not in order that he may perform virtuous
actions, but in order that he may become a virtuous
man, it follows that prudence will not be of any use
to virtuous people, nor indeed to people who are
destitute of virtue; for it will make no difference
whether they possess prudence themselves, or follow
the advice of others who possess it.   And, if so, we
may be content to treat prudence as we treat health;
for although we desire to be healthy, we do not study
medicine.

Again, it would seem paradoxical that prudence,
although inferior to wisdom should enjoy a higher
authority, *as it seems that it must;* for it is the
productive faculty which is the ruling and command-
ing faculty everywhere.

These are the questions which must be discussed;
at present we have merely raised difficulties in regard
to them.

Now the first remark to be made is that wisdom
and prudence will be necessarily desirable in themselves, inasmuch as each is a virtue of one of the two
parts of the soul, even if neither of them produces
anything.   And the second is that they *are* productive.   Thus wisdom is productive of happiness, not

indeed in the sense in which the medical art produces
health, but in the sense in which health[1] itself produces
it; that is to say, as wisdom is a part of complete
virtue, the possession and exercise of it make a man
happy.

Again, a man discharges his proper function when
he acts in accordance with prudence and moral virtue;
for while virtue) ensures the correctness of the end
which is in view, prudence ensures the correctness of
the means to it. (The fourth part of the soul, viz. the
vegetative part, possesses no moral virtue like the
other parts; it has no power of performing or not
performing moral action.)[2]

If it be said that prudence does not augment our
capacity of doing what is noble and just, let us go a
little further back and look at it in this way.

We admit that there are some people who, although they do what is just, are not yet themselves
just, e.g. if they do what the laws prescribe, but do it
either unwillingly or in ignorance, or for some secondary motive, and not for love of the thing itself,
although indeed they do what is right, and do all that

[1] The carelessness of language is conspicuous; but the meaning
seems to be that when the state of the body is healthy, it is
capable of a healthy activity or, as Mr Peters puts it, the ἕξις of
health produces the ἐνέργεια of health.

[2] This sentence, which I have bracketed as being parenthetical,
is an interruption of the argument. The soul (ψυχή) has been
divided into the rational (τὸ λόγον ἔχον) and the irrational (τὸ
ἄλογον) parts, and the rational part has been farther subdivided.
See p. 102, ll. 22—27. The virtues of these three parts have been
described, and there remains only the irrational or vegetative (τὸ
θρεπτικόν) which is here excluded from the conception of virtue.

a virtuous man ought to do. It follows as a corollary that a person may be good in all his actions, if he is in a particular moral state, at the time of acting, i.e. if he acts from moral purpose, and for the sake of the actions themselves.

Now, while it is virtue which ensures the correctness of the moral purpose, it is the function not of virtue but of a different faculty to decide upon such means as are natural in order to give effect to that purpose. But we must dwell upon this point with greater attention and exactness.

Cleverness.   There is a certain faculty which is called cleverness. It is the faculty of hitting upon and acting upon the means which conduce to a given object. If then the object be noble, the faculty is laudable, but if ignoble, it is unscrupulousness; hence we speak of prudent people and unscrupulous[1] people alike as clever.

Prudence is not cleverness, but neither can it exist without the faculty of cleverness. But this eye of the soul, *i.e. prudence,* does not attain its *perfect* condition without virtue, as has been already stated, and as is clear; for all such syllogisms as relate to action have this major premiss: "Since the end or supreme good is so and so," whatever it may be ; for the sake of argument it may be whatever we like. But the supreme good is not apprehended except by the good man, as vice distorts and deceives the mind in regard to the principles of action.

It is evident therefore that it is impossible for a man to be prudent unless he is good.

p. 199.

---

[1] The sense of the passage seems to require τοὺς πανούργους.

We must resume then the consideration of virtue.
For the case of virtue is much the same as that of
prudence in relation to cleverness. Prudence, al-
hough not identical with cleverness, is akin to it; Virtue
nd similarly natural virtue is akin to virtue proper, and
out is not identical with it. For it seems that the proper.
various moral qualities are in some sense innate in
everybody. We are just, temperate, courageous, and
he like, from our very birth. Nevertheless, when
we speak of the good, properly so called, we mean
something different from this, and we expect to find
these qualities in another form; for the natural moral
states exist even in children and the lower animals,
but apart from reason they are clearly hurtful. However this at least seems evident, that, as a strong
body, if it moves without sight, stumbles heavily,
because it cannot see, so it is with natural virtue;
but let it acquire reason, and its action becomes
excellent. When that is the case, the moral state
which before resembled virtue will be virtue properly
so called.

Hence, as in the sphere of opinion there are two
special forms, viz. cleverness and common sense, so in
that of the moral character there are two, viz. natural
virtue and virtue proper, and of these the latter is
impossible without prudence. Accordingly some
people hold that all the virtues are forms of prudence. Socrates *who was one of them* was partly
right and partly wrong in his researches; he was
wrong in thinking that all the virtues are forms of
prudence, but right in saying that they cannot exist
without prudence.

It is an evidence of this truth that at the present time everybody in defining virtue, after stating the subjects to which it relates, adds that it is the moral state which accords with right reason, and right reason is prudential reason. It seems then to be generally divined that such a moral state, viz. the moral state which is in accordance with prudence, is virtue, but it is necessary to make a slight change of expression. It is not only the moral state which is in accordance with right reason but the moral state which is under the guidance of right reason, i.e. virtue; but right reason in such matters is prudence.

While Socrates then considered the virtues to be forms of reason, as being all sciences, we consider them to be under the guidance of reason.

It is clear then from what has been said that goodness in the proper sense is impossible without prudence, and prudence without moral virtue. And *not only so*, but this is the answer to an objection which will perhaps be urged in argument, viz. that the virtues are found apart one from another; for the same person is not perfectly disposed to all the virtues; consequently he will already have acquired one virtue before he has acquired another. The answer is that, although this is possible in the case of the natural virtues, it is impossible in the case of such virtues as entitle a person to be called good in an absolute sense; for if the one virtue of prudence exist, all the others will co-exist with it.

It is clear that, even if prudence were not practical, it would be requisite as being a virtue of its part of the soul, and because the moral purpose will not

e right without prudence or virtue, as the one, *viz.*
irtue, leads to the attainment of the end, and the
ther, *viz. prudence,* to the choice of the right means.
.t the same time prudence is not the mistress of
'isdom or of the better part *of the soul,* any more
1an medicine is the mistress of health. For pru-
ence does not employ wisdom, but aims at producing
:; nor does it rule wisdom, but rules in wisdom's
1terest. And to say that prudence rules wisdom is
1uch the same thing as to say that statesmanship
1les the Gods, because it regulates all the institu-
ons, *and among them the religious observances,* of
1e State.

BOOK VII.

CHAP. I. **BUT** it is time to make a fresh start by laying it

Bad moral characters: down that there are three species of moral character

Vice, Incontinence, which ought to be avoided, viz. vice, incontinence,

Brutality. and brutality.

The opposites of the two first are clear. We call the one virtue, and the other continence. As the opposite of brutality it will be most appropriate to name the virtue which is above us, i.e. what may be called heroic or divine virtue, as when Homer makes Priam say of Hector, that he was exceeding good

"nor seemed
The son of mortal man, but of some god[1]."

If then it is true, as is often said, that apotheosis is the reward of preeminent human virtue, it is clear that the moral state which is opposite to the brutal, will be some such state of preeminent virtue; for as in a brute, so too in a God, there is no such thing as virtue or vice, but in the one something more honourable than virtue, and in the other something generically different from vice. But as it is rare to find a

---

[1] *Iliad* XXIV. 258, 259.

"divine man¹," if one may use the favourite phrase
of the Lacedaemonians when they admire a person
exceedingly, so too the brutal man is rare in the
world. Brutality is found chiefly among the barba- Brutality.
rians, although it is sometimes the result of disease
and mutilation; and if people are preeminently
vicious, we speak of them by the same opprobrious
name.

However, it will be right to say something about
this sort of disposition later on², and we have
already³ discussed vice. We must therefore now
speak of incontinence, effeminacy, and luxury *on the
one hand*, and of continence and steadfastness *on the
other;* for it would be wrong to regard these moral
states as respectively identical with virtue and vice,
or again as generically different from them.

It will be proper here, as in other cases, to state
the obvious or accepted views upon the subject, and
after thoroughly discussing them, to establish the
truth of all, or if not of all, of most, and the most
important, of the popular opinions in regard to these
emotions; for if the difficulties are solved, and the
popular opinions hold their ground, the proof of
them will be sufficient for our purpose.

It is the popular opinion then that continence and CHAP. II.
Continence
steadfastness are virtuous and laudable, incontinence and Incon-
and effeminacy wrong and censurable, and that the tinence.
Steadfast-
ness and
¹ σεῖος is the Laconian Doric for θεῖος. It appears from Plato, Effeminacy.
Meno, p. 99 D that the Lacedaemonians were fond of the word
"divine" as descriptive of personal excellence.

² In ch. 5.

³ In Books III. IV. V.

continent man is one who abides by his calculations, and the incontinent one who departs from them. *Also that* the incontinent man does what he knows to be wrong under the influence of emotion, but the continent man, knowing his desires to be wrong, is prevented by his reason from following them. Also that the temperate man is continent and steadfast; but while some people hold that the continent and steadfast man is always temperate, others deny it, and while some speak of the licentious man as incontinent, and of the incontinent man as licentious indiscriminately, others make a distinction between them. Again, it is sometimes said that the prudent man cannot be incontinent, and at other times that some men who are prudent and clever are incontinent. And lastly men are called incontinent in respect, *not of their sensual emotions only, but* of angry passion, honour, and gain.

CHAP. III.   Such are the views generally entertained.

Knowledge and Incontinence.   But the question may be raised, How is it that a person, if his conceptions *of duty* are right, acts incontinently?

Some people say that incontinence is impossible, if one has knowledge. It seems to them strange, as Socrates thought, that, where knowledge exists in a man, something else should master it and drag it about like a slave. Socrates was wholly opposed to this idea; he denied the existence of incontinence, arguing that nobody with a conception of what was best could act against it, and that, if he did so act, his action must be due to ignorance.

Now the Socratic theory is evidently at variance

with the facts of experience, and if ignorance be the cause of the passion, *i.e. of incontinence*, it is necessary to inquire what is the nature of the ignorance. For there can be no doubt that a person who acts incontinently, however he may act, does not think his action *to be right* until he has got into a condition of incontinence. But there are some people who agree in part with this theory, and in part dissent from it; they admit that there is nothing which can master or overcome knowledge, but do not admit that nobody acts against what has seemed best to him. Accordingly they hold that the incontinent man, when he is mastered by his pleasures, possesses not knowledge, but only opinion.

But it may be answered that, if this is opinion and not knowledge, if the resisting conception is not a strong, but a feeble one, as in cases where we hesitate how to act, a person is pardoned for not remaining true to it in the teeth of strong desires; whereas neither vice nor anything else that is censurable admits of pardon at all.

Is it then when prudence resists the desires [1] *that a person is censured for yielding to them?* For there is nothing so powerful as prudence. But that is an absurdity, as it implies that the same person is at once prudent and incontinent, and nobody will maintain that a prudent person can voluntarily do the basest deeds.

Moreover, it has been already shown that the p. 188. prudent person, whatever else he may be, is a man of

---

[1] There should be a mark of interrogation after ἀντιτεινούσης.

action, for he is one who concerns himself with ultimate *or particular* facts, and he possesses the

Continence and Temperance.

other virtues as well as prudence. Again, if the existence of strong and base desires is essential to continence, the temperate man will not be continent, nor the continent man temperate; for it is inconsistent with the character of the temperate man to have extravagant or wrong desires. Yet it must be so *with the continent man;* for if his desires were good, the moral state which prevents his following them would be wrong, and therefore continence would not, in all cases, be virtuous. If on the other hand they were feeble and not wrong, it would be no great credit, and if they were wrong and feeble, it would be no great triumph *to overcome them.*

Continence and Opinion.

Again, if continence inclines a man to adhere to every opinion, whatever it may be, it is wrong, e.g. if it inclines him to adhere to a false opinion; and if incontinence inclines him to abandon every opinion, whatever it may be, there will be what may be called a virtuous incontinence. Thus Neoptolemus in the *Philoctetes*[1] of Sophocles deserves praise for refusing to adhere to the line of action, which Odysseus had persuaded him to adopt, because of the pain which he felt at telling a lie.

Again, *if continence be defined as meaning that a person will adhere to his opinions at all costs*, the sophistical argument[2], fallacious as it is, is perplexing.

---

[1] The argument of Neoptolemus and Philoctetes, which illustrates this passage, occurs in the *Philoctetes* vv. 895 sqq.

[2] It appears that "the sophistical argument" is the argument relating to folly and incontinence given below.

The sophists, wishing to prove a paradox, and to be thought clever if they are successful in proving it, are fond of constructing a syllogism which perplexes their interlocutor. For he is caught in a logical trap, as he does not wish to acquiesce in a conclusion which is distasteful to him, and yet it is impossible for him to escape as he cannot refute the argument. One such argument is used to prove that folly and incontinence together make virtue. It is urged that, *if a person is foolish and incontinent,* his incontinence leads him to do the opposite of that which he conceives to be good; but he conceives that what is really good is evil, and that it is his duty not to do it; therefore he will do what is good and not what is evil.

Again, *if continence be so defined,* it would seem that he who does and pursues what is pleasant from conviction and deliberate moral purpose is better than he who does so not from calculation but from incontinence; for it is easier to cure the former, as he may be led to change his opinion. But the incontinent man is open to the proverbial saying "When water chokes you, what must you take to wash it down?" For if he had not already been convinced that his actions are wrong, he might have been converted and induced to give them up; but in point of fact, although he is convinced of what is right, nevertheless he does something else.

Again, if there is incontinence and continence in all things, who is the continent man in an absolute sense? For nobody exhibits all the forms of incontinence; yet there are people of whom we speak as incontinent in an absolute sense, *i.e. without qualification.*

CHAP. IV.   Such then more or less are difficulties which arise in regard to continence. Some of them we must explain away, others we must leave; for it is impossible to solve a difficulty except by discovering a truth.

It is necessary, then, to inquire (1) whether incontinent people can be said to act with knowledge or not, and if so, what is the nature of their knowledge; (2) what is to be regarded as the sphere of continence or incontinence, i.e. whether it be pleasure or pain universally, or certain definite pleasures and pains; (3) whether the continent and the steadfast person are the same, or different, and to deal similarly with all such other questions as are germane to the present inquiry.

Nature of continence and incontinence.   But the first step in the inquiry is to ask whether the continent and the incontinent person are distinguished by the sphere or by the manner of their operation; in other words, whether the incontinent person is so called merely as being incontinent in certain matters, or rather as being incontinent in a certain way, or on both grounds. And the next step is to ask whether the sphere of continence and incontinence is universal or not. For one who is incontinent in an absolute sense exhibits his incontinence not in any and every sphere of action but in the same sphere as one who is licentious. Nor does incontinence consist in a mere indefinite disposition to certain action—in which case incontinence would be the same thing as licentiousness—but in a disposition of a particular kind.

For the licentious person is led away of his own *Inconti-nence and* deliberate moral purpose, under the idea that he *Licentious-ness.* ought always to pursue the pleasure of the moment, but the incontinent person pursues it without any such idea.

As to the theory then that it is true opinion, and *Chap. V.* not knowledge, against which people offend in their *Whether inconti-* incontinence, it makes no difference to the argument; *nence is an offence* for some people who have only opinions do not feel *against* doubt, but suppose that they have accurate know- *knowledge and* edge. *opinion.*

If it be said then that people who have opinions are more likely, owing to the weakness of their conviction, to act against their conception of what is right than people who have knowledge, it may be answered that there is no such difference between knowledge and opinion; for some people are as strongly convinced of their opinions as others of their knowledge, as the example of Heraclitus[1] shows.

But we use the word "knowledge" in two distinct *Two senses of "know-* senses; we speak of a person as "knowing" if he *ledge."* possesses knowledge but does not apply it, and also if he applies his knowledge. There will be a differ-ence then between doing wrong, when one possesses knowledge, but does not reflect upon it, and so doing when one not only possesses the knowledge but reflects upon it. It is in the latter case that wrong

[1] The passages quoted by Sir A. Grant from Diogenes Laertius seem to show that Heraclitus was criticized in antiquity for his dogmatism upon subjects in which scientific knowledge was im-possible.

14—2

action appears strange, but not if it is taken without reflexion.

Again, as the premisses of the syllogism are of two modes, *the major premiss being universal and the minor particular*, there is nothing to prevent a person, although he has both premisses, from acting against his knowledge, if in spite of having both he applies the universal and not the particular premiss; for it is particulars which are matters of action. Nay, there is a distinction to be made in the universal or major premiss[1] itself; one part of it has reference to the person, the other part to the thing; thus, *the major premiss may be*, "Dry things are good for every man," and *the minor premiss* "So and so is a man," or "Such a thing is dry," but the fact that the particular thing is of a particular kind may either be not known or may have no effect *upon the mind*.

These different modes of the premisses of the syllogism constitute an immense difference *in the knowledge so acquired*. There is nothing paradoxical then in saying that the incontinent person possesses knowledge of one kind; but it would be surprising if he possessed knowledge of another. Again, it is possible for men to possess knowledge in a different manner from those which have just been described. For in a case where a person possesses knowledge

---

[1] Aristotle is fond of expressing moral or mental truth syllogistically; and as knowledge in his view takes the form of the syllogism, his point is here that in the syllogism it is possible to go wrong either by neglecting one of the two premisses or by neglecting one of the two factors of which the major premiss consists.

but does not apply it, we see that "possession" has a different meaning; in fact there is a sense in which he possesses knowledge and another sense in which he does not possess it, as e.g. in sleep or madness or intoxication. But this is the very condition of people who are under the influence of passion; for fits of anger and the desires of sensual pleasures and some such things do unmistakeably produce a change in the condition of the body, and in some cases actually cause madness.

It is clear then that we must regard incontinent people as being in much the same condition as people who are asleep or mad or intoxicated. Nor is it any proof of knowledge, *i.e. of knowledge in the full sense*, that they repeat such phrases as would seem to imply knowledge; for people who are mad or intoxicated repeat demonstrations and verses of Empedocles, and beginners in learning string phrases together, before they know their meaning. Assimilation is essential to *full* knowledge, and this is necessarily a work of time. We must suppose then that people in a state of incontinence repeat phrases in the same way as actors on the stage.

Again, we may consider the reason *of incontinence* by examining its nature[1], as follows: There is in the syllogism firstly an universal opinion, and secondly an opinion relating to particulars which fall under the dominion of sense. Now when a third opinion is formed from these two, it is necessary that

---

[1] Aristotle seems to mean by φυσικῶς an investigation into the special character or principle of ἀκράτεια.

the mind should on the one hand assent to the conclusion, and on the other should in practice give immediate effect to it. To take an example, if it is proper to taste everything that is sweet,—*which is a universal opinion*—and such or such a thing is sweet, —*which is a particular opinion*—it is necessary that one, who has the power and is not prevented, should at once act upon the conclusion, *i.e. should taste it*. When therefore there is in the mind one universal opinion which forbids tasting, and another which says that everything sweet is pleasant, *and ought to be tasted*, when *there is the particular opinion that* a certain thing is sweet, and this particular opinion is effective, and when there is the actual presence of desire, then, while the first universal opinion enjoins avoidance of the thing, desire impels to it; for desire has the faculty of setting every one of our members in motion. The result is that a person may be said in some sense to be led into incontinence by reason or opinion, but it is an opinion which is not intrinsically, but only accidentally, opposed *to right reason;* for it is *really* the desire and not the opinion which is opposed to right reason. Accordingly brutes are not said to be incontinent, because they have no universal conceptions, but only an image or recollection of particulars.

If it be asked how the incontinent person is delivered from ignorance and restored to knowledge, it may be answered, that the process is the same as in the case of one who is intoxicated or asleep; it is not peculiar to the condition of incontinence, and the proper authorities upon it are the physiologists. But as the minor premiss is an opinion of something that is an object of sensation, and as it determines actions, it follows that one who is in a condition of incontinence either does not possess an opinion, or possesses it in a sense in which possession, as we said, does not p. 213. mean knowledge but merely the repetition of phrases, as an intoxicated man may repeat the verses of Empedocles[1]. And as the minor term *or premiss* is not universal, and has apparently not the same scientific character as the universal, it seems too that the theory of Socrates[2] is really true; for it is not when knowledge properly so regarded is present to the mind that the condition of incontinence occurs, nor is it this knowledge which is twisted about by incontinence, but such knowledge only as is sensational *or depends on sensation.*

So much then for the question whether a person, CHAP. VI. when he acts incontinently, has knowledge or not, and in what sense it is possible for him to have knowledge.

The next thing is to state whether a person may Inconti-be incontinent in an absolute sense, or all people are nence ab-solute and incontinent in some particular sense, and, if there is a particular. person who is incontinent in the absolute sense, what is the sphere of his incontinence.

It is evident that pleasures and pains are the

---

[1] There should be a full stop after Ἐμπεδοκλέους in l. 11 and no stop after ὅρον in l. 13.

[2] The Socratic theory is that vice excludes knowledge; Aristotle, while asserting that it is consistent with knowledge of some kind, admits that it excludes knowledge in the full or proper sense of the word.

sphere in which the continent and steadfast, or the
incontinent and effeminate, display their characters.
But some things which produce pleasure are necessary, others are desirable in themselves but admit of
excess. By the former I mean physical processes, e.g.
the processes of nutrition and sexual love, and such
other physical processes as in our view afforded scope
for licentiousness and temperance. By the latter,
which although not necessary, are desirable in themselves, I mean e.g. victory, honour, wealth, and other
things of the same class which are good and pleasant.

Now, if it is in reference to these last things that
people transgress and exceed the limits of right
reason, we do not call them "incontinent" in an
absolute or unqualified sense, but we qualify the
word by saying that they are incontinent in respect
of money or gain or honour or angry passion. We
do not speak of them as incontinent in an absolute
sense, because they are different and are called
incontinent only by analogy as the victor in the
Olympian games was called Man[1]; for in his case the
general definition of "man" differed slightly from the
special definition but still was distinct. It is signifi-
cant of this difference that, while incontinence is
censured not as a mistake only, but as a vice, whether
a vice of an absolute or of some particular kind,
nobody is censured for being incontinent in respect
of money, gain, honour, and the like.

If we look at bodily enjoyments, in regard to

---

[1] I cannot make sense of the passage, unless it be supposed
that Ἄνθρωπος, like *Mann* in English, is here a proper name.
If so, it should be written Ἄνθρωπος rather than ἄνθρωπος.

which we commonly speak of a man as temperate or licentious, we see that one who pursues excessive pleasures, and avoids excessive pains, such as hunger, thirst, heat, cold, and the various sensations of the touch and taste, and who does so, not of deliberate purpose, but contrary to his purpose and intelligence, is called incontinent not with the qualification that he is incontinent in certain respects, as e.g. in respect of anger, but incontinent simply in an absolute sense. We may infer this to be the case, as people are similarly called effeminate in respect of pleasures and pains, but not in respect of wealth, gain, honour, and the like. This is the reason too why we class the incontinent man and the licentious man together, and again the continent man and the temperate man together, as being concerned more or less with the same pleasures and pains, while we do not place any of the others in the same class with them. They are concerned with the same things, but their attitude is different; the licentious act with deliberate purpose, but the incontinent do not. Hence we should call a person more licentious, if without desire or without any strong desire he pursues excessive pleasures and avoids moderate pains, than if he does so from a violent desire; for what (it may be asked) would such a person do if there should come upon him a fierce desire, and it were intensely painful to him to omit the gratification of his natural appetites?

But there are some desires and pleasures which are noble and virtuous of their kind; for according to our previous definition some pleasant things are naturally desirable, such as wealth, gain, victory, and honour, others the opposite of these, and others intermediate. In regard to all such things as are desirable or intermediate, it is not for feeling emotion, desire and affection for them, that people are censured, but for running into some kind of excess. Accordingly people are always censured, if they are unreasonably mastered by something that is naturally noble and good, or unreasonably pursue it, as e.g. if they are inordinately devoted to honour, or to children and parents; for children and parents are goods as well as honour, and devotion to them is laudable. But even here there is a possibility of excess, as e.g. if one should vie with the gods themselves like Niobe[1], or like Satyrus who was nicknamed "the filial" from his affection for his father, as it made him look exceedingly foolish.

It is true that these cases do not admit of vice, and the reason has been already assigned, viz. that the objects are all desirable in themselves, although excess in them is wrong, and ought to be avoided; nor again do they admit of incontinence, as incontinence is something that ought not only to be avoided but to be censured.

Still the similarity of the emotional condition leads us to use the term "incontinence" in these cases, although we do not use it without qualification, as when we speak of a person as "a bad doctor" or "a bad actor," although we should not call him "bad" in an absolute sense. As in that instance then *we do*

---

[1] The story of Niobe is well known; but Satyrus is only a name.

not use the term "bad" without qualification, because bad doctoring or bad acting is not badness or vice, but only analogous to a vice, so here it is evident that we must regard nothing as being continence or incontinence in a strict sense, but what has the same sphere as temperance or licentiousness, and must not apply the terms "continence" and "incontinence" to anger, except by analogy. Accordingly we add *a qualification* and say, that a person is incontinent in respect of angry passion in the same sense as in respect of honour or gain.

There are certain things which are naturally Bad moral pleasant, some of them being pleasant in an absolute states. sense and others pleasant to particular classes of animals or men, while there are other things which are not naturally pleasant but owe their pleasantness to physical defects or habits or to depravity of nature; and it is possible to discover moral states corresponding to each of these kinds of pleasures.

What I mean is that there are brutal states as Brutality. e.g. in the female creature who is said to rip up pregnant women and devour their children, or in some savage tribes near the Black Sea which are said to delight in such practices as eating raw meat or human flesh, or in cannibals who lend their children to one another to feast upon, or as the story tells of Phalaris[1]. And if these are brutal states, there are others which are produced in some people by disease and madness, as when a person sacrificed and ate his

---

[1] The "story" is the traditional belief that Phalaris ate his son in infancy. Cp. Bentley's *Dissertation upon the Epistles of Phalaris* xvi.

mother, or another person ate the liver of his fellow-slave. Other such states again are the results of a morbid disposition or of habit, as e.g. the practice of plucking out one's hair, or biting one's nails, or eating cinders and earth, or of committing unnatural vice; for these habits are sometimes natural, *when a person's nature is vicious*, and sometimes acquired, as e.g. by those who are the victims of outrage from childhood.

Now whenever nature is the cause of these habits, nobody would call people who give way to them incontinent, any more than we should call women incontinent for being not males, but females; and the same is the case with people in whom habit has produced a morbid condition.

These various habits, like brutality itself, lie beyond the pale of vice; but if a person in whom they exist becomes their master or slave, his conduct ought to be called *continence or* incontinence, not in an absolute, but in a metaphorical sense; just as if a person is mastered by his angry passions, he ought to be called incontinent in respect of anger, but not incontinent in an absolute sense. For all excess whether of folly, cowardice, incontinence, or savagery is either brutal or morbid. For if it is a person's nature to be frightened at everything, even at the noise of a mouse, he is such a coward as to be more like a brute beast than a human being; but it was disease which made the man[1] afraid of the weasel. Again, foolish people who are naturally irrational, and live a life of mere sensation, as e.g. some races of remote barbarians, are like brutes; but foolish people

[1] In allusion to some story now forgotten.

whose folly arises from disease e.g. from epilepsy, or from insanity, are in a morbid state.

A person may at times possess one of these habits without being mastered by it, as e.g. if Phalaris had restrained his desire of eating a child or his unnatural passions; or again he may not only possess it but be mastered by it.

As then human vice is sometimes called vice in an absolute sense, and at other times is qualified by the epithet "brutal" or "morbid," but is not called vice in an absolute sense, so it is clear that incontinence may be either brutal or morbid, but it is only incontinence in an absolute sense when it is coextensive with human licentiousness.

It is evident therefore that continence and inconti- CHAP. VII. nence have to do simply with the same matters as temperance and licentiousness, and that in other matters there is a different kind of incontinence which is called incontinence in a metaphorical, and not in an absolute, sense.

It must be observed too that the incontinence of Incontinence of angry passion is not so disgraceful as the incontinence passion and of the desires. For it is as if the passion heard reason incontinence of more or less, but misheard it, like hasty servants, who desire. run out before they have heard all that is said to them, and so mistake their orders, or like dogs who bark at a person, if only he makes a noise, without waiting to see if he is a friend. In the same way the temper from its natural heat and impetuosity hears something, but does not hear the voice of command, when it rushes to revenge. For when the reason or fancy indicates that an insult or slight has been

inflicted, the passion jumps, as it were, to the conclusion that it must do battle with the person who
inflicted it, and therefore gets into a fury at once.
Desire, on the other hand, rushes to the enjoyment of
a thing, if only reason or sensation says that it is
pleasant. Thus passion follows reason in a sense, but
desire does not. Desire is therefore the more disgraceful; for the man of incontinent temper is in a
sense the servant of reason, but the other is the
servant of desire and not of reason.

Again, there is more excuse for following natural
impulses, as indeed there is for following all such
desires as are common to all the world, and the more
common they are, the more excusable are they also.
But passion and rage are more natural than the
desires of excessive and superfluous pleasures, as
appears in the case of the man who defended himself
for striking his father by saying "Yes, for he struck
his own father before and his own father struck his
father," and pointing to his child " He too will strike
me when he becomes a man; it is in our blood." So
too the man, who was being dragged out of the house
by his son, told him to stop at the door, as he had
himself dragged his father so far but not beyond it.

Again, the greater the cunning, the greater is the
injustice of an action. Now a passionate man is not
cunning nor is passion cunning; it is open. Desire,
on the other hand, is cunning; thus Aphrodite is
called the

> "Goddess of the Cyprian isle,
> Artisan of many a wile[1],"

[1] The authorship of the phrase is unknown.

and Homer says of her embroidered girdle *that on it was*

"Guile that doth cozen wisest men of wit[1]."

Hence as this incontinence is more unjust and more disgraceful than incontinence of temper, it may be called incontinence in an absolute sense, and is in fact a species of vice.

Again, nobody feels pain when he commits a wanton[2] outrage. But anybody who acts in anger feels pain in his action, whereas wantonness is associated with pleasure. If then such things as are the most legitimate subjects of anger are properly regarded as the most unjust, it follows that the incontinence which is due to desire is more unjust *than the incontinence which is due to angry passion;* for there is nothing of wantonness in angry passion.

It is clear then that incontinence in respect of the desires is more disgraceful than incontinence in respect of angry passion, and that continence and incontinence are properly concerned with bodily desires and pleasures. But we have still to ascertain the differences in these desires and pleasures, for, as has been said at the outset, some are human and natural alike in kind and in degree, others are brutal, others again are the results of physical injuries and diseases. It is with the first of these alone that temperance and licentiousness are concerned. That is the reason why we do not speak of brutes as

Differences in desires and plea- sures. p. 219.

---

[1] *Iliad* xiv. 214—217.

[2] ὕβρις may here be represented in English by "wanton outrage" or "wantonness," as it is clearly such outrageous conduct as is the natural issue of desire.

temperate or licentious except metaphorically, and
where one kind of animal is absolutely distinguished
from another by peculiar wantonness, destructiveness,
voracity or the like; for animals do not possess moral
purpose or ratiocinative power, they merely get into
an unnatural state, like madmen.

Brutality
and Vice.

Brutality is not so bad a thing as vice, but it is
more formidable, for it is not the corruption of the
highest good in brutes as it is in men, but its non-
existence. The comparison then of brutality with
vice is like the comparison of inanimates with ani-
mates in respect of wickedness; for the depravity of
that which has no originative principle is always less
mischievous, and *brutes lack* reason, *which* is an
originative principle. (It is much the same then as a
comparison of injustice with an unjust man; there is a
sense in which each of them is worse than the other[1].)
For a bad man will do ten thousand times as much
evil as a brute.

Chap.VIII.

p. 216.

As to the pleasures and pains, desires and dislikes,
of touch and taste, with which licentiousness and
temperance, as has been already defined, are concerned, it is possible to be in such a moral state that
one is the slave of those of which most people are
masters, or again to be in such a moral state that one
is master of those of which most people are slaves.
According as a person's state is one or the other in
respect of pleasures he is continent or incontinent;

---

[1] There should be a full stop at κάκιον, and the sentence
παραπλήσιον οὖν...κάκιον should be regarded as virtually parenthetical, if indeed it has a right to a place in the text at all.

according as it is one or the other in respect of pains, he is courageous or effeminate. The moral state of the large majority of mankind lies between the two, even if they incline rather to the worse.

Inasmuch as some pleasures are necessary, and others are not necessary, or are necessary only up to a certain point, and as neither the excesses nor the deficiencies of these pleasures are necessary, and it is the same with desires and pains, it follows that, if a person pursues pleasures of an excessive character, or pursues *any pleasures* in an excessive degree, or pursues them from moral purpose for their own sake, and not for the sake of anything that results from them, he is licentious; for he is necessarily incapable of repentance and is therefore incurable, as to be incapable of repentance is to be incurable. The opposite state is the state of deficiency, the mean state is temperance. Similarly a person who avoids bodily pains, not from inability to endure them but from moral purpose, is also licentious. *Licentiousness.*

Where this moral purpose does not exist, a person may be moved either by pleasure or by avoidance of the pain resulting from desire. There is therefore a difference between these persons. But everybody will agree that a person is worse, if he does something disgraceful without desire, or without any strong desire, than if he does it at a time when his desire is violent, and worse, if he deals a blow in cold blood than when he is angry; for what, it may be said, would such a person do if he were in a passion? Hence the licentious person is worse than the incontinent. *Licentiousness and Incontinence.*

Of the characters which have been described the one, *viz. incontinence*, is rather a kind of effeminacy,

Continence and Steadfastness. the other is licentiousness. The opposite of the incontinent character is the continent, and of the effeminate the steadfast; for steadfastness consists in holding out against pain, and continence in overcoming pleasure, and it is one thing to hold out, and another to overcome, as it is one thing to escape being beaten and another to win a victory. Hence continence is preferable to steadfastness.

If a person gives in where people generally resist and are capable of resisting, he deserves to be called

Effeminacy. effeminate and luxurious; for luxury is a form of effeminacy. Such a person will let his cloak trail in the mud to avoid the trouble of lifting it up, or will give himself the airs of an invalid without considering himself miserable, although he resembles one who is miserable.

It is much the same with continence and incontinence. It is no wonder, if a person is mastered by strong and overwhelming pleasures or pains; nay, it is pardonable, if he struggles against them like Philoctetes when bitten by the snake in the play of Theodectes, or like Cercyon[1] in the *Alope* of Carcinus, or like people who in trying to suppress their laughter burst out in a loud guffaw, as happened to Xenophantus[2]. It is only unpardonable where a person is

[1] It is possible that the poet Carcinus represented in his *Alope* a struggle between the cruel disposition and the moral sense of Cercyon.

[2] The allusion is unknown.

mastered by things against which most people succeed in holding out, and is impotent to struggle against them, unless his impotence be due to hereditary constitution or to disease, as effeminacy is hereditary in the kings of Scythia, or as a woman is naturally weaker than a man.

If a person is fond of amusing himself, he is regarded as licentious, but he is really effeminate; for amusement, being a relaxation, is a recreation, and a person who is fond of amusing himself is one who carries his recreation to excess.

Incontinence assumes sometimes the form of impetuosity, and at other times that of weakness. Some men deliberate, but their emotion prevents them from abiding by the result of their deliberation; others again do not deliberate, and are therefore carried away by their emotion. For as people cannot be tickled, if they are themselves the beginners in a tickling match[1], so some people, if they anticipate or foresee what is coming, and have roused themselves and their reason to resist it before it comes, are not overcome by their emotion, whether it be pleasant or painful.

Forms of incontinence.

It is people of a quick and atrabilious temper whose incontinence is particularly apt to take the form of impetuosity; for the rapidity or the violence of their feeling prevents them from waiting for the guidance of reason, as they are easily led away by their imagination.

[1] The idea seems to be that, if a person anticipates tickling, he is in a sense armed against it; it depends for its effect upon surprise.

15—2

CHAP. IX.
p. 225.

The licentious person, as was said, is not disposed to repentance, as he abides by his purpose, but the incontinent person is always so disposed. The difficulty then which we raised does not exist. The former is incurable, the latter can be cured; for if vice may be compared to such a disease as dropsy or consumption, incontinence may be compared to epilepsy, the one being a chronic, the other an intermittent depravity. There is in fact an absolutely generic distinction between incontinence and vice; for vice may be, but incontinence cannot be, unconscious.

Incontinence and Vice.

Incontinence of two kinds.

There are two classes of incontinent people, and those who simply lose command of themselves are better than those who possess reason but do not abide by it, as they are not overcome by so violent an emotion, nor do they act without previous deliberation like the others. For an incontinent person may be compared to one who gets intoxicated with a little wine, i.e. with less wine than ordinary people.

It is evident then that incontinence is not vice (although there is, I think, a sense in which it is a vice), for the former is contrary, and the latter is conformable, to moral purpose. Still they come to much the same thing as regards actions; it is like the saying of Demodocus[1] about the Milesians, "The Milesians are not fools but they act just like fools"; so the incontinent are not unjust but they act unjustly.

The incontinent man then is the kind of person to

[1] The epigrammatist of Leros.

pursue such bodily pleasures as are excessive and contrary to right reason, although not from conviction *of their goodness*, but the vicious man is convinced *of their goodness* because he is the kind of person to pursue them; hence it is easy to convert the former, but not the latter. For virtue is preservative, and vice destructive, of principle; but in actions the object is a first principle[1], like the hypotheses or definitions in mathematics. In mathematics then it is not the reason which is capable of proving the first principle, nor is it in actions; it is the virtue, whether natural or acquired, of forming a right opinion about the first principle, *i.e. about the object of action.* A person who possesses this virtue then is temperate; a person who does not possess it is licentious.

But there are people who are apt to be so carried away by emotion as to act contrary to right reason; they are so far overcome by emotion as not to act in accordance with right reason, but not so far overcome as to be convinced that they ought to pursue such pleasures unreservedly. These are incontinent people; they are superior to the licentious, and not absolutely bad; for they have not lost the highest good, viz. the first principle. Opposite to these is another class of people who are capable of abiding by their principle and are not liable to be carried away, at least by emotion. It is evident from these considerations that the moral state of the former is vicious and that of the latter is virtuous.

---

[1] There is again a play upon the two senses of ἀρχή (1) a beginning, (2) a first principle or moral assumption.

CHAP. X.   *It remains to ask then,* Is a person continent, if he
Relation of abides by his reason and moral purpose, whatever
continence
to moral   they may be, or only if he abides by them when they
purpose.   are right? Is he incontinent, if he does not abide by
his moral purpose or reason, whatever they may be?
or is it only, if he does not abide by true reason and
right purpose[1]? This is a difficulty which has been
p. 208.   already raised. The answer seems to be that, although it may accidentally be any sort of reason or
purpose, yet essentially it is true reason and right
purpose, by which the one does, and the other does
not, abide. For if a person chooses or pursues a
thing which may be called *A* for the sake of something else which may be called *B*, it is *B* which he
pursues and chooses essentially, and *A* only accidentally. By "essentially" we mean "absolutely," and
therefore although in a certain sense it is any sort of
opinion by which the one abides, and from which the
other departs, yet in an absolute sense it is true
opinion.

Obstinacy.   There are certain people who are ready to abide
by their opinion at all costs; we call them obstinate.
They are people, I mean, who are hard to persuade,
and not easy to convert. Such people bear some
resemblance to continent people, as do prodigals to
liberal people, and foolhardy people to courageous,
but there are many points of difference. For while
the continent person does not veer about under the
influence of emotion and desire, *he is not immovable;*

---

[1] I follow Mr Bywater in reading ἢ ὁ τῷ μὴ ψευδεῖ λόγῳ καὶ
τῇ προαιρέσει τῇ ὀρθῇ.

it is easy to persuade him on occasion; but the obstinate person resists the persuasion of reason, since, as a matter of fact, such people may conceive desires, and are frequently led away by pleasure.

People who are self-opinionated, or ignorant, or boorish, are all obstinate. Self-opinionated people are so from motives of pleasure and pain; for they have a pleasant sense of victory in refusing to be convinced, and are pained, if their opinions, like bills before Parliament, are rejected. They are therefore more like incontinent than continent people. There are also some people who do not abide by their resolutions, but the reason is not incontinence; Neoptolemus in the *Philoctetes* of Sophocles is such a person. It was pleasure indeed which prevented him from abiding by his opinion, but it was a noble pleasure; for it was noble in his eyes to speak the truth, although he was persuaded by Odysseus to tell a lie. It is not everybody who acts from a motive of pleasure that is licentious or wicked or incontinent, but only if the pleasure be a disgraceful one.

There are people too whose character it is to take CHAP. XI. less pleasure than is right in bodily gratifications, and in virtue of their character not to abide by reason. The continent person then is intermediate between such people and the incontinent. For the reason why the incontinent person does not abide by reason lies in an excess, and the reason why the insensible person does not abide by it lies in a deficiency; but the continent person does abide by it, and is not affected either by the excess or by the deficiency.

But assuming that continence is virtuous, we must conclude that both the moral states which are opposed to it are vicious, as in fact they clearly are; but because one of these states, *viz. insensibility*, is seen only in few instances and on rare occasions, it seems that continence is the opposite of incontinence, as temperance of licentiousness.

Analogy is a frequent source of names. Such an expression then as "the continence of the temperate person" is a case of analogy. For it is the character both of the continent person and of the temperate person not to be induced by bodily pleasures to do anything that is contrary to reason; only the difference is that the former has, and the latter has not, bad desires, the former is the kind of person who will not feel such pleasure as is contrary to reason, the latter the kind of person who will feel such pleasure but who will not be led away by it.

The incontinent person and the licentious person resemble each other, although they are different. Both pursue bodily pleasures, but the former does not, and the latter does, regard it as right to pursue them.

Inconti-
nence and
Prudence.
It is impossible then for the same person to be at once prudent and incontinent; for it has been shown, that prudence implies a virtuous character. Again, prudence consists not merely in knowledge but in capacity for *moral* action, and the incontinent person is incapable of such action. But there is no reason why the clever person should not be incontinent. Hence it is that people are sometimes thought to be incontinent, although they are prudent, because

cleverness differs from prudence in the manner de- p. 200.
scribed in an early part¹ of this treatise, and, while it
is allied to it in intellectual ability, is different from
it in its moral purpose.

Nor again is the incontinent person like one who
has knowledge and reflexion, but like one who is
asleep or intoxicated. He acts voluntarily, for in a
certain sense he knows both what he is doing and
what is his object in doing it, but he is not wicked, as
his purpose is virtuous; he may therefore be said to
be only half wicked. Incontinent people too are not
unjust, as they are not cunning. They are either
incapable of abiding by the results of their deliberation, or they are atrabilious and incapable of deliberating at all. The incontinent person then, may be
compared to a State which passes all such bills as it
ought to pass, and has excellent laws, but. does not
carry them out, according to the taunt of Anaxan-
drides²

"'Twas the State's will; the State recks not of law."

The wicked man on the other hand may be compared
to a State which carries out its laws, but whose laws
are bad.

Incontinence and continence then have to do
with something that goes beyond the average moral
state of mankind; for the continent man abides more,
and the incontinent man less, by his moral purpose
than is in the power of ordinary people.

¹ Aristotle uses the phrase ἐν τοῖς πρώτοις λόγοις to denote
not the earliest—but any earlier—part of his book.

² The poet of the Middle Comedy, who is said to have
satirized the Athenians.

Various kinds of incontinence.
There are various kinds of incontinence, and the incontinence of the atrabilious is more easily curable than that of people who deliberate, but do not abide by the results of their deliberation. Again, it is easier to cure people who are incontinent by habit than by nature, as it is easier to change habit than to change nature. In fact the reason why habit is itself so difficult to change is that it resembles nature, as Evenus[1] says

"Practice, I say, endureth long, my friend,
And is a second nature in the end."

We have now discussed the nature of continence and incontinence, of steadfastness and effeminacy, and the mutual relations of these states of mind.

Chap. XII. Pleasure and pain.
The consideration of pleasure and pain belongs to the political philosopher. He is the architect who frames the idea of the end which we have in view in defining good and evil in an absolute sense.

There is another reason too why it is necessary to review pleasure and pain; we defined moral virtue and vice as having to do with pains and pleasures, and it is the general opinion that happiness implies pleasure[2].

Pleasure and good.
Now (1) there are some people who hold that no pleasure is a good, either essentially or accidentally, as good and pleasure are not the same thing. (2) Others hold that, while some pleasures are good, the

---

[1] The gnomic poet of Paros.

[2] A clause omitted in translation refers to the supposed etymological connexion between μακάριος (blessed) and χαίρειν (to rejoice).

majority are bad. (3) There is also a third opinion, that, even if every pleasure is a good, still the supreme good cannot possibly be pleasure.

(1) Speaking generally, we may say that pleasure is not a good, because every pleasure is a sensible process of coming to a natural state, and no process is akin to the ends, e.g. no process of building to a house. Another reason is that the temperate man eschews pleasures. Again, the prudent man pursues painlessness, but not pleasure. Pleasures too are an impediment to thoughtfulness, and the greater the pleasure, the greater is the impediment, as e.g. the pleasure of love, for thought is out of the question, while it lasts. Again there is no art of pleasure, but every good is a product of art. And lastly children and brute beasts pursue pleasures.

(2) In support of the view that it is not all pleasures which are virtuous, it is argued that there are some pleasures which are disgraceful and disreputable and injurious as well, for some things which are pleasant are dangerous to health.

(3) It is also argued that pleasure is not the supreme good, because it is not the end, but a process.

These are, in general, the views which are put CHAP. XIII. forward. But it does not follow that pleasure is not a good, or the supreme good, as is clear from the following considerations:

In the first place, as the good is of two kinds, Good. being either absolute or relative, natures and moral states, and therefore motions and processes too, will be consequently also of two kinds; and of those

which are called bad some are bad absolutely and
not bad relatively to the individual, but desirable for
him; some are not desirable for the individual, except
occasionally, and for a short time; others are not
pleasures at all, but only apparent pleasures, if they
involve pain and are remedial in their nature, as e.g.
the pleasures of the sick.

Nature of
pleasure.

Again, as the good may be either an activity or a
moral state, it is only in an accidental sense that such
processes as restore a person to his natural condition
can be said to be pleasant. In *the satisfaction of* the
desires there is the activity of the remaining part of
the state or nature[1], *i.e. of the part which does not
feel the desire; nor is desire a necessary condition of
pleasure;* for there are pleasures which are independent of pain or desire, as e.g. the activities of the
speculative life in which nature does not exhibit any
want. It is an indication of this fact that people do
not find delight in the same pleasure during the
process of satisfying their nature, as when their
nature is in its normal condition; when its condition
is normal, they find delight in such things as are
pleasures in an absolute sense, but during the process of satisfaction, in such things as are actually
opposite to these, for they find delight in things
which are acid and bitter, although no such thing is
either naturally or absolutely pleasant. These pleasures then are not natural or absolute pleasures; for
the pleasures resulting from pleasant things are
related to one another in the same way as the
pleasant things themselves.

[1] The expression is made clear by p. 138, l. 30.

Again, it is not necessary that there should be something else which is better than pleasure in the sense, as some people maintain, in which the end is better than the process which leads to it. For pleasures are not all processes nor concomitants of a process, but activities, and an end. We experience them not in the process *of acquiring certain powers* but in the exercise *of the powers when acquired.* Nor is it true that in all pleasures there is an end distinct from the pleasures themselves; it is true only of such pleasures as occur to people in the process of being brought to the consummation or complete realization of their nature.

It is wrong therefore to define pleasure as a "sensible process." It is better to define it as an "activity of the natural state of one's being," and to call it not "sensible" but "unimpeded." It is sometimes thought to be a process, as being a good in the proper sense of the term; for people suppose that an activity is a process, but they are really different. *Definition of pleasure.*

To say that pleasures are bad, because some things which are pleasant are injurious, is equivalent to saying that health is bad, because some things which are healthy are bad for money-making. It is true that in this sense both are bad, but this does not prove them to be bad *in themselves;* for study itself is at times injurious to health. But neither prudence nor any moral state is impeded by the pleasure which it produces; they are impeded only by alien pleasures, as the pleasures of study and learning will only make a person study and learn the more.

It is natural that pleasure should not be a product *No art of pleasure.*

of any art, for there is no art which produces any other activity. Art merely produces the faculty, although the art of the perfumer or the cook may be held to be *in a sense* productive of pleasure.

The objections that the temperate man avoids *pleasure*, that the prudent man pursues *not pleasure but* a painless life, and that children and brutes pursue pleasure, may all be met with the same answer. It has been stated in what sense all pleasures are good absolutely, and in what sense they are not good *absolutely*. It is pleasures of the latter kind that brutes and children pursue. It is painlessness in respect of them that a prudent man pursues. They are such pleasures as involve desire and pain or in other words bodily pleasures (for these involve desire and pain) and the excesses of pleasures which constitute the licentiousness of the licentious man. Hence the temperate man will avoid these pleasures, although he has pleasures of his own.

CHAP. XIV.

Pain an evil.

However, it is admitted that pain is an evil and that it ought to be avoided. It is an evil either absolutely or relatively, as causing some impediment to the individual. But the opposite of that which ought to be avoided, in the respect in which it ought to be avoided, and is bad, is good. It follows there-

Pleasure a good.

fore that pleasure is a good; for the objection of Speusippus, that pleasure is contrary to pain in the same way as the greater is contrary to the less as well as to the equal[1], cannot stand; for he would not

---

[1] If pleasure and pain were extremes and the good were intermediate between them, it would follow that pleasure is an evil.

maintain that pleasure is identical with some form of evil.

Nor does it follow that there is not some pleasure which is the supreme good, because there are some vicious pleasures, any more than it follows that some knowledge is not the supreme good although there are vicious kinds of knowledge. Indeed it is, I think, necessary, as every moral state admits of unimpeded activities, that, whether it be the activity of them all, or of some one of them, which is happiness, it should be most desirable, if it is unimpeded; but such un- impeded activity is pleasure. Hence it will be plea- sure of some kind which is the supreme good, although most pleasures are, it may be, in an absolute sense vicious. *Pleasure of some kind the supreme good.*

It is on this ground that everybody supposes a happy life to be pleasant, and happiness to involve pleasure; the supposition is reasonable, as no activity is perfect if it be impeded, and happiness is in its nature perfect. It follows that the happy man re- quires bodily goods, external goods and good fortune as accessories to his happiness, if his activity is not to be impeded. But to assert that a person on the rack, or a person plunged in the depth of calamities, is happy is either intentionally or unintentionally to talk nonsense. *Happiness and plea- sure.*

The fact that good fortune is a necessary adjunct to happiness leads some people to hold that good fortune is identical with happiness, but it is not so. It is an actual impediment to happiness, if it be excessive, and then perhaps should rightly cease to be called good fortune; for the definition *Happiness and good fortune.*

of good fortune depends on its relation to happiness.

Pleasure and the supreme good.

Again, the fact that all brutes and all men pursue pleasure is a certain indication of its being in some sense the supreme good; for

"No voice is wholly lost that is the voice of many men[1]."

But inasmuch as it is not the same nature or moral state that is, or is thought to be, the best, so it is not the same pleasure which is universally sought. Still it is pleasure. It may even be the case that all men *really* pursue not the pleasure which they fancy, or would say, they are pursuing, but a pleasure which is the same for all; for there is a divine instinct naturally implanted in all things. But bodily pleasures have usurped the title to the name "pleasure," as it is to them that people are most frequently diverted, and in them that everybody participates. These are then the only pleasures that people know, and they are therefore held to be the only pleasures that exist.

But it is evident that, unless pleasure or the *unimpeded* activity *which is pleasure* is a good, it will be impossible for the happy man to live pleasantly. For why should he want pleasure, if it is not a good, and if it is possible for him, *as it then would be*, to live painfully? For if pleasure is not an evil or a good, neither is pain. Why then should he avoid pain? Nor will the life of the virtuous man be pleasanter than that *of any one else*, unless his activities are pleasanter.

[1] Hesiod Ἔργα καὶ Ἡμέραι 761.

The investigation of bodily pleasures is necessary, Bodily pleasures. f we hold that some pleasures, if not all, are highly lesirable, i.e. noble pleasures but not bodily pleasures 1or the pleasures of the incontinent. It may be asked vhy, *if these pleasures are vicious*, the pains which are)pposite to them are vicious; for the opposite of evil s good. Is it to be said then that necessary pleasures tre only good in the sense that whatever is not evil s good? Or are they good up to a certain point?

In all moral states and motions in which it is mpossible to exceed the right limit of good, it is mpossible also to exceed the right limit of pleasure;)ut where there is a possible excess of good, there is tlso a possible excess of pleasure.

Now bodily goods admit of excess, and vice con- iists in pursuing the excess, not in pursuing the 1ecessary pleasures; for everybody finds a certain iatisfaction in rich meats or wines or the pleasures of pve, but not always the proper satisfaction. The :ontrary is the case with pain. People in general lo not avoid the excess of pain, but avoid pain tltogether; for such pain as is opposite to excessive)leasure is felt only by one who pursues that exces- iive pleasure.

It is right however to explain not the truth only CHAP. XV.)ut the cause of error also, as this explanation helps o produce belief. For when the reason why a thing vhich is not true appears to be true is seen and inderstood, it strengthens belief in the truth. We Bodily pleasures. 1ust therefore explain why it is that bodily pleasures ippear more desirable than other pleasures.

It is, firstly, then that such pleasure drives out

pain. The excesses of pain make people pursue excessive pleasure, and bodily pleasure generally, as a remedy. But the remedies *of severe diseases* are frequently severe, and people pursue them from their apparent contrast to the opposite pains.

p. 235.

(There are these two reasons, as has been said, why pleasure is thought not to be virtuous, viz. (1) That some pleasures are actions of a base nature, whether the baseness be congenital, as in a brute, or acquired, as in a vicious man. (2) That other pleasures are remedial, implying a want, and that the existence of the normal state is better than the process to that state; these pleasures then are felt only when we are coming to a *normal or* perfect state; they[1] are therefore only accidentally virtuous)[2].

Bodily pleasures too, as being violent, are pursued by people who are incapable of finding gratification in other pleasures. Thus people sometimes make themselves thirsty *in order to enjoy the pleasure of satisfying their thirst.* So long as these pleasures are harmless, there is no ground for censuring them (although it is wrong to pursue them, when they are harmful), for people who pursue them have no other objects of gratification, and a neutral state of the sensations is naturally painful to many people. For an animal is constantly labouring, as we read in books on physical science, where it is said that seeing and hearing are painful, but we have got accustomed to

---

[1] The stop after γίνεσθαι should be a colon.

[2] The passage which I have placed in brackets is an evident interruption of the argument.

hem by this time, as the saying is. Similarly in
outh people, because they are growing, are much
n the same state as drunken people, and youth is
leasant. Again, people of an atrabilious nature
equire constant medicine, as their temperament con-
tantly frets their body away, and thus they are
lways in a state of strong desire. But pain is ex-
elled either by the pleasure which is its opposite, or
y any pleasure if it be strong. This is why atra-
ilious people fall into licentiousness and wicked-
ess.

Such pleasures on the other hand as have no Natural
antecedent pains do not admit of excess; they are pleasures.
aturally, and not merely accidentally pleasant. By
accidental pleasures" I mean such as are remedial in
heir effect; for as we are cured by the action of the
emaining healthy part of our nature, the process of
ure is pleasant. By "natural pleasures" I mean
uch as produce action of our whole nature in a
ealthy state.

The same thing is never constantly pleasant to us,
s our nature is not simple, but there exists in us a
ort of second nature, which makes us mortal beings.
hus if one element is active, it acts against the
ature of the other, and when the two elements are
n equilibrium, the action appears to be neither
ainful nor pleasant. If there were a being, whose
ature is simple, the same action would always be
upremely pleasant to him. It is thus that God
njoys one simple pleasure everlastingly; for there is
n activity not only of motion but of immobility, and
leasure consists rather in rest than in motion. But

16—2

change, as the poet[1] says, is "the sweetest thing in the world," and the reason lies in a certain viciousness of our nature; for as the vicious man is fond of change, so too the nature which requires change is vicious, it is not simple or virtuous.

We have now discussed continence and incontinence, pleasure and pain, their nature and the reason why some of them are good and others bad. It remains to discuss friendship or love.

---

[1] Euripides, *Orestes*, v. 234, but the reading there is γλυκύ.

BOOK VIII.

Chap. I.
Friendship
or Love.
It is
(1) indis-
pensable;

It will be natural to discuss friendship[1] or love next, for friendship is a kind of virtue or implies virtue. It is also indispensable to life. For nobody would choose to live without friends, although he were in possession of every other good. Nay, it seems that if people are rich and hold official and authoritative positions, they have the greatest need of friends; for what is the good of having this sort of prosperity if one is denied the opportunity of beneficence, which is never so freely or so admirably exercised as towards friends? Or how can it be maintained in safety and security without friends? For the greater a person's importance, the more liable it is to disaster. In poverty and other misfortunes we regard our friends as our only refuge. Again, friends are helpful to us, when we are young, as guarding us from error, and when we are growing old, as taking care of us, and supplying such de-

[1] If it were necessary to choose one word for φιλία the best would be "friendship," but it corresponds as substantive to the meanings of the verb φιλεῖν and therefore rises at times in point of intensity to "love."

ficiencies of action as are the consequences of physical weakness, and when we are in the prime of life, as prompting us to noble actions, according to the adage

"Two come together";

for two people have a greater power both of intelligence and of action *than either of the two by himself.*

(2) natural;   It would seem that friendship or love is the natural instinct of a parent towards a child, and of a child towards a parent, not only among men, but among birds and animals generally, and among creatures of the same race towards one another, especially among men. This is the reason why we praise men who are the friends of their fellow-men or philanthropists. We may observe too in travelling how near and dear every man is to his fellow-man.

(3) social;   Again, it seems that friendship or love is the bond which holds states together, and that legislators set more store by it than by justice; for concord is apparently akin to friendship, and it is concord that they especially seek to promote, and faction, as being hostility to the state, that they especially try to expel.

If people are friends, there is no need of justice between them; but people may be just, and yet need friendship. Indeed it seems that justice, in its supreme form, assumes the character of friendship.

---

[1] *Iliad* x. 224. It is where Diomedes expresses his desire for a companion in invading the Trojan camp.

ἀλλ᾽ εἴ τίς μοι ἀνὴρ ἅμ᾽ ἕποιτο καὶ ἄλλος
μᾶλλον θαλπωρή, καὶ θαρσαλεώτερον ἔσται.
σύν τε δύ᾽ ἐρχομένω, καί τε πρὸ ὃ τοῦ ἐνόησεν.

Nor is friendship indispensable only; it is also noble. We praise people who are fond of their friends, and it is thought to be a noble thing to have many friends, and there are some people who hold that to be a friend is the same thing as to be a good man.

But the subject of friendship or love is one that affords scope for a good many differences of opinion. Some people define it as a sort of likeness, and define people who are like each other as friends. Hence the sayings "Like seeks like," "Birds of a feather," and so on. Others on the contrary say that "two of a trade never agree¹." Upon this subject *some philosophical thinkers* indulge in more profound physical speculations; Euripides asserting that

> "the parched Earth loves the rain,
> And the great Heaven rain-laden loves to fall
> Earthwards"²;

Heraclitus that "the contending tends together," and that "harmony most beautiful is formed of discords," and that "all things are by strife engendered;" others, among whom is Empedocles, taking the opposite view and urging that "like desires like."

The physical³ questions we may leave aside as not

---

¹ The allusion is to the proverbial quarrelsomeness of two potters, as in Hesiod's line

καὶ κεραμεὺς κεραμεῖ κοτέει καὶ τέκτονι τέκτων.
Ἔργα καὶ Ἡμέραι 25.

² The play from which these lines are taken is unknown.

³ "physical questions," i.e. questions relating to the constitution of the physical universe as contrasted with questions relating to the constitution of human nature.

being germane to the present enquiry. But let us investigate all such questions as are of human interest and relate to characters and emotions, e.g. whether friendship can be formed among all people, or it is impossible for people to be friends if they are vicious, and whether there is one kind of friendship or more than one.

Friendship of more kinds than one.

The idea that there is only one kind of friendship or love, because it admits of degrees, rests upon insufficient evidence; for things may be different in kind, and yet may admit of degrees. But this is a question which has been already discussed[1].

The lovable.

It is possible, I think, to elucidate the subject of friendship or love, by determining what it is that is lovable or an object of love. For it seems that it is not everything which is loved, but only that which is lovable, and that this is what is good or pleasant or useful. It would seem too that a thing is useful if it is a means of gaining something good or pleasant, and if so, it follows that what is good and what is pleasant will be lovable in the sense of being ends.

It may be asked then, Is it that which is good *in itself*, or that which is good relatively to us, that we love? For there is sometimes a difference between them; and the same question may be asked in regard to that which is pleasant. It seems then that everybody loves what is good relatively to himself, and that, while it is the good which is lovable in an

---

[1] There is no such discussion in the earlier part of the *Nicomachean Ethics*. Perhaps, as Sir A. Grant thought, the words εἴρηται δ' ὑπὲρ αὐτῶν ἔμπροσθεν are the interpolation of a copyist.

absolute sense, it is that which is good relatively to each individual that is lovable in his eyes. It may be said that everybody loves not that which is good, but that which appears good relatively to himself. But this is not an objection that will make any difference; for in that case that which is lovable will be that which appears to be lovable.

There being three motives of friendship or love, it must be observed that we do not apply the term "friendship" or "love" to the affection felt for inanimate things. The reason is (1) that they are incapable of reciprocating affection, and (2) that we do not wish their good; for it would, I think, be ridiculous to wish the good e.g. of wine; if we wish it at all, it is only in the sense of wishing the wine to keep well, in the hope of enjoying it ourselves. But it is admitted that we ought to wish our friend's good for his sake, and not for our own. If we wish people good in this sense, we are called well-wishers, unless our good wishes are returned; such reciprocal well-wishing is called friendship or love. *Limitation of friendship or love.*

But it is necessary, I think, to add, that the well-wishing must not be unknown. A person often wishes well to people whom he has not seen, but whom he supposes to be virtuous or useful; and it is possible that one of these persons may entertain the same feeling towards him. Such people then, it is clear, wish well to one another; but they cannot be properly called friends, as their disposition is unknown to each other. It follows that, if they are to be friends, they must be well-disposed to each other, and must wish each other's good, from one of the

motives which have been assigned, and that each of
them must know the fact of the other wishing him
well.

CHAP. III.   But as the motives of friendship are specifically
Different   different, there will be a corresponding difference in
kinds of
friendship   the affections and friendships.
or love.

The kinds of friendship therefore will be three,
being equal in number to the things which are lovable, *or are objects of friendship or love,* as every such
object admits of a reciprocal affection between two
persons, each of whom is aware of the other's love.

Motives   People who love each other wish each other's
of friend-
ship or   good in the point characteristic of their love. Accord-
love.   ingly those whose mutual love is based upon utility
do not love each other for their own sakes, but only
in so far as they derive some benefit one from another.
It is the same with those whose love is based upon
pleasure. Thus we are fond of witty people, not as
possessing a certain character, but as being pleasant
to ourselves. People then, whose love is based upon
utility, are moved to affection by a sense of their own
good, and people whose love is based upon pleasure,
by a sense of their own pleasure; and they love a
person not for being what he is in himself, but for
being useful or pleasant to them. These friendships
then are only friendships in an accidental sense; for
the person loved is not loved as being what he is, but
as being a source either of good or of pleasure.
Accordingly such friendships are easily dissolved, if
the persons do not continue always the same; for
they abandon their love if they cease to be pleasant
or useful to each other. But utility is not a perma-

nent quality; it varies at different times. Thus, when the motive of a friendship is done away, the friendship itself is dissolved, as it was dependent upon that motive. A friendship of this kind seems especially to occur among old people, as in old age we look to profit rather than pleasure, and among such people in the prime of life or in youth as have an eye to their own interest. Friends of this kind do not generally even live together; for sometimes they are not even pleasant to one another; nor do they need the intercourse of friendship, unless they bring some profit to one another, as the pleasure which they afford goes no further than they entertain hopes of deriving benefit from it. Among these friendships we reckon the friendship of hospitality, *i.e. the friendship which exists between a host and his guests.*

It would seem that the friendship of the young is based upon pleasure; for they love by emotion and are most inclined to pursue what is pleasant to them at the moment. But as their time of life changes, their pleasures are transformed. They are therefore quick at making friendships and quick at abandoning them; for the friendship changes with the object which pleases them, and friendship of this kind is liable to sudden change. Young men are amorous too, amorousness being generally a matter of emotion and pleasure; hence they fall in love and soon afterwards fall out of love, changing from one condition to another many times in the same day. But amorous people wish to spend their days and lives together, as it is thus that they attain the object of their friendship.

CHAP. IV.   The perfect friendship or love is the friendship or
Perfect
friendship
love of people who are good and alike in virtue; for
or love.   these people are alike in wishing each other's good,
in so far as they are good, and they are good in themselves. But it is people who wish the good of their
friends for their friend's sake that are in the truest
sense friends, as their friendship is the consequence
of their own character, and is not an accident. Their
friendship therefore continues as long as their virtue,
and virtue is a permanent quality.

(1) Its
moral
goodness.
Again, each of them is good in an absolute sense,
and good in relation to his friend. For good men
are not only good in an absolute sense, but serve each
(2) Its plea-
santness.
other's interest. They are pleasant too; for the good
are pleasant in an absolute sense, and pleasant in
relation to one another, as everybody finds pleasure
in such actions as are proper to him, and the like, and
all good people act alike or nearly alike.

(3) Its per-
manency.
Such a friendship is naturally permanent, as it
unites in itself all the proper conditions of friendship.
For the motive of all friendship or affection is good
or pleasure, whether it be absolute or relative to the
person who feels the affection, and it depends upon a
certain similarity. In the friendship of good men all
these specified conditions belong to the friends in
themselves; for other friendships *only* bear a resemblance to the perfect friendship. That which is good
in an absolute sense is also in an absolute sense
pleasant. These are the principal objects of affection,
and it is upon these that affectionate feeling, and
affection in the highest and best sense, depend.

(4) Its
rarity.
Friendships of this kind are likely to be rare; for

such people are few. They require time and familiarity too; for, as the adage puts it, it is impossible
for people to know one another until they have
consumed the proverbial salt together; nor can
people admit one another to friendship, or be friends
at all, until each has been proved lovable and trustworthy to the other.

People, who are quick to treat one another as
friends, wish to be friends but are not so really, unless
they are lovable and know each other to be lovable;
for the wish to be friends may arise in a minute, but
not friendship.

This friendship then is perfect in point of time CHAP. V.
and in all other respects; and each friend receives
from the other the same or nearly the same treatment in all respects, as ought to be the case.

The friendship which is based upon pleasure Friend-
presents a certain resemblance to this, as the good ships of
pleasure
are also pleasant to one another. It is the same with and utility.
the friendship which is based upon utility, as the
good are also useful to one another. But here again
friendships are most likely to be permanent in cases
where that which the two persons derive from one
another is the same thing, e.g. pleasure, and not only
the same thing in itself, but the same in the source
from which it comes, as in the case of two wits, and
not as in the case of a lover and his beloved. For
the lover and his beloved do not find pleasure in the
same things; the pleasure of the one is in seeing the
object of his love, and that of the other in being
courted by his lover. Thus it sometimes happens
that, when the beauty passes away, the affection

passes away too; for the lover finds no pleasure in the sight of his beloved, and the beloved object is not courted by his lover. But it often happens on the other hand that people remain friends if their characters are similar, and familiarity has inspired them with affection for each other's character.

People who in their love affairs give and receive not pleasure but profit are less true and less permanent friends. Friendships resting upon utility are dissolved as soon as the advantage comes to an end, for in them there is no personal love, but only a love of profit.

Friendships of the bad Thus for pleasure or profit it is possible that even bad people may be friends one to another, and good people to bad, and one who is neither good nor bad to either; but it is clearly none but the good who can be friends for the friend's own sake, as bad people do not delight in one another unless some profit accrues.

and of the good. It is only the friendship of the good which cannot be destroyed by calumnies. For it is not easy to believe what anyone says about a person whom we have tested ourselves for many years, and found to be good. The friendship of the good too realizes confidence, and the assurance that neither of the two friends will do injury to the other, and whatever else is implied in true friendship. But in other friendships there is no reason why calumnies and injuries should not occur.

Now the world recognizes friendships among men, where the friendship is based upon utility, in the same way as among states; for it seems that expediency is the motive with which alliances are contracted between states. It recognizes also friendships where the mutual affection is based upon pleasure as among children. This being the view of the world, it is perhaps right to recognize such friendships, and to say that there are various kinds of friendship, first friendship properly so called, i.e. the friendship of the good, *qua* good, and then other friendships which are so called by analogy; for in them people are friends in so far as they involve something that is good or like good, as pleasure itself is a good to people who are fond of pleasure. But these friendships do not altogether coincide, nor is it the same persons who become friends from motives of utility and pleasure; for these are accidental qualities, and such qualities are not always combined in the same person.

As friendship is divided into these kinds, it may CHAP. VI. be said that while bad people will be friends from motives of pleasure or utility and will so far resemble the good, the good will be friends from love of the persons themselves, i.e. from love of their goodness. While the good then are friends in an absolute sense, the others are friends only accidentally, and because of their resemblance to the good.

As in the case of the virtues it is sometimes a Friend-ship or moral state, and at other times an activity, which love cha-racterized entitles people to be described as good, so is it also by either in the case of friendship or love. For people who are (1) a moral state or living together delight in each other's society and do (2) an activity. each other good. But people who are asleep or who are separated by long distances, although they are not active, are in a state which disposes them to activity; for distances do not destroy friendship absolutely, they only destroy its active exercise. Still if the absence be prolonged, it is supposed to work oblivion of the friendship itself; whence the saying

"Many a friendship is dissolved by lack of converse[1]."

It does not appear that either old people or austere people form friendships readily. There is little in them that can give pleasure, and nobody can spend all his days in the company of what is painful or not pleasant ; for it appears that there is nothing which nature avoids so much as what is painful or desires so much as what is pleasant.

Friendship or love and social life.   If people tolerate one another, but do not live together, they are more like well-wishers than friends; for there is nothing so characteristic of friendship as living together. People who are in want of assistance long to spend their lives in company, nay, fortunate people themselves long to spend their days in company; for they of all people are the least suited to a solitary life. But it is impossible for people to live together always, unless they are pleasant to one another, and have the same pleasures; and this, it seems, is the characteristic of social intercourse.

Chap. VII.   It is the friendship of the good which is friendship in the truest sense, as has been said several times. For it seems that, while that which is good or pleasant in an absolute sense is an object of love and desire, that which is good or pleasant to each individual is an object of love or desire to him; but the love or desire of one good man for another depends upon such

[1] A proverbial saying of unknown authorship.

goodness and pleasantness as are at once absolute and relative to the good.

Affection resembles an emotion but friendship resembles a moral state. For while affection may be felt for inanimate as much as for animate things, the love of friends for one another implies moral purpose, and such purpose is the outcome of a moral state.

Affection (φίλησις) and friendship or love (φιλία).

Again, we wish the good of those whom we love for their own sake, and the wish is governed not by emotion but by the moral state. In loving our friend too, we love what is good for ourselves; as when a good man becomes a friend, he becomes a blessing to his friend. Accordingly each of two friends loves what is good for himself, and returns as much as he receives in good wishes and in pleasure; for, as the proverb says, equality is friendship.

These conditions then are best realized in the friendship or love of the good. Among austere and elderly people friendship arises less easily, as they are more peevish and less fond of society; for it is social intercourse which seems to be the principal element and cause of friendship. Thus it is that the young form friendships quickly, but old people do not, as they do not make friends with any body who is not delightful to them, nor do austere people. Such people, it is true, wish each other well; they desire each other's good, and render each other services; but they are not really friends, as they do not satisfy the principal condition of friendship by living together and delighting in each other's society.

Friendship or love of the good.

It is as impossible to be friends with a number of people in the perfect sense of friendship, as it is to be

in love with a number of people at the same time;
for perfect friendship is in some sense an excess, and
such excess of feeling is natural towards an individual,
but it is not easy for a number of people to give
intense pleasure to the same person at the same time,
or, I may say, to be good at all. Friendship too
implies experience and familiarity, which are very
difficult. But it is possible to find a number of
people[1] who are pleasant, as affording profit or
pleasure ; for people of this kind are numerous and
their services do not occupy much time.

Friendship
of pleasure.

Among such people the friendship which is based
upon pleasure more nearly resembles true friendship,
when each party renders the same services to the
other, and they are delighted with each other or with
the same things, as e.g. in the friendships of the
young; for a liberal spirit is especially characteristic
of these friendships.

Friendship
of utility.

The friendship which rests upon utility is commercial in its character. Fortunate people do not
want what is useful but what is pleasant. They want
people to live with; and although for a short time
they may bear pain, nobody would endure it continuously; nobody would endure the good itself
continuously, if it were painful to him. Hence it
is that they require their friends to be pleasant.
They ought perhaps to require them also to be good,
and not only so, but good in relation to themselves;
for then they will have all the qualities which friends
ought to have.

---

[1] Reading πολλοὺς with Ramsauer.

It appears that people in positions of authority make a distinction between their friends. Some are useful to them, and others are pleasant, but the same people are not in general both useful and pleasant. For they do not look for friends who are virtuous as well as pleasant, or who will help them to attain noble ends; they look partly for amusing people when they want to be pleased, and partly for people who are clever at executing their commands, and these qualities are hardly ever united in the same person.

It has been stated that a virtuous man is at once pleasant and useful; but such a man does not become the friend of one who is superior to him, unless he is himself superior[1] to that person in virtue. Otherwise there is no such equality as occurs when his superiority in virtue is proportionate to his inferiority in some other respect. Friendships of this kind however are exceedingly rare.

The friendships which have been described are based upon equality; for the services and sentiments of the two friends to one another are the same, or they exchange one thing for another, e.g. pleasure for profit. It has been already stated that friendships depending on exchange are less true and less permanent than others. As being at once similar and dissimilar to the same thing, such friendships may be said both to be and not to be friendships. They look like friendships in respect of similarity to the friendship which depends upon virtue; for the one

CHAP. VIII.
Different kinds of friendship or love. Friendships of equality. p. 253. Friendships of exchange.

---

[1] The subject of ὑπερέχηται must be ὁ ὑπερέχων.

17—2

possesses pleasure, the other utility, and these are characteristics of virtuous friendships as well. But as virtuous friendship is undisturbed by calumnies, and is permanent, while these are quickly changed, and as there are many other differences between them, it seems that their dissimilarity to virtuous friendship makes them look as if they were not friendships at all.

Friend-
ships of
superiority
and inferi-
ority.

There is another kind of friendship or love depending upon superiority, e.g. the friendship or love of a father for a son, or of any elder person for a younger, or of a husband for a wife, or of a ruler for a subject. These friendships are of different sorts; for the friendship or love of parents for children is not the same as that of rulers for subjects, nor indeed is the friendship or love of a father for a son the same as that of a son for a father, nor that of a husband for his wife the same as that of a wife for her husband. For in each of these there is a different virtue and a different function, and there are different motives; hence the affections and friendships are also different. It follows that the services rendered by each party to the other in these friendships are not the same, nor is it right to expect that they should be the same; but when children render to parents what is due to the authors of their being, and parents to children what is due to them, then such friendships are permanent and virtuous.

In all such friendships as depend upon the principle of superiority, the affection should be proportionate to the superiority; i.e. the better or the more useful party, or whoever may be the superior, should receive more affection than he gives; for it is when the affection is proportionate to the merit that a sort of equality is established, and this equality seems to be a condition of friendship.

But it is apparently not the same with equality in justice as with equality in friendship. In justice it is proportionate equality which is the first considera-tion, and quantitative equality which is the second, but in friendship quantitative equality is first and proportionate second. This is clearly seen to be the case, if there be a wide distinction between two persons in respect of virtue, vice, affluence, or any-thing else. For persons so widely different cease to be friends; they do not even affect to be friends. But it is nowhere so conspicuous as in the case of the Gods; for the Gods enjoy the greatest superiority in all good things. It is clear too in the case of kings; for people who are greatly inferior to them do not expect to be their friends. Nor again do worthless people expect to be the friends of the best or wisest of mankind. No doubt in such cases it is impossible to define exactly the point up to which friendship may be carried; it may suffer many deductions and yet continue, but where there is a great distinction, as between God and man, it ceases to be.

Chap. IX. Equality in justice and in friendship or love.

This is a fact which has given rise to the question whether it is true that friends do really wish the greatest good of their friends, e.g. whether they wish them to be Gods; for then they will lose them as friends, and will therefore lose what are goods, as friends are goods.

That being so, if it has been rightly said that a

friend wishes his friend's good for the friend's sake, it will be necessary that the friend should remain such as he is. He will wish his friend the greatest good as a man. And yet perhaps he will not wish him every good, as every one wishes good in the highest sense to himself.

It seems that ambition makes most people wish to be loved rather than to love others. That is the reason why most people are fond of flatterers; for a flatterer is an inferior friend, or pretends to be so, and to give more love than he receives. But to be loved seems to approximate to being honoured, and honour is a general object of desire. Not that people, as it appears, desire honour for its own sake, they desire it only accidentally; for it is hope which causes most people to delight in the honours paid them by persons of high position, as they think they will obtain from them whatever they may want, and therefore delight in honour as a symbol of prosperity *in the future*. But they who aspire to gain honour from persons of high character and wide information are eager to confirm their own opinion of themselves; they delight therefore in a sense of their own goodness, having confidence in the judgment so expressed upon it. But people delight in being loved for their own sake. Hence it would seem to follow that it is better to be loved than to be honoured, and that friendship or love is desirable in itself.

CHAP. X.

Loving rather than being loved essential

But friendship seems to consist rather in loving than in being loved. It may be seen to be so by the delight which mothers have in loving; for mothers sometimes give their own children to be brought up

by others, and although they know them and love
them, do not look for love in return, if it be
impossible both to love and to be loved, but are
content, as it seems, to see their children doing well,
and to give them their love, even if the children in
their ignorance do not render them any such service
as is a mother's due.

As friendship consists in loving rather than in
being loved, and people who are fond of their friends
receive praise, it is in some sense a virtue of friends
to love; hence where love is found in due proportion,
people are permanent friends, and their friendship is
permanent.

It is in this way that, even where people are
unequal, they may be friends, as they will be equalized.
But equality and similarity constitute friendship,
especially the similarity of the virtuous; for the
virtuous, being exempt from change in themselves,
remain unchanged also in relation to one another,
and neither ask others to do wrong nor do wrong
themselves to please others. It may even be said
that they prevent it; for good people neither do
wrong themselves nor allow their friends to do it.

But there is no stability in vicious friends; for
they do not remain like themselves, and if they
become friends it is only for a short time, and from
the gratification which they feel in each other's vice.

But if people are useful and pleasant to each
other, they remain friends for a longer time, i.e. they
remain friends so long as they afford each other
pleasure or assistance.

The friendship which is based upon utility seems

more than any other to be an union of opposites. It
is e.g. such friendship as arises between a poor man
and a rich man, or between an ignorant man and a
well informed man; for if a man happens to be in
want of something, his desire to get it makes him
give something else in exchange. We may perhaps
include a lover and his beloved, or a beautiful man
and an ugly man, in this class of friends. It is thus
that lovers sometimes make themselves look ridiculous
by expecting to be loved as much as they love others.
Such an expectation would perhaps be reasonable if
they were equally lovable; but if there is nothing
lovable about them, it is ridiculous. It is true, I
think, that one opposite does not desire another in
itself, but desires it only accidentally. What it
really longs for is the mean, as the mean is a good.
Thus it is good for what is dry not to become wet,
but to arrive at the mean state, and similarly for
what is hot, and so on.

But we may dismiss these questions as being more
or less foreign to our present purpose.

CHAP. XI.   It appears, as has been said at the outset, that
p. 246.   friendship and justice have the same occasions and
Friendship
or love   the same sphere; for every association seems to
and justice.   involve justice of some kind, and friendship as well.
At all events we address our fellow-sailors and fellow-
soldiers, and similarly the members of any other
association to which we belong, as friends. The
friendship too is coextensive with the association, for
so also is the justice. The proverbial saying, "Friends'
goods are common goods" is right, as friendship
depends upon association.

Brothers and comrades have all things in common. Other people have certain definite things in common, some more, some fewer; for some friendships go further than others. Justice too is of different kinds; it is not the same in the relation of parents to children as in that of brothers to each other, or in that of comrades and fellow citizens to each other, and similarly in other friendships. Injustice too assumes various forms in relation to these several classes. It is aggravating, if the friends whom it affects are nearer to each other. Thus it is a more dreadful thing to defraud a comrade of money than to defraud a fellow citizen, or to refuse help to a brother than to a stranger, or to assault a father than any body else.

Justice itself too naturally grows as friendship grows; for they have the same sphere and are equally extensive.

All associations are, as it were, parts of the political association; for when people take a journey together, it is from motives of interest and for the sake of gaining something that their life requires. It seems too that interest was the motive with which the political association was originally formed, and with which it is continued; for this is the goal which legislators have in view, and they describe the interest of the community as just. *Political association.*

Now all other associations aim at some particular interest or success. Thus sailors aim at a successful voyage in the hope of making money or something of the kind, fellow-soldiers in an army at a successful campaign, whether it be spoil or victory or the *Different friendships corresponding to different associations.*

capture of a city that is their aim, and it is much the same with members of a tribe or township. It seems too that some associations are formed on a basis of pleasure, as when people associate for a fête or a picnic; for there the object is sacrifice[1] and good fellowship. But these are all, as it were, subordinate to the political association; for the aim of the political association is the interest not of the moment but of all a life-time, in the sacrifices which people make and the meetings which they hold in connexion with the sacrifices, in the honours which they pay to the gods, and the pleasure and relaxation which they provide for themselves. For it appears that the ancient sacrifices and meetings take place after the ingathering of the fruits of the earth, e.g. the festival of the first-fruits, these having been the seasons of the greatest leisure.

It appears then that all these associations are parts of the political association, and the proper friendships will correspond to the associations.

CHAP. XII.   There are three kinds of polity and an equal
Three   number of perversions, or in other words corruptions,
kinds of
polity.   of these three kinds. The polities are kingship, aristocracy, and a third depending upon a property qualification, which it seems proper to describe as timocratic, but it is usually designated as a polity *in the limited sense.* Of these, kingship is the best and timocracy the worst.

The perversion of kingship is tyranny, both being monarchies although they are widely different, as the

---

[1] The connexion of festivity with religion is eminently characteristic of Greek thought.

tyrant considers his own interest, and the king
the interest of his subjects; for a king is not a Kingship.
king unless he is self-sufficient and superior to his
subjects in all that is good; but if he is such, there is
nothing more that he needs. Hence he will consider
not his own interest but the interest of his subjects;
for if he were not a king after this fashion, he would
be a sort of king of the ballot[1].

Tyranny is the opposite of kingship, as it pursues Tyranny.
the good of the tyrant himself. *It is clear that
kingship is the best form of polity; but* it is still
clearer that tyranny is the worst. The opposite of
the best is always worst.

A polity changes from kingship to tyranny; for Transformation of
tyranny is a vicious form of monarchy. Accordingly polities.
the vicious king becomes a tyrant. Kingship and

An aristocracy is converted into an oligarchy tyranny.
through the fault of the ruling class who make an Aristocracy and
unfair distribution of political honours, who reserve oligarchy.
all or nearly all the good things for themselves, and
who keep the offices of state continually in the same
hands, from the inordinate value that they set upon
wealth. The result is that it is only a few people
who hold office, and they are not the most virtuous,
but wicked people.

A timocracy is converted into a democracy; for Timocracy
they border closely upon each other, as timocracy cracy.
professes to have a democratic character, and all who and demo-
possess the requisite property qualification are equals
in a timocracy.

---

[1] The King-Archon (ἄρχων βασιλεύς) at Athens, when all
officers of state were appointed by ballot, might be so called.

Of the perversions democracy is the least vicious, as it departs but slightly from the character of the polity.

These are the ways in which polities are most easily transferred; for these are the least violent transformations.

Domestic associations.

It is possible to discover models, and so to say patterns, of these constitutions in households. For

(1) Father and children.

the association of a father with his sons takes the form of a kingship, as a father cares for his children. It is this care which makes Homer speak of Zeus as "father;" for kingship purports to be a parental rule. But in Persia the rule of the father is tyrannical; for there parents treat their sons as

(2) Master and slave.

slaves. The association of master and slave is also tyrannical, as it is the master's interest which is realized in it. Now the rule of a slave-master seems to be a right[1] form of tyranny, but the rule of a father in Persia seems to be a perverted form, as different people require to be ruled in different ways.

(3) Husband and wife.

The association of husband and wife seems to be aristocratical; for the husband's rule depends upon merit, and is confined to its proper sphere. He assigns to the wife all that suitably belongs to her. If the husband is lord of everything, he changes the association to an oligarchy; for then he acts unfairly, and not in virtue of his superior merit.

Sometimes again the wife rules, as being an heiress. Such rule is not based upon merit, but depends upon wealth or power as in oligarchies.

[1] Aristotle believes in a natural class of slaves. Cp. *Politics* i. ch. 5.

The association of brothers resembles a timocracy ; for they are equals except so far as they differ in years ; hence if the difference of years is very great, the friendship ceases to be fraternal.

A democracy is chiefly found in such households as have no master, where everybody is equal to everybody else, or where the head of the house is weak, and everybody can do as he chooses.

Now it appears that there is a friendship or love which is proper to each of these several polities in the same degree as there is a justice proper to each.

The friendship or love of a king to his subjects takes the form of superiority in benefaction. He treats his subjects well, as being good, and as caring for their welfare, like a shepherd for the welfare of his flock, whence Homer called Agamemnon "shepherd of the folk."

The love of a father for his child is similar in character, although it differs in the magnitude of the benefactions; for a father is the author of the child's existence, which seems to be the greatest of all benefactions, as well as of his nurture and education. These benefactions are ascribed also to ancestors, and it is Nature's law that a father should rule his sons, and ancestors their descendants, and a king his subjects.

These friendships imply superiority; hence parents are not only loved but honoured, as being superiors. Justice therefore in these cases implies not identical but proportionate treatment; for so too does friendship.

The friendship or love of husband and wife is the

same as exists in an aristocracy; for it depends upon
virtue. The better party gets the greater good, and
each gets what befits him or her, but this is equally
the rule of justice.

The friendship of brothers is like the friendship of
comrades; for they are equals and are persons of the
same age, and when this is the case, people are
generally alike in their feelings and characters. We
may compare with this the friendship or love which
is characteristic of a timocracy; for in a timocracy
the citizens profess to be equal and virtuous; hence
they hold office in turn and upon a principle of
equality, and accordingly their friendship follows the
same law.

But in the perverted forms of polity justice does
not go far, neither does friendship, and nowhere is
its range so limited as in the worst of them. Friendship does not exist, or hardly exists, in a tyranny; for
where there is nothing in common between ruler and
subject, there cannot be friendship between them, as
there cannot be justice either. The relation is like that
of an artisan to a tool, or of soul to body, or of master
to servant; for although all these are benefitted by
the people who use them, there is no possibility of
friendship or justice in the relation in which we stand
to inanimate things nor indeed in our relation to a
horse or an ox or to a slave *qua* slave. For there is
nothing in common between a master and his slave;
the slave is an animate instrument, and the instrument an inanimate slave. It is impossible therefore
to be friends with a slave *qua* slave, but not with a
slave *qua* man, for there would seem to be a possi-

bility of justice between every man and any one who is capable of participation in law and covenant, and therefore in friendship, in so far as he is man.

Friendships therefore and justice exist only to a slight extent in tyrannies and have only a narrow range. Their range is widest in democracies, as it is when people are equals that they have most in common.

All friendship then, as has been said, implies CHAP. XIV. association. Still it is proper to distinguish the Association essential to friendship of kinsmen and comrades from other friendship or love. friendships. The friendships of fellow-citizens, fellow-Special tribesmen, fellow-sailors and the like, have a greater friendship or love of resemblance to friendships of association, as they kinsmen appear to be based on a sort of compact. We may rades. and com-rank the friendship of hospitality with these.

The friendship of kinsmen too appears to be of various kinds, but to depend altogether upon the friendship or love of a parent for his child; for Parental and filial parents feel affection for their children as being a love. part of themselves, and children for their parents as the source of their being. But parents know their offspring better than the children know that they are sprung from them, and the author of another's being is more closely united to his offspring than the off-spring to the parent ; for that which proceeds from a person belongs to that from which it proceeds, as a tooth or a hair or anything to its possessor; but that from which a thing proceeds does not belong to that which proceeds from it, or does not belong to it in the same degree. There is a difference too in respect of time; for parents love their children as soon as they are born, but children do not love their parents until they are advanced in years and have gained intelligence or sense. It is evident from these considerations why mothers love their children more than fathers.

Parents then love children as themselves; for their offspring are like second selves—second, only in the sense of being separated—and children love parents,

Fraternal love.

as being born of them, and brothers one another, as being born of the same parents. For the identity of the children with their parents constitutes an identity between the children themselves. Hence we use such phrases as "the same blood" "the same stock" and so on, *in speaking of brothers and sisters.* They are therefore in a sense the same, although they are separate beings. It is a great help to friendship for people to have been brought up together, and to be of the same age; for "two of the same age agree," as the proverb says, and intimate friends become comrades; hence the friendship of brothers comes to resemble the friendship of comrades[1].

But cousins and all other kinsmen have the same bond of union to each other, as springing from the same source; they are more or less closely united according as their first ancestor is near or remote.

The friendship or love of children for parents, and of men for the Gods, may be said to be love for what is good and higher than themselves; for parents are

---

[1] It is an instance of the part which comradeship or *camaraderie* played in Greek life that the mutual love of two brothers should be assimilated to the mutual love of two comrades.

the authors of the greatest benefit to children, as to them children owe their existence and nurture and education from the day of their birth.

There is more pleasure and utility in such a friendship than in the friendship of strangers, as their life has more in common.

The characteristics of friendship among brothers are the same as among comrades; they are intensified when the brothers are virtuous, but they exist always in consequence of their likeness, inasmuch as brothers are more nearly related to each other than comrades and naturally love one another from birth, and as there is a greater similarity of character among people who are children of the same parents and are brought up together, and receive a similar education, nor is there any test so strong and sure as that of time.

The elements of love among other kinsmen are proportionate to the nearness of their kinship.

But the love of husband and wife seems to be a natural law, as man is naturally more inclined to contract a marriage than to constitute a state, inasmuch as a house is prior to a state, and more necessary than a state, and the procreation of children is the more universal function of animals. *Love of husband and wife.*

In the case of other animals this is the limit of their association; but men unite not only for the procreation of children but for the purposes of life. As soon as a man and a woman unite, a distribution of functions takes place. Some are proper to the husband and others to the wife; hence they supply one another's needs, each contributing his special gifts to the common stock. It is thus that utility and pleasure seem alike to be found in this friendship; but its basis will be virtue too, if the husband and wife are virtuous, as each of them has his or her proper virtue, and they will both delight in what is virtuous.

It seems too that children are a bond of union between them; hence such marriages as are childless are more easily dissolved, as children are the common blessing of both parents, and such community of interest is the bond of union between them.

To ask how husband and wife and friends in general should live together, is, it appears, nothing else than to ask how it is just for them to live; for justice is clearly not the same thing between one friend and another as towards a stranger or a comrade or a fellow-traveller.

CHAP. XV. There are three kinds of friendship, as has been said at the outset, and in each of them the friendship may be constituted upon terms either of equality or of superiority *and inferiority;* for people who are equals in goodness may become friends, or a better person may become the friend of a worse, and it is the same with pleasant people, and with people whose friendship rests upon utility, as their services may be either equal or different. It is proper then that those who are equals should show themselves equal by an equality of love and of everything else, and those who are unequal by such a feeling to others as is proportionate to the superiority of each.

Different kinds of friendship or love. p. 250.

Complaints and bickerings occur either exclusively or most frequently in a friendship which

Complaints and bickerings as

depends upon utility, and it is reasonable that this ^{disturbing} friendship. should be so. For where the basis of friendship is virtue, friends are eager to do good to one another as a mark of virtue and friendship. Where their rivalry takes this form, there is no room for accusations or bickerings; for nobody takes it ill that a person loves him and treats him well; on the contrary, if he is a man of good feeling, he requites a kindness. Nor will the superior person find fault with his friend, as he obtains his desire; for in such a friendship each of the friends desires the other's good.

Again, such quarrelling hardly ever arises in a friendship of which pleasure is the motive; for both parties get what they long for, if it is their great pleasure to live together. But one of them would make himself ridiculous if he were to complain of the other for not giving him pleasure, when he might leave off living in his company.

It is such friendship as is based upon utility that gives rise to complaints; for as the parties in their dealings with each other have an eye to profit, each of them always wants the larger share, and imagines himself to possess less than is his due, and complains of not obtaining all that he requires and deserves, when it is impossible for the benefactor to supply all that the recipient of the benefaction requires.

It seems that, as justice is twofold, being partly unwritten and partly embodied in law, the friendship Moral and which depends upon utility is either moral or legal, legal friend-*i.e. is based either upon character or upon convention.* ship. Complaints then occur most frequently, if the terms

18—2

of friendship are not the same when it is dissolved as
when it is formed. By legal friendship I mean such
as is formed on stated conditions, whether it be
absolutely commercial, demanding cash payments, or
more liberal in respect of time but still requiring a
certain covenanted *quid pro quo*. In this friendship
the debt is clear and indisputable, but the delay of
which it admits is an element of friendliness. Accordingly some states do not recognise actions for debt.
It is held that, if people have made a contract which
presupposes good faith on both sides, they must take
the consequences of making it. Moral friendship,
on the other hand, has no stated conditions. If a gift
or any other favour is bestowed upon a person, it is
bestowed upon him as a friend; but the giver expects
to receive as much or more in return, regarding it
not as a gift but as a loan. If he does not come out
of the contract as well off as he was when he entered
into it, he will complain. The reason of his complaint
is that, although all people, or nearly all people, wish
what is noble, they choose what is profitable, and it is
noble to do good without expecting a return, but it is
profitable to receive a benefaction.

If a man has the power, it is his duty to return
the full value of the services rendered to him, and to
return it voluntarily; for it is wrong to make a person
a friend against his will. If the will is lacking, then
we must suppose that we made a mistake in the first
instance, and were the recipients of a benefaction
from the wrong person i.e. not from a friend or some
one who meant to confer it; we must therefore dissolve the friendship, as if the service had been done

us on certain stated terms of repayment. In stipu-
lating to make the payment we must assume that it
will be in our power to make it; for if it is not, the
giver himself would not have expected to be repaid.
We must pay therefore, if we have the power, but
not otherwise. But it is our duty to consider in the
first instance who it is that is benefitted and what
are the terms of the benefaction, that so we may
agree to accept it or not.

It may be questioned whether the return is to be
measured by the benefit conferred upon the recipient,
and should be made proportionate to it, or should be
measured by the benevolent intention of the benefactor. For the recipients of a benefaction often
adopt a depreciatory tone, pretending to have received
from their benefactors services which did not cost the
benefactors much, or which might have been done
them by others. The benefactors, on the contrary,
urge that the services were the greatest which it was
in their power to render and such as could not have
been rendered by others, and that they were rendered
at a time of peril or some such urgent need.

If then the basis of the friendship be utility, it
would seem that the benefit done to the recipient is
the true measure of repayment; for it is the recipient
who asks for the boon, and the benefactor assists him
in the hope of receiving an equivalent. The service
done then has been commensurate with the benefaction received; hence it is the duty of the recipient
to repay the amount of his advance or even more, as
this is the nobler course.

But in such friendships as depend on virtue there

is no room for complaints; it is the moral purpose of
the benefactor which is, as it were, the measure of
repayment, for it is the moral purpose which determines virtue or character.

CHAP. XVI.   Differences occur also in the friendships in which
Unequal
friend-   one party is superior to the other, for in such friendships.   ships each party claims a larger share, and when he
gets it, the friendship is dissolved. The better of the
two friends thinks a larger share is his due, as a
larger share is a due of the good. So too does the
more helpful, as it is admitted that, if a person is
useless, he ought not to have so much as one who is
of use. The friendship (he says) ceases to be friendship and becomes mere public service, if the proceeds
of the friendship are not proportionate to the works
of the friends ; for people suppose, that as in a commercial association the larger contributors are the
larger recipients, so it ought to be in friendship.

The needy or inferior person takes an opposite
view. He argues that it is the part of a good friend
to assist the needy; for what (he says) is the good of
being the friend of a virtuous or powerful person, if
one is to derive no benefit from it?

It would seem that each is justified in his claim,
and that each ought to receive a larger share as the
result of the friendship, but not a larger share of the
same things. The superior person ought to receive
a larger share of honour, and the needy person a
larger share of profit, as honour is the reward of
virtue and beneficence, and money is the means of
relieving distress.

It appears that the same law holds good in politics. No honour is paid to the person who renders no service to the state; for that which the state has to give is commonly given to the benefactor of the state, and honour is that which the state has to give. For it is impossible for a person at one and the same time to make money out of the community, and to receive honour from it, as nobody will submit to inferiority in all respects. We pay honour then to one who suffers pecuniary loss by holding office, and we give money to one who is eager for a salary; for it is the principle of proportion which effects equality and p. 261. preserves friendship, as has been said.

This then is the true principle of association among unequals. If a person is benefitted by another in purse or character, he must repay him in honour, as this is the repayment which it is in his power to make. For friendship looks for what is possible, not for what is proportionate *or due to the merit of the friend;* for there are cases where a due return is out of the question, as in the honours paid to the Gods and to parents. In such cases while nobody could ever make a due return, a person is considered to be virtuous, if he pays such regard as lies within his power. Hence it may be held that a son has no right to disown his father, although a father may disown his son; for the son is a debtor, and must repay his debt, and as, whatever he does, it is not adequate to his obligation, he is a perpetual debtor. But the creditor may dismiss his debtor, and if so, then a father may dismiss his son. At the same time it seems, I think, that nobody would ever desert a son unless he were extraordinarily vicious; for apart from the natural affection *of father and son,* it is human nature not to reject such support as his son may afford him *in old age.* But the son, if he is vicious, will look upon the duty of assisting his father as one which he should avoid, or at all events not eagerly embrace; for the world in general wishes to receive benefits, but avoids the apparently unprofitable task of conferring them.

BOOK IX.

This may be regarded as a sufficient discussion of these questions. But in all heterogeneous[1] friendships it is the principle of proportion, as has been said, which equalizes and preserves the friendship. It is so in the political friendship or association, where a cobbler gets due value in exchange for his shoe, and so does the weaver and any other tradesman. In this case a common measure has been provided by the currency to which everything is referred, and by which everything is measured. But in the friendship of love it happens that the lover sometimes complains that, when he is passionately in love, his love is not returned, although it may be there is nothing lovable in him, or that the object of love complains, as often happens, that his lover was once lavish in his promises and now does not perform any of them.

Such cases occur because pleasure is the motive

---

[1] By "heterogeneous friendships," as the context shows, Aristotle means such friendships as that of a lover and his beloved, in which the parties, although they seek some pleasure or profit each from the other, do not seek the same pleasure or profit.

of the affection which the lover feels for the object of his love, and utility the motive of the affection which the other feels for his lover, and they do not both realize their desires. For when these are the motives of friendship, it is dissolved as soon as the expectations which induced the love are disappointed; for it was not the persons themselves, but their possessions, that inspired the affection, and, as the possessions are not permanent, neither are the friendships. But a friendship which is a friendship of character exists *per se*, and is permanent, as has been said.

p. 252.

Cause of differences arising between friends.

Again, differences arise between friends when one gets from the other something that is not what he desires; for it is like getting nothing at all, when a person does not get what he wants. For instance, there was once a person who promised a present to a harpist, and promised that the better he played, the larger should be his reward; but next day when the harpist asked him to fulfil his promises, he said he had given him one pleasure[1] in payment for another. Now if this were what both wished for, it would be satisfactory; but if the one wished for pleasure and the other for gain, and if the one has his wish and the other has not, the agreement between them will not be rightly carried out; for it is what a person happens to want that he sets his heart upon, and to get this, *but nothing else*, will he give the price.

Value of a benefaction: how

But it may be asked, Who is the proper person to settle the value of a benefaction? Is it he who was

---

[1] The pleasure which the harpist had received must be the pleasure of anticipating payment.

in the first instance the author, or he who was in the
first instance the recipient of the benefaction? It or by
whom to be
seems as if the author leaves it to the recipient to settled.
settle the value. This, they say, was the practice
of Protagoras, who, whenever he taught any subject,
would tell his pupils to estimate the value of the
knowledge in their own eyes, and would take just so
much payment and no more.

In such cases some people like the principle of "a
stated wage"[1]; but if a person first takes his fee, and
then does not fulfil any of his promises, because he has
promised a great deal more than he can perform, it
is reasonable to censure him for not carrying out his
professions. The practice of taking payment in
advance is probably forced upon the sophists, as
otherwise nobody would pay them a fee for the
knowledge which they impart. Such people then lie
open to reasonable censure, if they do not do the work
for which they receive payment. But it may happen
that there is no distinct agreement as to the service
rendered. Suppose A confers a benefaction upon B
for B's own sake[2], then A, as has been said, is not p. 252.
open to censure, as this is the character of a virtuous
friendship. The return made must be such as corresponds to the moral purpose of the benefactor, as it
is the moral purpose which constitutes a friend, or

---

[1] The words μισθὸς δ' ἀνδρί are taken from a line of Hesiod
which makes their meaning plain;

μισθὸς δ' ἀνδρὶ φίλῳ εἰρημένος ἄρκιος ἔστω.
῎Εργα καὶ ῾Ημέραι 368.

[2] Reading δι' αὐτούς.

constitutes virtue. It seems that the same principle
would apply to people who have been engaged *as
master and pupil* in philosophy. The value of philosophical teaching cannot be measured in money, nor
can an equivalent price be found for it. We must, I
think, be content if here, as in the worship of the
Gods or the respect shown to parents, we make such
return as is in our power. Suppose on the other
hand the gift is not disinterested, but is made on the
fixed condition of some return, it is, I think, right, if
it be possible, that the return made should be such
as in the eyes of both parties is proportionate to the
value of the gift, or, if this is impossible, it would
seem to be not only necessary but just that it should
be fixed by the original recipient. For whatever was
the amount of benefit which the recipient obtained,
or the amount which he would have paid for the
pleasure, the original benefactor, if he gets that
amount in return, will have his due value from the
recipient ; for this is clearly what takes place in the
market, and in some states there are laws prohibiting
such actions as arise out of voluntary contracts, on
the ground that if a person has once trusted another
he ought to conclude his contract with him in the
same spirit in which he originally made it. The idea
is that he who received credit has a better right to
settle the value of the service done than he who gave
it ; for as a rule people who possess a thing do not
set the same value on it as people who wish to
acquire it, as we always look upon the things which
we call our own and which we give away as being
exceedingly valuable. Nevertheless the amount of

the exchange must be regulated by the value which the recipient sets upon the gifts received. Still perhaps it ought not to be fixed at the value which he sets upon it when it is in his hands, but at the value which he set upon it before he had it.

There are still certain questions which present a difficulty. For instance, Is the respect and obedience due to a father unlimited? or ought a person, if he is ill, to obey a physician, and ought he to vote for the best soldier *rather than for his father* as general? Similarly, ought he to serve a friend rather than a virtuous man, and to repay a debt to a benefactor rather than make a present to a comrade, if he cannot do both?

Chap. II.
Questions of casuistry relating to friendship.

It is difficult perhaps to decide all such questions precisely, as the cases may vary indefinitely in importance or dignity or urgency. But it is evident at once that no one person can be entitled to unlimited respect. As a general rule, it is a duty to repay services which have been done to us rather than to confer favours on our comrades. We must behave as if we had incurred a debt, and must pay our creditors in preference to making a present to our comrade. But even this rule is possibly open to exceptions. Suppose e.g. a person has been ransomed from the hands of brigands; is it his duty to ransom his ransomer in turn, whoever he may be, or to repay him, even if he has not been taken prisoner, when he claims repayment? or is it his duty rather to ransom his own father? It would seem that he ought rather to ransom his father.

The general rule then, as has been said, is that

the repayment of our debt is a duty, but that if the honour, or urgent need, of making a present outweighs it, we must decide in favour of making the present rather than of repaying the debt. For it sometimes happens that there is an actual unfairness in requiting the original service, when *A* has done a service to *B*, knowing him to be virtuous, and *B* is called to repay *A*, whom he believes to be a rascal. For there are times when it is actually not right to do so much as lend money in return to one who has lent money to us. For it may happen that *A* lent money to *B*, who is an honest man, expecting to get it back again, but that *B* knows *A* to be vicious, and therefore does not expect to get his money back. If then this be the true state of the case, the claim which *A* makes for a loan in return is not an equal or fair claim ; or if this is not the true state of the case, but the parties think it to be so, his conduct could not be called unreasonable.

pp. 3, 37. We can only repeat then the remark, which has been made several times before, viz. that arguments relating to human emotions and human actions, admit of a neither greater nor less precision than the subjects with which they deal.

Different forms or degrees of respect appropriate to different persons. It is clear enough then that all people cannot rightly claim the same respect, nor can a father claim an unlimited respect, as Zeus himself does not receive unlimited sacrifices. But as the claims of parents, brothers, comrades, and benefactors are all different, it is our duty to render to each class of people such respect as is natural and appropriate to them. This is in fact the principle upon which we seem to act ;

for we invite our relations to a wedding, as they are concerned in the family, and therefore in all events of family interest, and we look upon relations for the same reason as having the best right to meet at funerals in the family.

It would seem to be an especial duty to afford our parents the means of living, as we owe it to them, and as it is more honourable to afford this kind of support to the authors of our being than to ourselves. It is a duty too to pay honour to parents, as to the Gods, but not to pay it indiscriminately. The same honour is not due to a father as to a mother, nor again is the same honour due to them as to a philosopher or a general, but the honour of a father or a mother, as the case may be. Again, it is a duty to pay our elders such honour as is due to their age, by rising to greet them, or by giving them the place of honour at the table and so on. To our comrades and brothers on the other hand we should speak our mind frankly, and give them a share of everything that belongs to us. Again, in our relation to our kinsfolk, our fellow-tribesmen, our fellow-citizens, and all other people, we should do our best to render them their due, and to estimate their claims by considering the nearness of their connexion with us, and their character, or the services they have done us. It is comparatively easy to make such an estimate where people belong to the same class, but it is more troublesome where they belong to different classes. Still this is not a reason for giving up the attempt, we must make such a distinction as is possible.

Duty of supporting and honouring parents.

CHAP. III.   Another question which presents a difficulty is
Dissolution whether we ought, or ought not, to dissolve friend-
of friend-
ship.   ships with people whose character is no longer what
it once was.

It appears that, if the motive of the friendship was
utility or pleasure, then when the utility or the
pleasure comes to an end, there is nothing unreasonable in dissolving the friendship. For it was the
utility or the pleasure that we loved, and when they
have ceased to exist, it is only reasonable that our
love should come to an end. But there would be
ground for complaint, if a person, whose affection was
due to utility or pleasure, pretended that it was due
p. 250.   to character. For as we said at the outset, differences
arise between friends most frequently when the actual
reason of the friendship is not the same as they
suppose it to be.

Now if a person *A* deceives himself into imagining
that it is his character which wins him *B*'s affection,
although there is nothing in *B*'s conduct which
warrants such an idea, he has only himself to blame;
but if he is imposed upon by *B*'s pretence, he has
a right to complain of him as an impostor and to
complain of him still more strongly than of a person
who utters counterfeit coin, inasmuch as the felony
affects what is more precious than a mere pecuniary
interest.

But there is this further question. If we admit a
person to our friendship, believing him to be a good
man, and he turns out and is seen to be a rascal, is it
still our duty to love him? But love, it may be
answered, is an impossibility, as it is not everything,

but only the good that is lovable. A wicked person
is not lovable, nor ought he to be loved; for it is not
right for us to be lovers of the wicked, or to make
ourselves like bad men ; but it has been already said p. 247.
that like loves like.

Is it right in such circumstances to dissolve a
friendship at once? Perhaps not in all cases, but
only where the vice is incurable. If there is a
possibility of reforming the friend who has gone
wrong, it is a duty to help him in respect of his
character even more than in respect of his property,
inasmuch as character is a better thing than property,
and enters more closely into friendship. It would be
admitted that, if a person dissolves a friendship in
these circumstances, his action is not at all unreasonable. He was not a friend of the person as that
person is now, and therefore if his friend has been
metamorphosed, and it is impossible to restore him,
he abandons the friendship.

Again, suppose A retains his original character,
and B becomes more moral or vastly superior to A in
virtue; is it right for B to treat A as a friend? It is
impossible, I think, for him to treat him so. The
case becomes clearest, if there is a wide discrepancy
between the two friends. It may happen so in the
friendships of boyhood; for if one of two friends
remains a boy in mind, and the other is a fully
developed man, how can they be friends, if they do
not sympathise with each other in their tastes or in
their pleasures and pains ? There will be no personal
sympathy between them, and without sympathy it is p. 257.
impossible, as we saw, to be friends, as it is impossible

for two people to live together. But this is a point which has been already discussed.

Is it right then, *when two friends cease to be sympathetic,* for one to treat the other as not being in any sense more an alien than if he had never become a friend? The answer seems to be that we must not forget the old intimacy, but as we think it a duty to gratify friends rather than strangers, so we ought to show some consideration for old friends in virtue of the past friendship, provided that the dissolution of friendship is not due to some extraordinary vice.

CHAP. IV.   The origin of friendly relations to our friends and of the characteristic marks of friendship seems to lie in our relation to ourselves. For a friend may be defined as one who wishes and does what is good, or what seems to be good, to another for the other's sake, or who wishes the existence and life of his friend for the friend's sake. This is the feeling of mothers towards their children, and of friends who have had a quarrel towards each other. Or again, a friend may be defined as one who lives with another and shares his desires, or as one who sympathises with another in his sorrows and joys, as is preeminently the case with mothers *in relation to their children.* But it is one or the other of these characteristics which constitutes the definition of friendship. They are all found in the relation of the virtuous man to himself, and in the relation of other men to themselves, in so far as they affect to be good. For it seems, as has been said, that virtue and the virtuous man are the measure of everything; for the virtuous man is at unity with himself, and desires

Love of friends an expansion of self-love.

p. 72.

the same things with his whole heart. He therefore wishes what is good or what appears to be good for himself, and effects it, as a good man naturally carries out what is good, and he does so for his own sake, i.e. for the sake of the intellectual part of his nature, which seems to be in every man his true self. Also he wishes his own life and preservation, and especially the life and preservation of the part of himself by which he thinks. For existence is a good thing for the virtuous man, and everybody wishes what is good for himself; but nobody desires to lose his personality even on condition that nothing should be wanting to his new personality, *although this condition is not inconceivable*, as God even now possesses the supreme good; he desires it only on condition of being whatever he now is, and it would seem that the thinking faculty is the man's true self, or is more nearly his true self than anything else is.

Such a person wishes to live with himself. It is pleasant for him to do so; for the memories of the past are pleasant, and he has good hopes, i.e. pleasant hopes, of the future. His mind too is full of speculations, he sympathises with himself preeminently in pain and pleasure; for the same things are pleasant or painful to him always, they do not vary, as he experiences, it may be said, few regrets. As then all these conditions are realized in the relation of a virtuous man to himself and as he has the same relation to his friend as to himself (for his friend is a second self) it seems that friendship consists in one or other of these conditions, and that they in whom these conditions are realized are friends.

19—2

Self-love. Whether it is possible or not for a man to be a friend of himself is a question which may be left for the present. It would seem to be possible in so far as two or more of the specified conditions exist, and because the friendship of one man for another in its extreme form is comparable to the friendship or love of a man for himself. On the other hand it appears that these conditions exist in the majority of people, although they are bad people. Perhaps then we may conclude that these conditions are found in such people only so far as they please themselves, and

Self-love impossible to the wicked. suppose themselves to be good. For if a person is utterly bad and impious, these conditions do not exist; they do not even appear to exist. But it may be said practically that they do not exist in any bad people; for such people are at variance with themselves, and while desiring one set of things, wish for something else. They are e.g. incontinent people; they choose, not what seems to themselves good, but what is pleasant, although it is injurious, or they are so cowardly and lazy that they abstain from doing what they think to be best for themselves, or they are people whose moral depravity has led them to commit terrible crimes, and they hate and shun life and put an end to themselves.

Vicious people seek companions to spend their days with and try to escape from themselves; for when they are alone, there are many disagreeable things which they recall, and others which they anticipate, but when they are in the company of other people, they forget them. There is nothing lovable in them, and therefore they have no feeling of love for themselves, nor do such people sympathise with themselves in joy or sorrow; for their soul is divided against itself, one part being pained—so vicious is it—at abstaining from certain things, and the other part being pleased, one part pulling this way, and the other that way, as if they would tear the man asunder. Or if it is impossible to feel pain and pleasure simultaneously, it is not long at all events before the vicious man is pained at having been pleased and could have wished that he had not enjoyed such pleasures; for the wicked are full of regrets.

It appears then that the wicked man has not a friendly disposition even to himself, as there is nothing lovable in him, and it follows that if this condition is a condition of extreme misery, we must strain every nerve to avoid wickedness, and must make it our ambition to be virtuous; for then we shall stand in a friendly relation to ourselves, and shall become the friends of others.

Goodwill resembles friendship, but it is not the same thing; for goodwill, unlike friendship, may be directed towards people who are unknown to us, and who do not know that we wish them well, as has been already said. CHAP. V. Goodwill and friendship.

p. 249.

Again, goodwill is not the same thing as affection; for it does not imply intensity of feeling or desire, which are concomitants of affection. Goodwill and affection.

Again, while affection implies familiarity, the feeling of goodwill may arise in a moment, as e.g. when we feel goodwill towards competitors in the games. We wish them well and we sympathise with them, but we should not think of giving them practical help; for as we said, goodwill arises in a moment, and it implies no more than a superficial regard.

Goodwill then may be said to be the germ of friendship, as the pleasure which we feel in looking upon a person is the germ of love. Nobody falls in love, unless he has first felt delight in the beauty of the person whom he loves; but it does not follow that one who feels delight in a person's beauty falls in love, unless he longs for him even in absence and desires his presence. So too it is impossible for people to be friends, unless they have come to feel goodwill to each other; but it does not follow that, if people wish each other well, they are friends; for we merely wish the good of those to whom we feel goodwill, we should not think of giving them practical help or of taking serious trouble in their behalf. It may be said then metaphorically[1] that goodwill is unproductive friendship, but by lapse of time and familiarity it may become friendship, although not

Origin of goodwill.

such friendship as is based on utility or pleasure; for neither utility nor pleasure is a possible basis of goodwill. It is true that if A has received a benefaction from B, he renders his goodwill to B as a return for the services done him, and it is only right for him to make such a return. But if A wishes to confer a benefaction on B in the hope of gaining some advantage by his help, it seems that he does not wish well to B, but rather to himself, as in fact he is

---

[1] A "metaphor" in Aristotle's sense is any use of a word that is not perfectly natural and straightforward.

not *B*'s friend, if his motive in courting him is the
desire to get something out of him. On the whole
however it may be said that goodwill, when it arises,
depends on some sort of virtue or goodness. It arises
when we look on a person as noble or brave and so
on, as we said in the case of competitors in the p. 293.
games.

Unanimity too, appears to be a mark of friend- Chap. VI.
ship; but if so, unanimity is not mere unity of Unanimity as a mark
opinion, as this may exist among people even if they of friend-ship.
do not know one another. Nor do we speak of
persons who are united in judgment on any subject,
e.g. on astronomy, as unanimous; for unanimity on
these subjects is not a mark of friendship; but we
speak of states as unanimous when they are united in
judgment upon their interests, and have the same
purposes and pursue a common policy.

It is thus when people agree upon practical
matters that they are said to be unanimous, especially
when they agree upon such practical matters as are
important and as are capable of belonging to both
parties or to all. Thus a state is unanimous when all Unanimity of a state.
the citizens are in favour of making the offices of
state elective, or of forming an alliance with the
Lacedaemonians, or of electing Pittacus governor,
Pittacus himself having been at the time willing to
govern.

But when each of two parties wishes to be
governor like *Eteocles and Polynices* in the *Phoenissae*[1], there is not unanimity but discord; for

---

[1] The scene in the *Phoenissae* of Euripides beginning at v. 586
will sufficiently explain this allusion.

unanimity does not mean that both parties entertain the same view whatever it may be, but that they entertain the same view as to the way of carrying it out, as when the masses and the upper classes agree in desiring the government of the best citizens; for then they all gain their desire.

Unanimity then[1] appears to be political friendship, and indeed it is often so described, as it touches the interests and concerns of life. Such unanimity can exist only among the virtuous; for they are unanimous both in themselves[2] and in their relation to each other. They are anchored, as it were, immovably, as their wishes are permanent, and do not ebb and flow like the Euripus; the objects of their wishes are just and profitable, and they all agree in desiring these objects.

It is impossible for bad men to be unanimous, as it is impossible for them to be friends, except to a slight extent; for each desires an advantage over the other in all profits, and seeks to avoid his share of labours and public services, and while each person wishes to gain unfair advantage and to escape a fair share of duty, he criticizes and thwarts his neighbours' actions; for unless they keep an eye upon each other, their community is destroyed. The consequence is that they are always in a state of discord, each insisting that the other shall do what is just, and neither wishing to do it himself.

---

[1] Reading δή.

[2] To speak of a person as "unanimous in himself" is rather a Greek than an English mode of expression.

It seems that benefactors are better friends to
recipients of their benefactions than are the recipi
to their benefactors, and as this is a surprising fact,
people try to account for it.

The usual explanation is that the benefactors are
creditors and the recipients debtors. Hence as in the
case of loans the debtors would be glad if their
creditors ceased to exist, but the creditors look
anxiously to the safety of the debtors, so benefactors
desire the existence of the recipients of their benefactions, in the hope of receiving a return for the
favours they have done them, but the debtors are not
anxious to repay the debt.

Supposing this to be the explanation, Epicharmus
would perhaps say that to give it is to take a low
view of mankind; but it seems to be true to human
nature, as people have generally short memories, and
are more eager to receive benefits than to confer
them.

It would seem, however, that the reason lies
deeper down in the nature of things. It is not like
the reason which makes creditors care for their
debtors; for they have no affection for their debtors,
and if they feel a wish for their safety, it is only in
the hope of recovering the debt. But people who
have conferred benefactions upon others feel love and
affection for the recipients of their benefactions, even
if these recipients do not and cannot do them any
service. The same law holds good among artisans.
Every artisan feels greater affection for his own work,
than the work, if it were endowed with life, would
feel for him. But nowhere I think is it so true as in

...p of the authors and reci-pients of benefac-tions.

the case of poets; they have an extraordinary affection
for their own poems, and are as fond of them as if
they were their children.

It seems to be much the same with benefactors.
The recipient of the benefaction is their work, and
therefore they feel a greater affection for their work,
than the work feels for its author. The reason is that
existence is an object of desire and love to everybody,
but we exist by activity i.e. by living and acting; the
author of a work then may be said to exist by
activity; he is therefore fond of his work, because he
is fond of existence.

This affection of the author for his work is a
natural law; for that which exists potentially is
proved by the work to exist actively. It is also true
that in the eyes of the benefactor the performance of
his action is noble; he therefore delights in the
person who affords him the opportunity of displaying
it. The recipient of the benefaction, on the other
hand, finds no nobleness, but at the best only profit,
in its author, and profit is less pleasant and lovable
than nobleness.

Again, it is activity in the present which is
pleasant, hope for the future, and recollection of the
past; but nothing is so pleasant or so lovable as the
exercise of activity. Now a person who has conferred
a benefit finds that his work is permanent, for nobleness is longlived. But if he receives a benefaction,
the profit is transitory. The memory too of noble
deeds is pleasant, but that of useful deeds is less
pleasant, if pleasant at all. It seems to be just the
opposite with the expectation. Again, the feeling of

affection is a sort of active, but the receiving of it a sort
of passive, condition, and the feeling and exercise of
affection naturally accompany superiority in the action.

Again, we are all most fond of such things as
have cost us trouble. Thus people who have made
money are always fonder of it than people who have
inherited it. Accordingly, as it takes no trouble to
receive a benefaction, but is hard work to confer one,
benefactors are more affectionate *than the recipients
of benefactions*. This is the reason why mothers are
more devoted to their children than fathers; it is
that they suffer more in giving them birth and are
more certain that they are their own. But this
certainly belongs also to benefactors.

It is often asked whether one ought to love
oneself or somebody else most.

We censure people who are exceedingly fond of
themselves, and call them "lovers of self" by way of
reproach; for it seems that a bad man has an eye to
his own interest in all that he does, and all the more
in proportion to his greater viciousness. Accordingly
it is a charge against him that he does nothing
without an eye to his own interest. The virtuous
man, on the other hand, is moved by a motive of
nobleness, and the better he is, the more strongly he
is so moved; he acts in the interest of his friend,
disregarding his own.

The facts of life are at variance with these theories
as indeed we might expect; for we ought, it is said,
to love our best friend best; but the best friend is he
who, when he wishes the good of another, wishes it
for the other's sake, and wishes it even if nobody will

CHAP.VIII.
Should a
person love
himself or
somebody
else most?

know his wish. But these conditions and all such others as are characteristic of friendship, are best realized in the relation of a man to himself; for it has been said that all the characteristics of friendship in the relation of a man to other men are derived from his relation to himself. All the proverbial sayings agree with this view, such as "Friends have one soul," "Friends' goods are common goods," "Equality is friendship," and "Charity begins at home"; for all these conditions exist preeminently in relation to oneself, as every one is his own best friend, and therefore must love himself best.

It is not unnatural to ask, Which of these two lines of argument ought we to follow, as there is something convincing in both? Perhaps then it will be well to analyse them and to determine how far and in what sense they are respectively true. Now the truth will I think become clear, if we ascertain the meaning of the word "self-love" in them both. When people use it as a term of reproach, they give the name "lovers of self" to people who assign themselves a larger share of money, honours, and bodily pleasures than belongs to them. These are the objects of desire to men in general. It is these that they conceive to be the highest goods, on these that they set their hearts, and it is for these therefore that they contend. Thus people who are eager to get an undue share of these things gratify their desires and emotions generally, or, in other words, the irrational parts of the soul. This is the character of men in general, and hence as men in general are bad, the term "self-love" has come to be used in a

p. 291.

Nature of
self-love.

bad sense. It is right then to censure people who are lovers of self in this sense. It is easy to see that people ordinarily apply the term "self-love" to those who assign themselves an undue share of such things as money, honour, and pleasure; for if a person were to set his heart always on preeminence in doing what is just or temperate or virtuous in any other respect, and were always and by all means to reserve to himself the noble part, nobody would accuse him of self-love or censure him for it. Yet it would seem that such a person is conspicuously a lover of self. At all events he assigns to himself what is in the highest sense good, and gratifies the supreme part *of his nature* and yields it an unqualified obedience. But as it is the supreme part of a state or any other corporation which seems to be in the truest sense the state or corporation itself, so it is with a man. Accordingly he is in the truest sense a lover of self, who loves and gratifies the supreme part of his being.

Again, a person is called continent and incontinent according as reason is, or is not, the ruling faculty in his being. But to say this is to say that the reason is the man. Also it is when we act most rationally that we are held in the truest sense to have acted ourselves, and to have acted voluntarily.

It is perfectly clear then that it is the rational part of a man which is the man himself, and that it is the virtuous man who feels the most affection for this part. It follows that the virtuous man is a lover of self, although not in the sense in which a man who is censured for self-love is a lover of self, but in a sense differing from it as widely as a life directed by reason differs from a life directed by emotion, and as the desire for what is noble differs from a desire for what seems to be one's interest.

Now if people set their hearts preeminently upon noble actions, we all approve and applaud them; but if all people were eager in pursuit of what is noble and exerted themselves to the utmost to do the noblest deeds, then the state would have all its wants supplied, and an individual citizen would have the greatest of all goods, assuming that virtue is the greatest good. We conclude then that a good man ought to be a lover of self, as by his noble deeds he will benefit himself and serve others, but that the wicked man ought not to be a lover of self, as he will injure himself and other people too by following his evil passions.

In the bad man then there is a discrepancy between what he ought to do and what he does, whereas the virtuous man does what he ought to do; for reason always chooses what is best for itself, and the good man is obedient to his reason.

It is true of the virtuous man that he will act often in the interest of his friends and of his country, and, if need be, will even die for them. He will surrender money, honour, and all the goods for which the world contends, reserving only nobleness for himself, as he would rather enjoy an intense pleasure for a short time than a moderate pleasure long, and would rather live one year nobly than many years indifferently, and would rather perform one noble and lofty action than many poor actions. This is true of one who lays down his life for another; he chooses great nobleness for his own. Such a man will surrender riches gladly if only he may enrich his friends; for then while his friend gets the money, he gets the nobleness, and so assigns the greater good to himself.

It is the same with honour and offices of state. All these he will surrender to his friend, but the surrender is noble and laudable in his eyes.

It is reasonable then to call such a man virtuous, as he prefers nobleness to everything. He may even surrender the opportunity of action to his friend. It may be nobler for him to inspire his friend to act than to act himself.

Wherever then the virtuous man deserves praise, it is clear that he assigns to himself a preponderant share of noble conduct. In this sense then it is right to be a lover of self, but not in the sense in which ordinary people love themselves.

Another question in dispute is whether the happy man will need friends or not.

CHAP. IX.
Does the happy man need friends?

It is sometimes said that people, whose lives are fortunate and independent, have no need of friends, as they are already in possession of all good things. As being independent then they have no need of anything more, whereas a friend is like a second self, who supplies what it is not in our own power to supply. Hence the saying

"Let but God bless us, what's the good of friends?[1]"

But it looks absurd to assign all good things to

---

[1] Euripides, *Orestes* 667.

the happy man, and yet not to assign friends—the greatest as it seems of all external goods. If it is more a friend's part to do good than to receive it, if beneficence is the part of the good man or of virtue, and if it is nobler to do good to one's friends than to strangers, the virtuous man will need somebody to do good to. Accordingly it is sometimes asked whether we need friends more in times of prosperity or in times of adversity, the idea being that an unfortunate man needs somebody to do him a service, and a fortunate man somebody for him to do good to. Again, it is I think absurd to place the fortunate man in solitude, as nobody would choose to possess all good things by himself. For man is a social being, and disposed to live with others. It follows that the fortunate man must live in society, as he possesses all natural goods. But it is clearly better to spend one's days with friends and virtuous people than with strangers, who may not be virtuous. It follows therefore that the happy man has need of friends.

What is the meaning then of the first view[1], and in what sense is it true? It may be suggested that in the ordinary view friends are regarded as people who can be useful. Now the fortunate man will not need friends of this kind, as he already possesses all that is good, nor will he need friends to give him pleasure, or he will need them but little; for as his life is pleasant *in itself*, it has no need of adventitious pleasure. But as he does not need friends of this kind, it looks as if he did not need friends at all.

---

[1] i.e. the view that the happy man has no need of friends.

But this, I think, is not true, for it has been stated at p. 16. the outset that happiness is a form of activity, and it is clear that an activity is always coming into being, and does not already exist, like a piece of property. But if happiness consists in life and activity, and the activity of the good man is virtuous and pleasant in itself, as has been said at the outset, if there is a p. 20. pleasure in the sense that a thing is our own, and if we are better able to contemplate others than ourselves, and to contemplate the actions of others than our own, it follows that the actions of virtuous people, if they are friends, are pleasant to the good, as they contain both the elements[1] which are naturally pleasant. The fortunate man then will need friends of this kind, as it is his choice to contemplate such actions as are good and belong to himself; for the actions of the good man who is his friend answer to this description.

Again, it is supposed that the happy man must have a pleasant life. Now life is hard, if it be lived in solitude, as it is difficult for a man easily to maintain a constant activity by himself, but it is comparatively easy in the society of others and in relation to them.

The activity *in relation to others* then will be more continuous, and it is pleasant in itself. It ought to be so in the case of the fortunate man; for a virtuous man *qua* virtuous man delights in virtuous

---

[1] The two elements are (1) that our friend's actions are good, (2) that they belong to us, our friend being, as Aristotle says, "a second self."

actions, but is offended at vicious actions, as a
musician feels pleasure in good music and pain at
bad music.

There is a certain discipline too in virtue which
may be derived from living in good society, as
Theognis[1] says.

But if we look more deeply into the nature of
things, it seems that a virtuous friend is naturally

p. 20.   desirable to a virtuous man; for that which is
naturally good, as has been said, is good and pleasant
Essential   in itself to the virtuous man. But while life among
nature of   the lower animals is defined by the faculty of sensa-
life.   tion, it is defined among men by the faculty of
sensation or thought. But a faculty is *intelligible
only* by reference to its activity. It is upon the
activity that the faculty essentially depends. It
seems then that life consists essentially in sensation
or thought.

Again, life is a thing that is good and pleasant in
itself, for it possesses the definiteness[2] which is of the
nature of the good; but that which is naturally good
is good also to the virtuous man. It is as being a
natural good that life seems to be pleasant to
everybody. But in speaking of life as pleasant, we
must not take a vicious or corrupt life, or a life of
pain; for such a life is indefinite, as are its conditions.
But we will try to clear up the subject of pain

---

[1] The saying of Theognis ἐσθλῶν μὲν γὰρ ἄπ᾽ ἐσθλά, which is
quoted p. 179, l. 19, may be taken as illustrating this opinion.

[2] The idea of "definiteness" or "limitation" as a characteristic
of the good is Pythagorean. Cp. τὸ γὰρ κακὸν τοῦ ἀπείρου, ὡς οἱ
Πυθαγόρειοι εἴκαζον, τὸ δ᾽ ἀγαθὸν τοῦ πεπερασμένου, p. 29, ll. 32—34.

hereafter. Life itself is good and pleasant. It seems to be so from the fact that it is desired by people, and especially by the virtuous and fortunate; for it is to them that life is most desirable, as it is theirs which is the most fortunate life. One who sees perceives that he sees, and one who hears that he hears, and one who walks that he walks, and similarly in all our activities there is something in us which perceives that we exercise the activity; and if so, it follows that we can perceive that we perceive, and understand that we understand. But to *perceive or understand* that we perceive or understand, is to *perceive or understand* that we exist[1]; for existence consists, as we said, in perceiving or understanding.

But the perception or sensation of life is a pleasure in itself; for life is naturally a good, and it is a pleasure to perceive good existing in oneself. Life is an object of desire, and to none so desirable as to the good, because existence is to them good and pleasant; for they feel a pleasure in their consciousness of what is good in itself. But the virtuous man stands in the same relation to his friend as to himself; for his friend is a second self. As then everyone desires his own existence, so or similarly he desires the existence of his friend. But the desirableness of existence, as p. 291. we saw, lies in the sense of one's own goodness, such a sensation being pleasant in itself. We require therefore the consciousness of our friend's existence,

---

[1] Sir A. Grant justly regards this statement of "the absolute unity of existence with thought" as anticipating the Cartesian formula, *Cogito, ergo sum.*

and this we shall get by living with him and associating with him in conversation and thought; for it would seem that this is what we mean when we speak of living together in the case of men, we do not mean, as in the case of cattle, merely occupying the same feeding-ground.

If the fortunate man then finds existence desirable in itself, as being naturally good and pleasant, and if a friend's existence is much the same as one's own, it follows that a friend will be a desirable thing. But that which is desirable a man ought to possess, or, if he does not possess it, he will be so far deficient. We conclude therefore that, if a person is to be happy, he will need virtuous friends.

CHAP. X.
Proper number of friends.

Is it our duty then to make the largest possible number of friends? or is it with friendship generally, as with the friendship of hospitality, where it has been neatly said

"Give me not many friends, nor give me none[1],"

i.e. will it here too be proper neither to be friendless nor again to have an excessive number of friends?

In the case of friends whose friendship we make from a motive of expediency the rule is a perfectly proper one, as it is a laborious task to return the services of a number of people, nor is life long enough for the task. A larger number of such friends then than are sufficient for one's own life would be superfluous and prejudicial to noble living; they are therefore unnecessary.

Again, of those whom we make friends as being

[1] Hesiod, Ἔργα καὶ Ἡμέραι, 713.

pleasant or sweet to us, few are enough, as a little sweetening is enough in our diet.

But if we take the case of virtuous friends it may be asked, Should they be as numerous as possible, or is there a fixed limitation to the size of a circle of friends, as there is to the size of a state? For ten people would not be enough to compose a state; on the other hand, if the population rose to a hundred thousand, it would cease to be a state. It may be suggested, however, that the number of citizens is not a single fixed amount, but may be anything within certain definite limits. So too there will be a definite limit to the number of friends. It will, I think, be the highest number with whom a person could live. For it is community of life which we saw to be the especial characteristic of friendship, and it is easy to see that a person cannot live with a number of people and distribute himself among them.

Again, a person's friends must themselves be friends of each other, if they are all to pass their days together, and this is a condition which can hardly exist among a number of people. It is hard for a person to sympathise fittingly with a number of people in their joys and sorrows; for it will probably happen that at the very time when he is called upon to rejoice with one he will be called upon to sorrow with another.

Perhaps it is well then not to try to have the largest possible number of friends, but to have only so many as are sufficient for community of life, as it would seem to be impossible to be a devoted friend of a number of people. Hence it is impossible to be

in love with several people; for love is in its intention
a sort of exaggerated friendship, and it is impossible
to feel this exaggerated friendship except for an
individual. So too it is impossible to be the devoted
friend of more than a few people. This is what
seems to be practically the case. We do not find
that people have a number of friends who are as
intimate with them as comrades. The classical
friendships[1] of story too have all been friendships
between two persons.

People who have a host of friends, and who take
everybody to their arms, seem to be nobody's friends,
unless indeed in the sense in which all fellow-citizens
are friends; and if they have a host of friends, we call
them complaisant people.

Although then as a fellow-citizen it is possible for
one to be the friend of a number of people and yet
not to be complaisant, but to be truly virtuous, it is
impossible to be the friend of a number of people as
being virtuous and deserving of friendship for their
own sake. We must be content if we can find only a
few people who deserve such friendship.

CHAP. XI.
Whether
friends
are more
needed in
prosperity
or in ad-
versity.

It remains to ask, Is it in times of prosperity or in
times of adversity that friends are more needed?
We require them at both times; for in adversity we
need assistance, and in prosperity we need people to
live with and to do good to, as it is *presumably* our
wish to do good.

Friendship then is more necessary in times of

---

[1] Such as the friendship of Achilles and Patroclus or of
Damon and Pythias.

adversity; therefore in adversity we want friends to help us; but it is nobler in times of prosperity; therefore in times of prosperity we look for good people, as it is more desirable to do them services and to live in their society. For the mere presence of friends is pleasant even in adversity, as pain is alleviated by the sympathy of friends. Accordingly it may be doubted whether they take part of the burden as it were upon themselves, or it is rather the pleasure of their presence, and the thought of their sympathy, which diminishes the pain we feel.

We need not now discuss whether this or something else is the cause of the alleviation. It is clear, at all events, that the fact is as we state it. But it seems that the presence of friends is a source partly of comfort and partly of pain. There is a pleasure in the mere sight of friends, especially when one is in adversity, and something too of support against sorrow; for the look and voice of a friend are consoling to us if he be a person of tact, as he knows our character and the sources of our pleasure and pain. On the other hand it is painful to perceive that a person is pained at our own adversity, as everybody avoids being a cause of pain to his friends. Accordingly people of a courageous nature shrink from involving their friends in their pain, and such a person, unless he be extraordinarily indifferent to pain, cannot endure the pain which he causes them, nor can he in any way put up with people whose sympathy takes the form of lamentation, as he is not fond of indulging in lamentation himself. It is only weak women and effeminate men who take delight in such people as display their sympathy by their groans and who love them as friends and sympathisers in their sorrow. But it is evident that we ought always to imitate one who is better than ourselves.

The presence of friends in seasons of prosperity is a pleasant means of passing the time, and not only so, but it suggests the idea that they take pleasure in our own goods. It would seem a duty then to be forward in inviting friends to share our good fortune, as there is a nobleness in conferring benefactions, but to be slow in inviting them to share our ill fortune, as it is a duty to give them as small a share of our evils as possible, whence the saying

"Enough that I am wretched[1]."

But the time when we should be most ready to call them to our side is the time when it is probable that at the cost of but slight personal inconvenience they will have a chance of doing us a great service.

On the other hand, it is, I think, proper for us to go to our friends when they are in trouble, even if they do not send for us, and to make a point of going, as it is a friendly act to do good, especially to those who are in need and have made no claim upon us; for this is the nobler and pleasanter course for both. It is proper too to be forward in helping them to enjoy themselves, as this again is a service that friends may render, but to be less forward in seeking

---

[1] The words of Jocasta in the *Oedipus Tyrannus* 1061

ἅλις νοσοῦσ' ἐγώ,

are in sense, though not exactly in form, the same as this quotation.

to get enjoyment for ourselves, as there is nothing noble in being forward to receive benefits. Still we must, I think, be on our guard against seeming churlish, as sometimes happens, in rejecting their services.

It appears then that the presence. of friends is universally desirable.

Nothing is so welcome to people who are in love CHAP. XII. as the sight of one another. There is no sense that Commu-nity of they choose in preference to this, as it is upon this life as essential to more than upon anything else that the existence and friendship creation of their love depends. May we not say then or love. that there is nothing which friends desire so much as community of life? For the essence of friendship is association.

Again, a man stands in the same relation to his friend as to himself; but the sense of his own existence is desirable; so too then is that of the existence of his friend. The activity of friends too is realized in living together. It is only reasonable therefore that they should desire community of life.

Again, whatever it is that people regard as con-stituting existence, whatever it is that is their object in desiring life, it is in this that they wish to live with their friends. Accordingly some people are com-panions in drinking, others in gambling, others in gymnastic exercises, or in the chase or in philosophy, and each class spends its days in that for which it cares more than for anything else in life; for as it is their wish to live with their friends, they do the things and participate in the things which seem to them to constitute a common life.

Thus the friendship of the bad proves to be vicious; for as they are unstable, they participate in what is bad, and become vicious by a process of mutual assimilation. But the friendship of the virtuous is virtuous; it grows as their intercourse grows, and they seem to be morally elevated by the exercise of their activity and by the correction of each other's faults; for each models himself upon the pleasing features of the other's character, whence the saying

"From good men learn good life[1]."

This may be regarded as a sufficient discussion of friendship or love. We will proceed to discuss pleasure.

[1] A saying of Theognis. Cp. p. 174 l. 31.

BOOK X.

It is natural, I think, to discuss pleasure next; for it seems that there is, in a preeminent degree, an affinity between pleasure and our human nature, and that is the reason why, in the education of the young, we steer their course by the rudders of pleasure and pain. It seems too that there is no more important element in the formation of a virtuous character than a rightly directed sense of pleasure and dislike; for pleasure and pain are coextensive with life, and they exercise a powerful influence in promoting virtue and happiness of life, as we choose what is pleasant and avoid what is painful.

Considering, then, the importance of these questions, it would seem to be clearly a duty not to pass them over, especially as they admit of much dispute. For some people say that the good[1] is pleasure; others, on the contrary, that pleasure is something utterly bad, whether, as is possible, they are convinced that it really is so, or they think it better in the interest of human life to represent pleasure as an evil, even if it is not so, feeling that men are generally inclined to pleasure, and are the slaves of their

---

[1] Aristotle in this book speaks of "the good" (τἀγαθόν), meaning the highest good or *summum bonum.*

pleasures, and that it is a duty therefore to lead them
in the contrary direction, as they will so arrive at the
mean *or proper* state.

But I venture to think that this is not a right
statement of the case. For in matters of the emotions
and actions theories are not so trustworthy as facts;
and thus, when theories disagree with the facts of
perception, they fall into contempt, and involve the
truth itself in their destruction. For if a person
censures pleasure and yet is seen at times to make
pleasure his aim, he is thought to incline to pleasure
as being entirely desirable; for it is beyond the
power of ordinary people to make distinctions. It
seems then the true theories are exceedingly useful,
not only as the means of knowledge but as guides of
life; for as being in harmony with facts, they are
believed, and being believed they encourage people
who understand them to regulate their lives in
accordance with them.

Enough then of such considerations; let us review
the various doctrines of pleasure.

CHAP. II.
Theory of
Eudoxus.
Pleasure
the good.

Eudoxus held that pleasure was the good, because
he saw that all things, whether rational or irrational,
make pleasure their aim. He argued that in all
cases that which is desirable is good, and that which
is most desirable is most good; hence the fact of all
things being drawn to the same object is an indication
that that object is the best for all, as everything
discovers what is good for itself in the same way as
it discovers food; but[1] that that which is good for all,
and is the aim of all, is the good.

1 Reading δέ.

His theories were accepted, not so much for their intrinsic value as for the excellence of his moral character; for he was regarded as a person of exemplary temperance. It seemed then that he did not put forward these views as being a votary of pleasure, but that the truth was really as he said. He held that this truth resulted with equal clearness from a consideration of the opposite *of pleasure*; for as pain is something which everybody should avoid, so too its opposite is something which everybody should desire. He argued that a thing is in the highest degree desirable, if we do not desire it for any ulterior reason, or with any ulterior motive, and this is admittedly the case with pleasure; for if a person is pleased, nobody asks the further question, What is his motive in being pleased? a fact which proves that pleasure is desirable in itself. And further that the addition of pleasure to any good, e.g. to just or temperate conduct, renders that good more desirable, and it follows that if the good is augmented by a thing, that thing must itself be a good.

It seems then that this argument proves pleasure to be a good, but not to be a good in a higher sense than anything else; for any good whatever is more desirable with the addition of another good than when it stands alone. It is by a precisely similar argument that Plato tries to prove that pleasure is not the good. Pleasure (he says) is not the chief good, for the pleasant life is more desirable with the addition of prudence than without it; but if the combination is better, pleasure is not the good, as

Pleasure and good.

the good itself cannot be made more desirable by any addition.

But it is clear that, *if pleasure is not the good,* neither can anything else be which is made more desirable by the addition of any absolute good. What is it then which is incapable of such addition, but at the same time admits of our participating in it? For it is a good of this kind which is the object of our research.

Desire and good.

People who argue on the other hand that that which all things aim at is not a good may be said to talk nonsense; for we accept the universal opinion as true, and one who upsets our trust in the universal opinion will find it hard to put forward any opinion that is more trustworthy. If it were only unintelligent beings that longed for pleasure, there would be something in what he says; but if intelligent beings also long for it, how can it be so? It is probable that even in the lower creatures there is some natural[1] principle which is superior to the creatures themselves, and aims at their proper good.

Arguments against pleasure being a good.

Nor does it seem that these people fairly meet the argument drawn from the opposite of pleasure. They say it does not follow that, if pain is an evil, pleasure is a good, as not only is one evil opposed to another, but both are opposed to that which is neither one nor the other, *but a neutral state.* This is true enough, but it does not apply to pleasure and pain. For if both pleasure and pain were evil, it would have been a duty to avoid both, and if neither

---

[1] I cannot help thinking that ἀγαθόν ought to be omitted from the text.

were evil, it would have been a duty not to avoid
either, or not to avoid one more than the other;
whereas in fact it is clear that people avoid one as an
evil, and desire the other as a good. It follows then
that pleasure and pain are opposed to each other as
good and evil.

Nor again does it follow that, if pleasure is not a
quality, neither is it a good, for the activities of virtue
are not qualities, nor is happiness.

It is argued too that good is definite, but pleasure
is indefinite, as it admits of degrees.

Now if the ground of this opinion is that it is
possible to be pleased *in a greater or a less degree,*
the same thing is true of justice and the other
virtues. For here it is evident that we speak of
persons as possessing the several virtues in a greater
or less degree; some people are just and courageous
in a greater *or less* degree than others, and it is
possible to act with a greater or less degree of
justice and temperance.

If however the meaning is that the indefiniteness
resides in the pleasures, this is, I think, not the true
explanation, supposing that some pleasures are mixed
and others unmixed[1].

Again[2], health is definite, yet it admits of degrees;
and why should it not be so with pleasure? For
health is not the same symmetry or proportion of

---

[1] Aristotle, following Plato's theory of "mixed" and "unmixed" pleasures, argues that it is only such pleasures as are
"mixed" which can be said to possess the character of "indefiniteness." Cp. *Philebus* p. 52.

[2] Reading καὶ τί κωλύει.

elements in all people, nor is it always uniform in the same person; it admits of relaxation up to a certain point, and of different degrees, without ceasing to be health. Something of the same kind then may be also true of pleasure.

Again, *the opponents of pleasure*, looking upon the good as perfect or complete, and the processes of movement and production as imperfect or incomplete, try to prove that pleasure is motion or production. But they are wrong, I think, nor is pleasure a motion at all. For quickness and slowness are characteristic, it seems, of every motion, either absolutely, as of the motion of the universe, or else relatively, but neither of them is a condition inherent in pleasure. It is possible to *become* pleased, as it is to *become* angry, quickly, but not to *be* pleased quickly or relatively, *i.e. in comparison with somebody else*, as it is to walk or to grow quickly and so on. The transition then, to a state of pleasure may be quick or slow, but the active experience of pleasure, i.e. the state of being pleased, cannot be quick.

Pleasure not a process of production.

In what sense, too, can pleasure be a process of production? It is apparently not the case that anything can be produced out of anything; it is the case that a thing is resolved into that out of which it is produced. Also, pain is the destruction of that of which pleasure is the production. It is said too that pain is a deficiency of the natural state, and pleasure its satisfaction. But this deficiency and this satisfaction are emotions of the body. If, then, pleasure is a satisfaction of the natural state, it follows that the part which is the seat of the satisfaction will feel pleasure i.e. the body. But this seems not to be the case. We conclude therefore that pleasure is not a satisfaction of the natural state, although one may feel pleasure while the process of satisfaction is going on, as he may feel pain while undergoing[1] an operation.

This view of pleasure, *viz. that it is a process of satisfaction*, seems to have originated in the pleasures and pains of eating and drinking, as in them we first feel a deficiency and an antecedent pain, and then feel pleasure at the satisfaction. But this is not true of all pleasures; the pleasures of mathematics e.g. have no such antecedent pain, nor among the pleasures of the senses have those of the smell, nor again many sounds and sights, memories and hopes. What is there then of which these will be processes of production? For in them there has been no deficiency to be satisfied.

But if the instance of immoral pleasures be adduced *to prove that pleasure is a bad thing*, we may answer that these are not really pleasant. They may be pleasant to people who are in a bad condition, but it must not be inferred that they are pleasant except to such people, any more than that things are healthful or sweet or bitter in themselves, because they are so to invalids, or that things are white, because they appear so to people who are suffering from ophthalmia.

Perhaps the truth may be stated thus: Pleasures are desirable, but not if they are immoral in their

[1] It is hardly likely that τεμνόμενος is the true reading; but I have tried to give such sense as can be made of it.

origin, just as wealth is pleasant, but not if it be obtained at the cost of turning traitor to one's country, or health, but not at the cost of eating any food, however disagreeable. Or it may be said that pleasures are of different kinds, those which are noble in their origin are different from those which are dishonourable, and it is impossible to enjoy the pleasure of the just man without being just, or that of the musician without being musical, and so on. The distinction drawn between a friend and a flatterer seems to bring out clearly the truth that pleasure is not a good, or that there are pleasures of different kinds; for it seems that while the object of the friend in social intercourse is good, that of the flatterer is pleasure, and while the flatterer is censured, the friend for his disinterestedness is praised.

Again, nobody would choose to live all his life with the mind of a child, although he should enjoy the pleasures of childhood to the utmost, or to delight in doing what is utterly shameful, although he were never to suffer pain for doing it. There are many things too upon which we should set our hearts, even if they brought no pleasure with them, e.g. sight, memory, knowledge, and the possession of the virtues; and if it be true that these are necessarily attended by pleasures, it is immaterial, as we should desire them even if no pleasure resulted from them. It seems to be clear then that pleasure is not the good, nor is every pleasure desirable, and that there are some pleasures which are desirable in themselves, and they differ in kind or in origin from the others.

We may regard this as a sufficient account of such views as are held in regard to pleasure and pain.

But the nature or character of pleasure will be more clearly seen, if we resume our argument from the beginning. ^{CHAP. III.} *Nature of pleasure.*

It seems that the act of sight is perfect or complete at any time; it does not lack anything which will afterwards be produced, and will make it perfect of its kind. Pleasure appears to resemble sight in this respect; it is a whole, nor is it possible at any time to find a pleasure which will be made perfect of its kind by increased duration.

It follows that pleasure is not a motion; for every motion takes a certain time, and aims at a certain end. Thus the builder's art is perfect or complete when it has accomplished its object. It is complete, either in respect of the whole time which the building took, or in respect of the moment *when it was completed.* But in the various parts of the time the various processes or motions are imperfect and different in kind from the whole and from one another; for the setting of the stones is different from the fluting of the pillar, and both from the building of the temple *as a whole,* and whereas the building of the temple is complete, nothing being wanting to the object proposed, that of the basement and the triglyph is incomplete, as each is only the building of a part of the temple. These processes or motions are therefore different in kind, and it is impossible at any time *when the building is going on* to find a motion which is complete or

Pleasure not a motion or process of production.

perfect of its kind. Such a motion, if found at all, will be found only in the whole time.

It is much the same with walking or any other process. For here again, although all locomotion is a motion from one place to another, there are different kinds of locomotion, such as flying, walking, jumping, and the like. And not only so, but walking itself is of different kinds; for the starting-point and the goal are not the same in the whole course, and in a part of it, or in one part of the course and in another; nor is it the same thing to cross one line as to cross another; for it is not only that a person crosses a line, but the line which he crosses is in a certain place, and one line is in a different place from another.

The subject of motion has been accurately discussed in another treatise[1]. Motion is apparently not complete in any and every period of time; on the contrary, most motions are incomplete and different in kind, inasmuch as the starting-point and the goal constitute a difference of kind. Pleasure on the other hand seems to be complete or perfect of its kind in any and every period of time.

It is clear then that motion and pleasure must be distinct from one another, and that pleasure is something which is whole and perfect.

Another reason for holding this view is that motion is impossible except in a period of time, but pleasure is not; for the pleasure of a moment is a whole.

---

[1] φυσικὴ ἀκρόασις, Books III. sqq.

It is clear from these considerations that pleasure is not rightly described as a motion or process of production, for such a description is not appropriate to all things but only to such as are divisible into parts and are not wholes. For there is no process of production in an act of sight or in a mathematical point or in a unit, nor is any one of these things a motion or a process of production. It follows that there is no such process in pleasure, as it is a whole.

Again, every sense exercises its activity upon its own object, and the activity is perfect only when the sense itself is in a sound condition, and the object is the noblest that falls within the domain of that sense; for this seems to be preeminently the character of the perfect activity. We may say that it makes no difference whether we speak of the sense itself or of the organ in which it resides as exercising the activity; in every instance the activity is highest when the part which acts is in the best condition, and the object upon which it acts is the highest of the objects which fall within its domain. Such an activity will not only be the most perfect, but the most pleasant; for there is pleasure in all sensation, and similarly in all thought and speculation, and the activity will be pleasantest when it is most perfect, and it will be most perfect when it is the activity of the part being in a sound condition and acting upon the most excellent of the objects that fall within its domain.

Pleasure perfects the activity, but not in the same way in which the excellence of the sense or of the object of sense perfects it, just as health is the cause of our being in a healthy state in one sense and the doctor is the cause of it in another.

It is clear that every sense has its proper pleasure; for we speak of pleasant sights, pleasant sounds and so on. It is clear too that the pleasure is greatest when the sense is best, and its object is best; but if the sentient subject and the sensible object are at their best, there will always be pleasure so long as there is a subject to act and an object to be acted upon.

When it is said that pleasure perfects the activity, it is not as a state *or quality* inherent in the subject but as a perfection superadded to it, like the bloom of youth to people in the prime of life.

So long then as the object of thought or sensation and the critical or contemplative subject are such as they ought to be, there will be pleasure in the exercise of the activity; for this is the natural result if the agent and the patient remain in the same relation to each other.

Impossibility of continuous pleasure.

It may be asked then, How is it that nobody feels pleasure continuously? It is probably because we grow weary. Human beings are incapable of continuous activity, and as the activity comes to an end, so does the pleasure; for it is a concomitant of the activity. It is for the same reason that some things give pleasure when they are new, but give less pleasure afterwards; for the intelligence is called into play at first, and applies itself to its object with intense activity, as when we look a person full in the face *in order to recognize him*, but afterwards the activity ceases to be so intense and becomes remiss, and consequently the pleasure also fades away.

It may be supposed that everybody desires pleasure, for[1] everybody clings to life. But life is a
species of activity and a person's activity displays
itself in the sphere and with the means which are
after his own heart. Thus a musician exercises his
ears in listening to music, a student his intellect in
speculation, and so on.

But pleasure perfects the activities; it therefore[2]
perfects life, which is the aim of human desire. It is
reasonable then to aim at pleasure, as it perfects life
in each of us, and life is an object of desire.

Whether we desire life for the sake of pleasure or
pleasure for the sake of life, is a question which may
be dismissed for the moment. For it appears that
pleasure and life are yoked together and do not
admit of separation, as pleasure is impossible without activity and every activity is perfected by pleasure.

CHAP. V.
Pleasure
and life.

If this be so, it seems to follow that pleasures are
of different kinds, as we hold that things which are
different in kind are perfected by things which are
themselves different in kind. For this is apparently
the rule in the works of nature or of art, e.g. animals,
trees, pictures, statues, a house, or a piece of furniture.
Similarly we hold that energies which are different in
kind are perfected by things which are also different
in kind.

Pleasures
of different
kinds.

Now the pleasures of the intellect are different
from the pleasures of the senses, and these again are
different in kind from one another. It follows that

---

[1] Reading ὅτι.   [2] Reading δή.

the pleasures which perfect them will also be different.

This conclusion would appear also to result from the intimate connexion of each pleasure with the activity which it perfects. For the activity is increased by its proper pleasure, as if the activity is pleasant, we are more likely to arrive at a true judgment or an accurate result in any matter. It is so e.g. with people who are fond of geometry; they make better geometricians and understand the various problems of geometry better than other people. It is so too with people who are fond of music or architecture or any other subject; their progress in their particular subject is due to the pleasure which they take in it. Pleasure helps to increase activity, and that which helps to increase a thing must be closely connected with it. Where things then are different in kind, the things which are closely connected with them will also be different in kind.

Pleasure and activity. This becomes still clearer when we observe that the pleasures which spring from one activity are impediments to the exercise of another. Thus people who are fond of the flute are incapable of attending to an argument, if they hear somebody playing the flute, as they take a greater pleasure in flute-playing than in the activity which they are called to exercise at the moment; hence the pleasure of the flute-playing destroys their argumentative activity. Much the same result occurs in other cases, when a person exercises his activity on two subjects simultaneously; the pleasanter of the two drives out the other, especially if it be much the pleasanter, until the activity of the other disappears. Accordingly, if we take intense delight in anything, we cannot do anything else at all. It is only when we do not care much for a thing that we do something else as well, just as people who eat sweetmeats in the theatres do so most when the actors are bad.

As the pleasure then which is proper to an activity refines it and gives it greater permanence and excellence, while alien pleasures impair it, it is clear that there is a wide difference between these pleasures. It may almost be said that the pleasures which are alien to it have the same effect as the pains which are proper to it; for the pains which are proper to an activity destroy it, as, when a person finds writing or thinking unpleasant and painful, he does not write or does not think, as the case may be. Pleasures and pains proper to activities.

The pleasures and pains then which are proper to an activity have opposite effects upon it. I mean by "proper" such as are the consequences of the activity *per se*. But it has been already stated that alien pleasures have much the same effect as pain; they are destructive of the activity, although not destructive of it in the same way.

Again, as the activities differ in goodness and badness, some being desirable, some undesirable, and some neither the one nor the other, so it is with pleasures, as every activity has its proper pleasure. Thus the pleasure which is proper to a virtuous activity is good, and that which is proper to a low activity is vicious. For the desires of what is noble are themselves laudable, the desires of what is disgraceful are censurable; but the pleasures which

reside in the activities are more strictly proper to
them than the desires, as the latter are distinct[1] from
the activities in time and nature, but the former are
closely related in time to the activities, and are so
difficult to distinguish from them that it is a question
whether the activity is identical with the pleasure.

It seems however that pleasure is not the same
thing as thought or sensation; it would be strange if
it were so; but the impossibility of separating them
makes some people regard them as the same.

As the activities then are different, so are the
pleasures.   Sight is different from or superior to
touch in purity, hearing and smell are superior to
taste; there is a corresponding difference therefore
in their pleasures.   The pleasures of the intellect too
are different from or superior to these, and there are
different kinds of pleasures of the senses or of the
intellect.   It seems that there is a pleasure, as there
is a function, which is proper to every living thing,
viz. the pleasure inherent in its activity.   If we
consider individual living things, we see this is so;
for the pleasures of a horse, a dog, and a man are
different, and as Heraclitus says, "a donkey would
choose a bundle of hay in preference to gold; for
fodder is pleasanter to donkeys than gold."

As the pleasures then of beings who are different
in kind are themselves different in kind, it would be
reasonable to suppose that there is no difference
between the pleasures of the same beings.   But there

---

[1] The desire is distinct from the activity in time, as being
antecedent to it, and in nature, as being less complete in itself.

is a wide difference, at least in the case of men; the same things give pleasure to some people and pain to others, to some they are painful and hateful, to others pleasant and lovable. This is true of sweet things; the same things do not seem sweet to a person in a fever and to a person in good health, nor does the same thing seem hot to an invalid and to a person in a good physical condition. It is much the same with other things as well.

But in all these cases it seems that the thing really is what it appears to the virtuous man to be. But if this is a true statement of the case, as it seems to be, if virtue or the good man *qua* good is the measure of everything, it follows that it is such pleasures as appear pleasures to the good man that are really pleasures, and the things which afford him delight that are really pleasant. It is no wonder if what he finds disagreeable seems pleasant to somebody else, as men are liable to many corruptions and defilements; but such things are not pleasant except to these people, and to them only when they are in this condition. *Relation of pleasure and virtue.*

It is clear then that we must not speak of pleasures which are admitted to be disgraceful as pleasures, except in relation to people who are thoroughly corrupt. But the question remains, Among such pleasures as are seen to be good, what is the character or nature of the pleasures that deserve to be called the *proper* pleasures of Man? It is plain, I think, from a consideration of the activities; for the activities bring pleasures in their train. Whether then there is one activity or there are several belonging to the perfect and fortunate man, it is the pleasures which perfect these activities that would be strictly described as the *proper* pleasures of Man. All other pleasures are only in a secondary or fractional sense the pleasures of Man, as are all other activities.

CHAP. VI
Happiness.

p. 5.

After this discussion of the kinds of virtue and friendship and pleasure it remains to give a sketch of happiness, since we defined happiness as the end of human things. We shall shorten our account of it if we begin by recapitulating our previous remarks.

We said that happiness is not a moral state; for, if it were, it would be predicable of one who spends his whole life in sleep, living the life of a vegetable, or of one who is utterly miserable. If then we cannot accept this view if we must rather define

Happiness
an acti-
vity.

p. 16.

happiness as an activity of some kind, as has been said before, and if activities are either necessary and desirable as a means to something else or desirable in themselves, it is clear that we must define happiness as belonging to the class of activities which are desirable in themselves, and not desirable as means to something else; for happiness has no want, it is self-sufficient.

Again, activities are desirable in themselves, if nothing is expected from them beyond the activity. This seems to be the case with virtuous actions, as the practice of what is noble and virtuous is a thing desirable in itself. It seems to be the case also with such amusements as are pleasant, we do not desire them as means to other things; for they often do us harm rather than good by making us careless about our persons and our property. Such pastimes are generally the resources of those whom the world calls happy. Accordingly people who are clever at such pastimes are generally popular in the courts of despots, as they make themselves pleasant to the despot in the matters which are the objects of his desire, and what he wants is to pass the time pleasantly.

The reason why these things are regarded as elements of happiness is that people who occupy high positions devote their leisure to them. But such people are not, I think, a criterion. For a high position is no guarantee of virtue or intellect, which are the sources on which virtuous activities depend. And if these people, who have never tasted a pure and liberal pleasure, have recourse to the pleasures of the body, it must not be inferred that these pleasures are preferable; for even children suppose that such things as are valued or honoured among them are best. It is only reasonable then that, as men and children differ in their estimate of what is honourable, so should good and bad people.

As has been frequently said, therefore, it is the things which are honourable and pleasant to the virtuous man that are really honourable and pleasant. But everybody feels the activity which accords with his own moral state to be most desirable, and accordingly[1] the virtuous man regards the activity in accordance with virtue as most desirable.

Happiness then does not consist in amusement. It would be paradoxical to hold that the end of

[1] Reading δή.

human life is amusement, and that we should toil and
suffer all our life for the sake of amusing ourselves.
For we may be said to desire all things as means to
something else except indeed happiness, as happiness
is the end *or perfect state.*

It appears to be foolish and utterly childish to
take serious trouble and pains for the sake of
amusement. But to amuse oneself with a view to
being serious seems to be right, as Anacharsis says;
for amusement is a kind of relaxation, and it is
because we cannot work for ever that we need
relaxation.

Relaxation.   Relaxation then is not an end. We enjoy it as a
means to activity; but it seems that the happy life is
a life of virtue, and such a life is serious, it is not
one of mere amusement. We speak of serious[1]
things too *(for serious things are virtuous)* as better
than things which are ridiculous and amusing, and of
the activity of the better part of man's being or of
the better man as always the more virtuous. But
the activity of that which is better is necessarily
higher and happier. Anybody can enjoy bodily pleasures, a slave can enjoy them as much as the best of
men; but nobody would allow that a slave is capable
of happiness unless he is capable of life[2]; for happiness consists not in such pastimes as I have been
speaking of, but in virtuous activities, as has been
already said.

----

[1] The argument depends upon the connexion between σπουδή
"seriousness" and σπουδαῖος, which here hovers in meaning between "serious" and "virtuous."

[2] i.e. the life of a free Athenian citizen.

If happiness consists in virtuous activity, it is only Chap. VII.
reasonable to suppose that it is the activity of the Happiness
a virtuous
highest virtue, or in other words, of the best part of activity.
our nature. Whether it is the reason or something
else which seems to exercise rule and authority by a
natural right, and to have a conception of things
noble and divine, either as being itself divine or as
relatively the most divine part of our being, it is the
activity of this part in accordance with its proper
virtue which will be the perfect happiness.

It has been already stated[1] that it is a speculative Happiness
activity, *i.e. an activity which takes the form of* a specula-
tive acti-
contemplation. This is a conclusion which would vity.
seem to agree with our previous arguments and with
the truth itself ; for the speculative is the highest
activity, as the intuitive reason is the highest of our
faculties, and the objects with which the intuitive
reason is concerned are the highest of things that can
be known. It is also the most continuous; for our
speculation can more easily be continuous than any
kind of action. We consider too that pleasure is an
essential element of happiness, and it is admitted
that there is no virtuous activity so pleasant as the
activity of wisdom or philosophic reflexion; at all
events it appears that philosophy possesses pleasures
of wonderful purity and certainty, and it is reasonable
to suppose that people who possess knowledge pass

---

[1] The reference is not clear; Sir A. Grant suggests, p. 21,
ll. 16—18; but the general drift of Aristotle's argument in Book
VI. has tended to show the speculative or intellectual nature of
happiness.

their time more pleasantly than people who are seekers after truth.

Self-sufficiency too, as it is called, is preeminently a characteristic of the speculative activity; for the wise man, the just man, and all others, need the necessaries of life; but when they are adequately provided with these things, the just man needs people to whom and with whom he may do justice, so do the temperate man, the courageous man and everyone else; but the wise man is capable of speculation by himself, and the wiser he is, the more capable he is of such speculation. It is perhaps better for him in his speculation to have fellow-workers; but nevertheless he is in the highest degree self-sufficient.

It would seem too that the speculative is the only activity which is loved for its own sake as it has no result except speculation, whereas from all moral actions we gain something more or less besides the action itself.

Happiness and leisure.   Again, happiness, it seems, requires leisure; for the object of our business is leisure, as the object of war is the enjoyment of peace. Now the activity of the practical virtues is displayed in politics or war, and actions of this sort seem incompatible with leisure. This is absolutely true of military actions, as nobody desires war, or prepares to go to war, for its own sake. A person would be regarded as absolutely bloodthirsty if he were to make enemies of his friends for the mere sake of fighting and bloodshed. But the activity of the statesman too is incompatible with leisure. It aims at securing something beyond and apart from politics, viz. the power and honour or at least the happiness of the statesman himself and his fellow citizens, which is different from the political activity and is proved to be different by our search for it *as something distinct.*

If then political and military actions are pre-eminent among virtuous actions in beauty and grandeur, if they are incompatible with leisure and aim at some end, and are not desired for their own sakes, if the activity of the intuitive reason seems to be superior in seriousness as being speculative, and not to aim at any end beyond itself, and to have its proper pleasure, and if this pleasure enhances the activity, it follows that such self-sufficiency and power of leisure and absence of fatigue as are possible to a man and all the other attributes of felicity are found to be realized in this activity. This then will be the perfect happiness of Man, if a perfect length of life is given it, for there is no imperfection in happiness. But such a life will be too good for Man. He will enjoy such a life not in virtue of his humanity but in virtue of some divine element within him, and the superiority of this activity to the activity of any other virtue will be proportionate to the superiority of this divine element in man to his composite *or material* nature.

If then the reason is divine in comparison with *the rest of* Man's nature, the life which accords with reason will be divine in comparison with human life in general. Nor is it right to follow the advice of people who say that the thoughts of men should not be too high for humanity or the thoughts of mortals

Happiness and intuitive reason.

too high for mortality; for a man, as far as in him lies, should seek immortality and do all that is in his power to live in accordance with the highest part of his nature, as, although that part is insignificant in size, yet in power and honour it is far superior to all the rest.

It would seem too that this is the true self of everyone, if a man's true self is his supreme or better part. It would be absurd then that a man should desire not the life which is properly his own but the life which properly belongs to some other being. The remark already made will be appropriate here. It is what is proper to everyone that is in its nature best and pleasantest for him. It is the life which accords with reason then that will be best and pleasantest for Man, as a man's reason is in the highest sense himself. This will therefore be also the happiest life.

CHAP. VIII.
Speculative and non-speculative virtue.

It is only in a secondary sense that the life which accords with other, *i.e. non-speculative*, virtue can be said to be happy; for the activities of such virtue are human, *they have no divine element.* Our just or courageous actions or our virtuous actions of any kind we perform in relation to one another, when we observe the law of propriety in contracts and mutual services and the various moral actions and in our emotions. But all these actions appear to be human affairs. It seems too that moral virtue is in some respects actually the result of physical organization and is in many respects closely associated with the emotions. Again, prudence is indissolubly linked to moral virtue, and moral virtue to prudence, since the principles of prudence are determined by the moral virtues, and moral rectitude is determined by prudence. But the moral virtues, as being inseparably united with the emotions, must have to do with the composite or *material* part *of our nature,* and the virtues of the composite part *of our nature* are human, *and not divine,* virtues. So too therefore is the life which accords with these virtues; so too is the happiness *which accords with them.*

But the happiness *which consists in the exercise* of the reason is separated *from these emotions.* It must be enough to say so much about it; for to discuss it in detail would take us beyond our present purpose. It would seem too to require external resources only to a small extent or to a less extent than moral virtue. It may be granted that both will require the necessaries of life and will require them equally, even if the politician devotes more trouble to his body and his bodily welfare than the philosopher; for the difference will not be important. But there will be a great difference in respect of their activities. The liberal man will want money for the practice of liberality, and the just man for the requital of services which have been done him; for our wishes, *unless they are manifested in actions,* must always be obscure, and even people who are not just pretend that it is their wish to act justly. The courageous man too will want physical strength if he is to perform any virtuous action, and the temperate man liberty, as otherwise it will be impossible for him or for anybody else to show his character.

But if the question be asked whether it is the

purpose or the performance that is the surer determinant of virtue, as virtue implies both, it is clear that both are necessary to perfection. But action requires various conditions, and the greater and nobler the action, the more numerous will the conditions be.

In speculation on the other hand there is no need of such conditions, at least for its activity; it may rather be said that they are actual impediments to speculation. It is as a human being and as living in society that a person chooses to perform virtuous actions. Such conditions then will be requisite if he is to live as a man.

That perfect happiness is a species of speculative activity will appear from the following consideration among others. Our conception of the Gods is that they are preeminently happy and fortunate. But what kind of actions do we properly attribute to them? Are they just actions? But it would make the Gods ridiculous to suppose that they form contracts, restore deposits, and so on. Are they then courageous actions? Do the Gods endure dangers and alarms for the sake of honour? Or liberal actions? But to whom should they give money? It would be absurd to suppose that they have a currency or anything of the kind. Again, what will be the nature of their temperate actions? Surely to praise the gods for temperance is to degrade them; they are exempt from low desires. We may go through 'the whole category of virtues, and it will appear that whatever relates to moral action is petty and unworthy of the Gods.

Yet the Gods are universally conceived as living

Happiness of the Gods.

and therefore as displaying activity; they are certainly not conceived as sleeping like Endymion. If then action and still more production is denied to one who is alive, what is left but speculation? It follows that the activity of God being preeminently blissful will be speculative, and if so then the human activity which is most nearly related to it will be most capable of happiness.

It is an evidence of this truth that the other animals, as being perfectly destitute of such activity, do not participate in happiness; for while the whole life of the Gods is fortunate or blessed, the life of men is blessed in so far as it possesses a certain resemblance to their speculative activity. But no other animal is happy, as no other animal participates at all in speculation.

We conclude then that happiness is coextensive with speculation, and that the greater a person's power of speculation, the greater will be his happiness, not as an accidental fact but in virtue of the speculation, as speculation is honourable in itself. Hence happiness must be a kind of speculation.

Man, as being human, will require external prosperity. His nature is not of itself sufficient for speculation, it needs bodily health, food, and care of every kind. It must not however be supposed that, because it is impossible to be fortunate without external goods, a great variety of such goods will be necessary to happiness. For neither self-sufficiency nor moral action consists in excess; it is possible to do noble deeds without being lord of land and sea, as moderate means will enable a person to act in

Chap. IX. Happiness and external goods.

accordance with virtue. We may clearly see that it
is so; for it seems that private persons practise
virtue not less but actually more than persons in
high place. It is enough that such a person should
possess as much as is requisite for virtue; his life
will be happy if he lives in the active exercise of
virtue. Solon[1] was right perhaps in his description
of the happy man as one " who is moderately supplied
with external goods, and yet has performed the
noblest actions,"—such was his opinion[2]—" and had
lived a temperate life," for it is possible to do one's
duty with only moderate means. It seems too that
Anaxagoras did not conceive of the happy man as
possessing wealth or power when he said that he
should not be surprised if the happy man proved a
puzzle in the eyes of the world; for the world judges
by externals alone, it has no perception of anything
that is not external.

The opinions of philosophers then seem to agree
with our theories. Such opinions, it is true, possess
a sort of authority; but it is the facts of life that are
the tests of truth in practical matters, as they possess
a supreme authority. It is right then to consider the
doctrines which have been already advanced in
reference to the facts of life, to accept them if they
harmonize with those facts, and to regard them as
mere theories if they disagree with them.

Happiness   Again, he whose activity is directed by reason
and reason.

---

[1] It is possible that Aristotle alludes to the story in Herodotus i. ch. 30.

[2] The words ὡς ᾤετο come in strangely; Lambinus conjectured
ὡς οἷόν τε.

and who cultivates reason, and is in the best, *i.e. the most rational*, state of mind is also, as it seems, the most beloved of the Gods. For if the Gods care at all for human things, as is believed, it will be only reasonable to hold that they delight in what is best and most related to themselves, i.e. in reason, and that they requite with kindness those who love and honour it above all else, as caring for what is dear to themselves and performing right and noble actions.

It is easy to see that these conditions are found preeminently in the wise man. He will therefore be most beloved of the Gods. We may fairly suppose too that he is most happy; and if so, this is another reason for thinking that the wise man is preeminently happy.

Supposing then that our sketch of these subjects and of the virtues, and of friendship too, and pleasure, has been adequate, are we to regard our object as achieved? Or are we to say in the old phrase that in practical matters the end is not speculation and knowledge but action? It is not enough to know the nature of virtue; we must endeavour to possess it, and to exercise it, and to use whatever other means are necessary for becoming good.

Now, if theories were sufficient of themselves to make men good, they would deserve to receive any number of handsome rewards, as Theognis said, and it would have been our duty to provide them. But it appears in fact that, although they are strong enough to encourage and stimulate youths who are already liberally minded, although they are capable of bringing a soul which is generous and enamoured of nobleness under the spell of virtue, they are impotent

CHAP. X.
Knowledge and practice of virtue.

to inspire the mass of men to chivalrous action; for
it is not the nature of such men to obey honour but
terror, nor to abstain from evil for fear of disgrace
but for fear of punishment. For, as their life is one
of emotion, they pursue their proper pleasures and
the means of gaining these pleasures, and eschew the
pains which are opposite to them. But of what is
noble and truly pleasant they have not so much as a
conception, because they have never tasted it. Where
is the theory or argument which can reform such
people as these? It is difficult to change by argument the settled features of character. We must be
content perhaps if, when we possess all the means by
which we are thought to become virtuous, we gain
some share of virtue.

Formation
of a virtu-
ous charac-
ter.
Some people think that men are made good by
nature, others by habit, others again by teaching.

Now it is clear that the gift of Nature is not in
our own power, but is bestowed through some divine
providence upon those who are truly fortunate. It is
probably true also that reason and teaching are not
universally efficacious; the soul of the pupil must
first have been cultivated by habit to a right spirit of
pleasure and aversion, like the earth that is to
nourish the seed. For he whose life is governed by
emotion would not listen to the dissuasive voice of
reason, or even comprehend it, and if this is his state,
how is it possible to convert him? Emotion, it
seems, never submits to reason but only to force. It
is necessary then to presuppose a character which is
in a sense akin to virtue, which loves what is noble
and dislikes what is dishonourable. But it is difficult
for one to receive from his early days a right inclina-

tion to virtue, unless he is brought up under virtuous laws; for a life of temperance and steadfastness is not pleasant to most people, least of all to the young. It follows that the nurture and pursuits *of the young* should be regulated by law, as they will not be painful, if he becomes used to them.

But it is not enough, I think, that we should receive a right nurture and control in youth; we must practise what is right and get the habit of doing it when we have come to man's estate. We shall need laws then to teach us what is right, and so to teach us all the duty of life; for most people are moved by necessity rather than by reason, and by the fear of punishment rather than by the love of nobleness.

Accordingly it is sometimes held that legislators should on the one hand invite and exhort men to pursue virtue because it is so noble, as they who have been already trained in virtue will pay heed to them, and on the other hand, if they are disobedient and degenerate, should inflict punishments and chastisements on them and utterly expel them, if they are incurable; for so the good man who lives by the rule of honour will obey reason, and the bad man whose aim is pleasure must be chastened by pain like a beast of burden. Hence too it is said that the pains ought to be such as are most opposed to a person's favourite pleasures.

If then, as has been said, he who is to be a good man should receive a noble nurture and training and then should live accordingly in virtuous pursuits and never voluntarily or involuntarily do evil, this result will only be attained if we live, so to say, in accordance with reason and right order resting upon force.

Now the authority of a father does not possess such force or compulsion, nor indeed does that of any individual, unless he is a king or some such person. But the law has a compulsory power, as being itself in a sense the outcome of prudence and reason; and whereas we hate people who oppose our inclinations, even if they are right in so doing, we do not feel the law to be grievous in its insistence upon virtue.

The state and education.

It is only in the state of Lacedaemon and a few other states that the legislator seems to have undertaken to control the nurture and pursuits of the citizens. In the great majority of states there is an absolute neglect of such matters, and everybody lives as he chooses, "being lawgiver of wife and children" like the Cyclops[1].

It is best then that the state should undertake the control of these matters and should exercise it rightly and should have the power of giving effect to its control. But if the state altogether neglects it, it would seem to be the duty of every citizen to further the cause of virtue in his own children and friends, or at least to set before himself the purpose of furthering it. It would seem too from what has been said that he will be best able to do this, if he has learnt the principles of legislation; for the control of the state is clearly exercised through the form of laws, and is good if the laws are virtuous. Whether they are written or unwritten laws, and whether they are suited to the education of an individual or

[1] Homer's description of the Cyclopean life (to which Aristotle frequently refers) is found in the *Odyssey* ix. 114, 115.

of a number of people is apparently a matter of indifference, as it is in music or gymnastic or other studies. For as in a state it is law and custom which are supreme, so in a household it is the paternal precepts and customs, and all the more because of the father's relationship to the members of his family, and of the benefits which he has conferred upon them; for the members of a family are naturally affectionate and obedient to the father from the first.

Again, there is a superiority in the individual as against the general methods of education; it is much the same as in medicine where, although it is the general rule that a feverish patient needs to be kept quiet and to take no food, there may perhaps be some exceptions. Nor does a teacher of boxing teach all his pupils to box in the same style.

Individualism in education.

It would seem then that a study of individual character is the best way of perfecting the education of the individual, as then everyone has a better chance of receiving such treatment as is suitable. Still the individual case may best be treated, whether in medicine or in gymnastic or in any other subject, by one who knows the general rule applicable to all people or to people of a particular kind; for the sciences are said to deal, and do deal, with general laws. At the same time there is no reason why even without scientific knowledge a person should not be successful in treating a particular case if he has made an accurate, although empirical, observation of the results which follow from a particular course of treatment, as there are some doctors who seem to be excellent doctors in their own cases, although they would be unable to relieve anybody else.

Need of
principles
of legisla-
tion.

Nevertheless if a person wishes to succeed in art or speculation, it is, I think, his duty to proceed to a universal principle and to make himself acquainted with it as far as possible; for sciences, as has been said, deal with universals. ⌈Also it is the duty of any one who wishes to elevate people, whether they be few or many, by his treatment, to try to learn the principles of legislation, if it is laws that are the natural means of making us good. So in education it is not everybody—it is at the most only the man of science—who can create a noble disposition in all who come to him as patients, as it is in medicine or in any other art which demands care and prudence.

Is it not then our next step to consider the sources and means of learning the principles of legislation? It may be thought that here as elsewhere we must look *to the persons who practise the principles, i.e.* to statesmen; for legislation, as we

p. 346.

saw, is apparently a branch of politics. But there is this difference between politics and all other sciences and faculties. In these it is the same people who are found to teach the faculties and to make practical use of them, e.g. doctors and painters; whereas in

Sophists.

politics it is the sophists who profess to teach, but it is never they who practise. The practical people are the active statesmen who would seem to be guided in practical life by a kind of faculty or experience rather than by intelligence; for we see that they never write or speak on these subjects, although it is perhaps a nobler task than the composition of forensic or parliamentary speeches, nor have they ever made their own sons or any other people whom they care for into statesmen. Yet it might be expected that they should do so, if it were in their power, for they could not have bequeathed any better legacy to their state, nor is there anything which they would have preferred for themselves or their dearest friends to such a faculty. Still it must be admitted that experience does much good; otherwise people could not be made statesmen by familiarity with politics. It follows that, if people desire to understand politics, they need experience as well as theory.

These sophists however who are lavish in their professions appear to be far from teaching *statesmanship;* in fact they are absolutely ignorant of the sphere or nature of statesmanship. If it were not so they would not have made statesmanship identical with, or inferior to, rhetoric; they would not have thought it easy work to form a legislative code by merely collecting such laws as are held in high repute; they would not have supposed that all they have to do.is to make a selection of the best laws, as if the selection itself did not demand intelligence, and as if a right judgment were not a thing of the greatest difficulty in legislation no less than in music. For it is only such persons as possess experience of particular arts who can form a correct judgment of artistic works, and understand the means and manner of executing them, and the harmony of particular combinations. Inexperienced persons on the other hand are only too glad if they are alive to the fact that a work has been well or badly executed, as in painting. But laws are like the artistic works of political science. How then should *a mere collection of* laws make a person capable of legislating, or of deciding upon the best laws? It does not appear that *the study* of medical books makes people good doctors; yet medical books affect not only to state methods of treatment, but to state the way of curing people, and the proper method of treating particular cases by classifying the various states of health. But all this, although it seems useful to the experienced, is useless to those who are ignorant of medical science. It may be supposed then that collections of laws and polities would be useful to those who are capable of considering and deciding what is right or wrong, and what is suitable to particular cases; but if people who examine such questions have not *the proper* frame of mind, they will find it impossible to form a right judgment unless indeed by accident, although they may gain a more intelligent appreciation of them.

As previous writers have failed to investigate the subject of legislation, it will perhaps be better to examine it ourselves, and indeed to examine the whole subject of politics[1], in order that the philosophy of human life may be made as complete as possible.

Let us try then, first of all, to recount such particular opinions as have been rightly expressed by our predecessors, then, in view of the polities which we have collected, to consider the preservatives and destructives of states and of particular polities, and the reasons why some polities are good and others bad. For when we have considered these, it will perhaps be easier to see what kind of polity is best, and what is the best way of ordering it and what are its laws and customs.

[1] Aristotle thus paves the way for his *Politics*, a treatise published later than the *Nicomachean Ethics*.

INDEX.

CAMBRIDGE: PRINTED BY C. J. CLAY, M.A. & SONS, AT THE UNIVERSITY PRESS.

MESSRS MACMILLAN & CO.'S PUBLICATIONS.

BY THE SAME AUTHOR.

THE POLITICS OF ARISTOTLE. Translated with an analysis and critical notes by J. E. C. WELLDON, Litt.D., Fellow of King's College, Cambridge, and Head Master of Harrow School. Crown 8vo. 10s. 6d.

SATURDAY REVIEW. "Mr Welldon, we may say at once, has produced a version as English and idiomatic in style, as transparent with regard to meaning, as the difficulties of the task permit. He has ingeniously broken up and arranged the sprawling sentences of his author. He has supplied necessary links in the thought (when these links are omitted by Aristotle), inserting glosses in italics. We think that anyone who is already familiar with Aristotle and his little ways can read Mr Welldon's translation with some rapidity, though not, of course, without concentrated attention. We know no other version of which so much can be said."

ACADEMY. "Mr Welldon has provided an excellent version of the *Politics* of Aristotle. Those who want assistance in coping with the Greek will find him very faithful and exact, and the general reader has every reason to be satisfied with so readable a version of a difficult Greek author...It remains faithful to the general style of the Greek, though it is distinguished throughout by a high degree of accuracy... A translation of Aristotle which is exact, and which at the same time hardly reads like a translation must be good."

THE RHETORIC OF ARISTOTLE. Translated with an analysis and critical notes by J. E. C. WELLDON, Litt.D., Fellow of King's College, Cambridge, and Head Master of Harrow School. Crown 8vo. 7s. 6d.

THE GUARDIAN. "Mr Welldon's version of the *Rhetoric*, taken as a whole, is excellent. It is the work of a scholar who understands his Aristotle, and who has taken great pains to make Aristotle intelligible to his readers."

SATURDAY REVIEW. "It is a book to be used. The scholar who knows his *Rhetoric* and the student who wishes to know it are placed under obligations to Mr Welldon's judgment and research. Page after page is a faultless reflection of Aristotle's thought...In his rendering of isolated expressions, and especially of the many proverbs which Aristotle has scattered about the Rhetoric, Mr Welldon is often felicitous. But he is seen at his best in the numerous places of real doubt and difficulty. He possesses the merit of knowing his own mind and being able to express his own meaning. Nor does the clearness of his insight make him dogmatical...He is careful to record the more important variations in the text. An elaborate analysis of the subject-matter is prefixed to the translation, which will be useful to serious students of the Rhetoric."

MACMILLAN AND CO., LONDON.

MESSRS MACMILLAN & CO.'S
CLASSICAL TRANSLATIONS.

ARISTOTLE—ETHICS. By J. E. C. WELLDON, M.A.
Crown 8vo.
— *THE POLITICS.* By the same. Crown 8vo. 10s. 6d.
— *THE RHETORIC.* By the same. Crown 8vo. 7s. 6d.
— *ON THE CONSTITUTION OF ATHENS.*
Translated by E. POSTE, M.A., Fellow of Oriel College, Oxford.
Second Edition. Cr. 8vo. 3s. 6d.
CICERO—SELECT LETTERS. Translated from
Watson's Edition. By G. E. JEANS, M.A. 10s. 6d.
— *ACADEMICS.* By J. S. REID, M.L., Litt.D. 8vo. 5s. 6d.
HERODOTUS. By G. C. MACAULAY, M.A. *THE
HISTORY.* 2 vols. Cr. 8vo. 18s.
HOMER—ODYSSEY. By Prof. S. H. BUTCHER, M.A.,
and A. LANG, M.A. 6s.
— *ILIAD.* By A. LANG, M.A., W. LEAF, Litt.D., and
E. MYERS, M.A. 12s. 6d.
— *THE ODYSSEY, BOOKS I—XII.* By the EARL
OF CARNARVON. 8s. 6d.
HORACE. By J. LONSDALE, M.A., and S. LEE, M.A. 3s. 6d.
JUVENAL—THIRTEEN SATIRES. By A. LEEPER,
M.A. Crown 8vo. 3s. 6d.
LIVY—BOOKS XXI—XXV. By A. J. CHURCH, and
W. J. BRODRIBB. 7s. 6d.
PINDAR—ODES. By ERNEST MYERS, M.A. Second
Edition. 5s.
PLATO—REPUBLIC. By J. L. DAVIES, M.A., and
D. J. VAUGHAN, M.A. 2s. 6d. net.
— *EUTHYPHRO, APOLOGY, CRITO, AND
PHÆDO.* By F. J. CHURCH. 2s. 6d. net.
— *PHÆDRUS, LYSIS, AND PROTAGORAS.* By
J. WRIGHT, M.A. 4s. 6d.
POLYBIUS—THE HISTORIES. By E. S. SHUCK-
BURGH, M.A. 2 vols. 21s.
SALLUST—CATILINE AND JUGURTHA. By
A. W. POLLARD, B.A. 6s. *CATILINE* separately, 3s.
TACITUS. By A. J. CHURCH, M.A. and W. J. BRODRIBB,
M.A. *HISTORY*, 6s. *ANNALS*, 7s. 6d. *AGRICOLA AND
GERMANIA*, 4s. 6d.
THEOCRITUS, MOSCHUS, AND BION. By A.
LANG, New Edit. 18mo. 4s. 6d.
VIRGIL—ÆNEID. By J. W. MACKAIL, M.A. 7s. 6d.
XENOPHON. By H. G. DAKYNS, M.A. 4 vols. Cr. 8vo.
Vol. I. 10s. 6d.

MACMILLAN AND CO., LONDON.

www.ingramcontent.com/pod-product-compliance
Lightning Source LLC
Chambersburg PA
CBHW032309280326
41932CB00009B/759